I0042644

Raising a Cautionary Flag

Raising a Cautionary Flag

Educational Malpractice and the Professional Teacher

Todd A. DeMitchell, Richard Fossey, and Terri A. DeMitchell

ROWMAN & LITTLEFIELD
Lanham • Boulder • New York • London

Published by Rowman & Littlefield
An imprint of The Rowman & Littlefield Publishing Group, Inc.
4501 Forbes Boulevard, Suite 200, Lanham, Maryland 20706
www.rowman.com

86–90 Paul Street, London EC2A 4NE

Copyright © 2022 by Todd A. DeMitchell, Richard Fossey, and Terri A. DeMitchell

All rights reserved. No part of this book may be reproduced in any form or by any electronic or mechanical means, including information storage and retrieval systems, without written permission from the publisher, except by a reviewer who may quote passages in a review.

British Library Cataloguing in Publication Information Available

Library of Congress Cataloging-in-Publication Data

Names: DeMitchell, Todd A., author. | Fossey, Richard, author. | DeMitchell, Terri A., author.
Title: Raising a cautionary flag : educational malpractice and the professional teacher / Todd A. DeMitchell, Richard Fossey, and Terri A. DeMitchell.
Description: Lanham, Maryland : Rowman & Littlefield Publishers, [2022] | Includes bibliographical references and index.
Identifiers: LCCN 2022027775 (print) | LCCN 2022027776 (ebook) | ISBN 9781475866759 (cloth) | ISBN 9781475866766 (paperback) | ISBN 9781475866773 (ebook)
Subjects: LCSH: Teachers—Malpractice—United States. | Tort liability of school districts—United States.
Classification: LCC KF1310 .D46 2022 (print) | LCC KF1310 (ebook) | DDC 344.73/075—dc23/eng/20220831
LC record available at https://lccn.loc.gov/2022027775
LC ebook record available at https://lccn.loc.gov/2022027776

Contents

Chapter 1

Introduction

The Teacher and Educational Malpractice—a Paradox and a Conundrum

> The concept that every person who enters into a learned profession under-
> takes to bring to the exercise of a reasonable degree of care and skill dates
> back to the laws of ancient Rome and England.[1]

What teachers do matters. This simple declarative statement captures the importance of teachers. It could equally be said that what physicians and attorneys do matters. If their work matters, what happens when their work, which matters, causes harm? The answer for physicians and attorneys may be a suit of negligence commonly called malpractice, in which the injured parties seek damages for their injuries caused by the substandard work. However, this is not true for educators; they currently cannot be sued for negligent instruction. A near half-century-long wall has been constructed protecting teachers and school districts from malpractice liability; is it cracking? Should a cautionary flag be raised?

Educational malpractice, sometimes referred to as instructional negligence, is both a paradox and a conundrum. It is a paradox, in that educators are basically immune from negligence lawsuits for their essential professional act of teaching, while other professionals—physicians, attorneys engineers, accountants, and the like—can be held liable for damages if they are negligent in the performance of their professional services and their negligence causes a harm. Plaintiffs essentially argue "that because courts have found malpractice in other professions to be legally compensable, courts should apply malpractice standards to the education profession."[2]

Should teachers be held accountable to the students they harm by their instructional actions and/or inactions? Is it contradictory for educators to be afforded professional status and yet be immune from one of the protections the public is afforded when other professionals provide substandard services?

1

Teachers can be dismissed for incompetent instruction and unprofessional conduct, but they cannot be sued for damages caused by their substandard teaching. They may be disciplined, even dismissed by their employing school district, but they cannot be sued for injurious teaching by their students. Should teachers, who hold themselves as professionals, be sued for malpractice in teaching? Therein is the paradox.

Educational malpractice also presents a conundrum. To recognize a cause of action for educational malpractice raises difficult problems. How should substandard or negligent teaching be defined? In malpractice cases, a central question is what professional practices are accepted by the profession as "usual and customary,"[3] and which professional practices are negligently applied or not applied in the classroom. After all, there are multiple pedagogical styles in the teaching profession, and students respond differently to various teaching practices. Can it be said with any degree of certainty that a particular manner of teaching is negligent or constitutes educational malpractice?

In addition, educational malpractice claims must identify specific actions at a point in time—the school day or the school year—when the negligent act(s) occurred. If a high school student graduates but reads at a fifth-grade level, when exactly did negligent instruction take place, and which specific educator was negligent and what acts or omissions were negligent? Did a single teacher commit malpractice when teaching the student or were multiple teachers responsible for the student's failure to read at an adult level? What impact did the makeup of the class have, or the culture of the school, or its resources?

Adding to the difficulty of recognizing educational malpractice as a cause of action for damages is the difficult issue of comparative negligence. Does a student bear part of the responsibility for failing to learn? Was the student a diligent scholar who regularly turned in homework assignments and conscientiously studied for exams? Was the student contributorily negligent for the harm suffered?

Do parents bear part of the responsibility for ensuring that their children are adequately educated? Does the home life of a student support the student's education? If so, what share of liability should be imposed upon the parents if their child fails to read at grade level or graduates from high school with substandard math skills?

Thus, the conundrum for educator malpractice is how to sort through the thicket of questions about who is liable for any malfeasance or nonfeasance that occurs. Individuals injured by medical malpractice may receive monetary relief and negligent members of a learned profession may be sanctioned by their profession (e.g., suspended license and license revocation). However, a student injured through poor, unacceptable instruction has no individual recourse for relief. The only current recourse is for the school district to discipline the teacher, usually for incompetence.[4]

THE SURGERY AND THE HIGH SCHOOL GRADUATION: FAILURES OF PRACTICE?

The Surgery Scenario

George Stamatis, a spokesperson for the University Hospitals in Cleveland, Ohio, acknowledged that on July 2, 2021, a kidney was transplanted into the wrong patient. Two kidney transplants had been scheduled for the same day. While the patient who received the wrong kidney was lucky that there was a match with the donated kidney and seemed to be doing well soon after the transplant, the intended recipient had to go back on the transplant list and undergo more dialysis and surgeries.[5] The spokesperson's statement read:

> *We have offered our sincerest apologies to these patients and their families. We recognize they entrusted us with their care. The situation is entirely inconsistent with our commitment to helping patients return to health and live life to the fullest.[6]*

The hospital placed two, undesignated, employees on administrative leave and the hospital launched an investigation. The United Network for Organ Sharing was notified of the medical mistake. The hospital is an experienced transplant center. Most likely, a lawsuit for medical negligence, typically known as medical malpractice, will be filed which, if negligence is sustained, will result in money damages and other potential "make whole" awards for the plaintiff.[7]

"The law has recognized professional malpractice actions when a professional demonstrates misconduct or an unreasonable lack of skill."[8] "Judicial intervention in the specific professions of medicine and law has largely molded the malpractice law applied to all professionals."[9] Medical malpractice is a well-known type of negligence lawsuit and perhaps the first example of professional malpractice that comes to mind when hearing the term malpractice.

One of the most concise statements regarding the requisite standard of care for physicians was established by a Kentucky Court of Appeals in *Blair v. Eblen*, holding, "[A physician is] under a duty to use that degree of care and skill which is expected of a reasonably competent practitioner in the same class to which he belongs, acting in the same or similar circumstances."[10]

TEXTBOX 1.1

If doctors, lawyers, architects, engineers, and other professionals are charged with a duty owing to the public whom they serve, it could be said that nothing in the law precludes similar treatment of professional educators.

Donohue v. Copiague Union Free School District, 391 N.E.2d 1352, 1353 (1979).

The Graduation Scenario

The plaintiff in this action was an eighteen-year-old male who had recently graduated from the San Francisco Unified School District after having been enrolled in the school system for a period of approximately twelve years. He claimed that although he had graduated from high school he possessed only a fifth-grade reading ability. He asserted, in part, that the school district negligently and carelessly:

(1) failed to identify his reading disabilities,
(2) assigned him to classes in which he could not read the books and materials,
(3) allowed him to pass and advance from a course or grade level with knowledge that he had not acquired the skills necessary for him to succeed or benefit from subsequent courses,
(4) assigned him to classes in which the instructors were unqualified or which were not "geared" to his reading level, and
(5) permitted him to graduate from high school although he was unable to read above the eighth-grade level, as required by the existing California Education Code, thereby depriving him of additional instruction in reading and other academic skills.[11]

Consequently, he asserted, that his limited ability to read and write rendered him unqualified for any gainful employment except labor, which typically had limited employment requirements for reading level and writing ability. The plaintiff, Peter W., lost, thus setting the table for future educational malpractice cases.[12]

Therefore, while medical professionals and attorneys can be held accountable through malpractice suits when their professional actions fail to conform to accepted practices resulting in an injury, to date, educational malpractice has failed as a theory of recovery.[13] Currently, educators are not required under threat of malpractice and the awarding of potential damage awards, as other professionals are required, to perform their duties in accordance with the standard of care observed by their profession.

The reasons for refusing to recognize educational malpractice Centers around both legal issues and public policy issues. Legal issues include the difficulty in establishing the elements of a tort, such as determining that educators have a duty to educate students non-negligently, recognizing a standard of care in education, proving that a breach of the standard of care is the caused the student's injury, and determining that a student was harmed.

Policy issues include a judicial policy of noninterference in educational matters for which judges may not be equipped to navigate. In addition, the courts have raised a concern that allowing educational malpractice suits to be brought could open floodgates of litigation, resulting in massive damages awards that could bankrupt school systems and embroil them in ongoing litigation.

However, at least some of the assumptions relied upon by the courts for refusing to recognize the tort of educational malpractice may no longer be valid. As standardized testing becomes more sophisticated and more prevalent in American schools, it has become possible to recognize students' learning deficiencies during their twelve-year journeys through the schools. Thus, it can be determined that a particular student is falling behind in reading or mathematics while still in elementary school.

The Focus of the Book

Professional malpractice law as applied to educators is the focus of this book. Some commentators have argued that the courts should recognize educational malpractice, asserting that "the courts' justification for their refusal to recognize educational malpractice claims is fundamentally flawed."[14] Our book does not advocate for the courts to recognize the viability of educational malpractice claims. Instead, it explores the foundation and issues that inform the discussion about the viability of such a tort for negligence. Is the long-standing barrier to educational malpractice giving way or as DeMitchell and DeMitchell asked, "Is a crack forming in the educational malpractice wall?"[15] It is an issue of growing concern for judges, lawyers, educators, and policymakers.[16]

PROFESSIONAL MALPRACTICE

Professionals who engage in alleged professional misconduct or who allegedly lack appropriate skill, which results in injury, may be liable for malpractice.

Prosser and Keeton note that the earliest appearance of negligence "was in the liability of those who professed to be competent in certain 'public' callings."[17] Generally, the key to malpractice cases is whether the professional performed in accordance with the standard of care observed by members of the profession (*mala praxis*[18]). In other words, the standard of care is used to measure the competence of the professional. Malpractice is defined as

> professional misconduct or unreasonable lack of skill. . . . [It is the] failure of one rendering professional services to exercise the degree of skill and learning commonly applied under all the circumstances of the community by the average prudent reputable member of the profession with the result of injury, loss or damage to the recipient of those services or to those entitled to rely upon them. It is any professional misconduct, unreasonable lack of skill or fidelity in professional or fiduciary duties, evil practice, or illegal or immoral conduct.[19]

Professionals who engage in professional misconduct or who lack the appropriate skills of their professions may be liable in damages for malpractice if an injury occurs. Thus, malpractice is a tort of negligence for which courts may provide a remedy for the damages suffered at the hands of another. Malpractice is usually equated with the failure to provide the quality of service based on their superior knowledge and training that a competent professional is reasonably expected to render to a person relying on those services.

Most professionals are held accountable through malpractice "for failure to perform in accordance with skills that define their jobs."[20] They are expected to utilize a standard of care recognized by their profession as appropriate, based on the training received and the commonly held set of practices associated with the service rendered. Failure to exercise the accepted standard of care may form the basis for a malpractice claim, if the negligent delivery of the service is the legal cause for an injury suffered.[21]

Medical literature often uses the term "medical errors" to cover a range of adverse outcomes. The European Union Patient Safety and Care Expert Group use the following definitions of error:

- An Error of Execution: The failure of a planned sequence of mental and physical activities to accomplish the desired effect, provided that this failure cannot be attributed to random factors.
- An Error of Planning: The selection and implementation of an incorrect plan for the achievement of the desired effect.[22]

It is worthwhile noting that these error definitions could also be applied to a definition of educational errors, with the possible addition of other errors to account for the unique circumstances of education.

Failure to exercise the accepted standard of care may form the basis for malpractice claim, if the negligent delivery of the service is the legal cause for an injury suffered due to the lack of an appropriate standard of care. In medicine, a surgeon may operate on a patient and follow all of the commonly accepted procedures for the operation and yet the patient dies. The death of the patient is not the measure of malpractice; the delivery of the standard of care concerning the operation is instead dispositive. In other words, a malpractice suit will not prevail if the patient dies despite the surgeon doing everything expected in the delivery of the professional service.

EDUCATORS AND MALPRACTICE

As stated earlier, the courts have historically been reluctant to hold educators accountable for their failure to properly educate their students: Thus, the paradox is being a professional but not being held legally accountable for their negligence as other professionals are for their negligence.

TEXTBOX 1.2

What then is a teacher? As teachers we use many sources of professional knowledge, skill, and experience at our disposal to engage the minds and hearts of children and youth by teaching and inspiring them. And once we mess with minds and hearts, we are prepared to take responsibility for the messes we have made, the dreams we inspired, the minds we have brought to life, the prejudices we have forestalled, and the society to which we have given hope.

Lee Schulman, *What Teachers Should Know and Be Able to Do* (Preface) (Arlington, VA: National Board for Professional Teaching Standards, 2016): 5.

A school district can discipline or dismiss a teacher for incompetence or unprofessional conduct.[23] But a student who is injured due to a teacher's pedagogical incompetence has no legal recourse in a suit for damages. In other words, a school district has a remedy if it has an incompetent teacher on its payroll; it can fire the teacher. But a student who receives negligent academic instruction[24] by a teacher, or perhaps by a series of teachers, is not entitled to a remedy in a malpractice action. In fact, in most jurisdictions, suits for educational malpractice are routinely dismissed prior to trial as being against public policy.[25]

Lawsuits for educational malpractice have consistently failed, but as the profession faces heightened scrutiny through accountability mechanisms and the formulation of research-based best practices, the tort of educational malpractice may be reexamined. While the education profession has had codes of conduct and ethics codes[26] for more than half a century, codes of accepted and expected practice of instruction lag. What instructional practices and skills has the profession identified as part of its professional preparation?

As educators continue to professionalize their practice, they may be opening the door to judicial recognition of educational malpractice. As Cooper stated, "We will know that teaching is a profession when a malpractice suit becomes plausible."[27] Professors Ethan L. Hutt (education) and Aaron Tang (law) have argued that common law torts such as negligence and malpractice are sensitive to changing times and that advances in data on student learning and teacher effectiveness, especially value-added modeling (VAM), "requires courts to revisit the initial rationales used to reject education malpractice claims."[28] Given the changes that education has undergone and will continue to undergo, a conversation about educational malpractice is timely and prudent.

It is not far-fetched to believe that one day courts and public policy will dictate that educators be held accountable for the professional services they render, particularly as the profession establishes standards for pedagogical practice. Some commentators have asserted that the use of scientifically accepted practices in the classroom can resolve any concerns about the difficulty of establishing a reasonable standard of care for educators.[29]

Who can be held responsible for what, and what can be done to help ensure that proper, accepted practices are clearly identified and consistently implemented in the classroom? In addition, what defenses are available to protect educators from unfair judgments against them and their schools? Is a tort for educational malpractice good policy? These are questions that this book explores.

THE BOOK: RAISING A CAUTIONARY FLAG OVER THE MALPRACTICE WALL

Who teaches our children matters, and how well that teacher teaches matters as well. Educators are consequential in the education and lives of children. They stand at the crossroads of education. It is largely through their efforts that the goals of education are achieved, neglected, or thwarted. At the core of their work, teachers provide instruction, structure learning activities, and assess the works of students. What deviations from prudent instructional practices constitute negligence? Are those practices clearly defined and widely accepted in the schools and are those practices taught in schools of education?

TEXTBOX 1.3

The very fact that school systems are specifically designed and usually required to educate students provides the argument that failure to do so is a clear example of unreasonable and socially harmful conduct. However, individuals are legally responsible only for acts and omissions which the law recognizes as unjustified. The courts must initially find that the failure to educate is a justified claim.

Frank D. Aquila, "Educational Malpractice: A Tort En Ventre," *Cleveland State Law Review* 39 (1991): 323–355, 326.

The importance of teachers to the education of students is not a subject of debate: it is well settled. As teacher-education scholar Richard M. Ingersoll observed, "The quality of teachers and teaching is undoubtedly among the most important factors shaping the learning and growth of students."[30] Teachers occupy the central position in every school by providing instruction, structuring their pupils' learning activities, and assessing the works of students. Succinctly stated, "Teacher quality matters. In fact, it is the most important school-related factor influencing student achievement."[31] Consequently, substandard practice negatively impacts the education of students and their future prospects for becoming prosperous and productive citizens.

Our book explores the legal and policy concepts that shape the conundrum of the failure of a cause of action for educational malpractice.[32] The book is divided into three sections with two chapters in each section.

The first section is "Professional Malpractice: A Tort of Negligence." This section first explores what it means to be a professional (chapter 2, "The Paradox of the Teacher as a Professional and Education as a Profession"). In common usage, how is the term professional used? What constitutes a profession? Are educators professionals in the same sense that other professionals are subject to malpractice?[33] The Educators Descriptors Study of the Profession developed for this book is explored. Figure 2.1 displays a Four-Phase and Influences Template for a Learned Society and the unique context of education. The context of education is applied to the four-phase template.

In the next chapter (chapter 3, "Malpractice: A Tort of Negligence"), the legal concept of tort liability for negligence is explored. This chapter lays the foundation for understanding the legal concepts of malpractice.

The second section, titled "Emerging Tort Actions," reviews malpractice cases in K–12 and higher education. Chapter 4, "The Early Educational Malpractice Suits: A Failed Tort," begins with an analysis of *Peter W. v. San Francisco Unified School District*,[34] a seminal case in which the California Supreme Court emphatically rejected the tort of educational malpractice. This chapter then analyzes several of the critical cases that followed in the wake of *Peter W.* and established the foundation for future educational malpractice cases.

The next chapter, "Higher Education Malpractice and Breach of Contract in the Time of the Pandemic," discusses higher education malpractice cases within the context of COVID-19 tuition-reimbursement litigation. It starts with a discussion of the seminal higher education malpractice case *Ross v. Creighton University*.[35] Next it reviews cases involving universities' decisions to close their campuses and switch all classes from a classroom setting to online formats in response to the COVID-19 pandemic.

Students filed more than 300 lawsuits against higher education institutions, arguing that the online instruction they received was inferior to face-to-face instruction. Students sued in both state and federal courts, seeking to get refunds for tuition and fees they paid after the universities terminated classroom teaching in an effort to protect both instructors and students from being infected by COVID.

Many of these cases included a claim for educational malpractice, in addition to breach of contract claims and claims of unjust enrichment. Although several courts allowed these cases to go to trial, most rejected the argument that students stated a claim for educational malpractice. Rather the courts generally concluded that the students' damages claims were essentially claims for breach of contract or unjust enrichment.[36]

Thirty years ago, in the seminal case of *Ross v. Creighton University*,[37] the Seventh Circuit rejected the viability of educational malpractice claims against postsecondary institutions. Have the courts' views about educational malpractice changed since that decision was rendered?

The last section, section III, "A Viable Tort? Law and Policy Responses," starts with chapter 6, "Are Cracks Forming in the Educational Malpractice Wall? Viability, Gag Orders, and VAM," which lays out the possible responses to a malpractice suit. First, the chapter explores recent research (Educational Malpractice Viability Survey [EMVS]) conducted by Todd A. DeMitchell, Stefanie King, and Terri A. DeMitchell on educational malpractice.[38]

The study uses a judgmental or expert sampling technique, whereby the researchers selected potential respondents based on their knowledge and professional judgment. It is a mixed methods study of quantitative and qualitative research. The research has sections on the viability educational malpractice, factors that impact the viability of educational malpractice, and who should be liable for malpractice suits. It also has two open-ended qualitative questions on school district responses to educational malpractice suits.

The chapter continues with a discussion of legislation and litigation that may reveal a crack in the wall that bars educational malpractice suits. A duty owed for curriculum and instruction may be emerging through legislative enactments and potential litigation akin to malpractice. A 1998 California ballot initiative titled "English Language in Public Schools" is discussed as well as the challenging lawsuit *California Teachers Association v. Davis*.[39]

Next, the negligence prong of causation is explored. VAM is a quantitative assessment tool that purportedly translates student outcome scores to teacher effectiveness. This accountability mechanism garnered significant national attention. If applied in an educational malpractice suit, it may provide a vehicle for overcoming the concern that causation cannot be demonstrated. However, there has been significant pushback on the use of VAM in high-stake settings.[40]

The last chapter raises a cautionary flag regarding viable educational malpractice lawsuits and explores various potential responses to educational malpractice suits. The discussion continues the exploration of the EMVS, focusing on the responses of the expert sample on the prompts of defenses to educational malpractice suits and developing proactive protective responses to viable lawsuits for malpractice. Potential unintended consequences of a viable tort for malpractice follow. We ask whether education is the right fit for the malpractice template, given the unique context of education. Rationales for flying a cautionary flag are presented to conclude the chapter and the book.

It is clear that children can be harmed by an inadequate education. Indeed, educational attainment has long been recognized as a good predictor of success in the labor market. Stream-of-earnings analyses over a worker's lifetime have consistently shown that the higher the level of the education, the higher the income. It is far from clear that educational malpractice is the proper vehicle for improving student outcomes.

Not quite a half century after *Peter W.* was decided, educational malpractice may be closer to becoming a cognizable cause of action for students who suffered educational harm at the hands of educators and the schools. It is important to understand the possible ramifications of such a major shift in policy and practice. Whether or not we believe that judicial oversight through a tort of educational malpractice is appropriate, the potential reality carries significant ramifications for American education.

Our book explores the history of educational malpractice by comparing how the negligent actions of other professionals can give rise to successful malpractice suits while malpractice suits against educators are barred. In recent years, at least some of the legal objections to a cause of action for educational malpractice seem less valid. Although courts were once per-suaded by public policy arguments against educational malpractice, more recent policy arguments maintain that the tort of educational malpractice might improve the quality of instruction while granting money as damages to students who were negligently educated.

Moreover, the standards of teaching practice are being established and articulated such that it is at least theoretically possible for a plaintiff to estab-lish that a particular teacher's pedagogical practices were negligent. A 2022 study investigated the "black box" of effective teaching asking, "What teach-ing practices matter for student achievement?"[41] These types of developments may break the wall of judicial prejudice against educational malpractice.

A change in the law that would allow negligence suits based on educa-tional malpractice would have profound consequences for educators, school districts, and the public purse. The book ends with a clear caution about a rush to securing a private cause of action for educational malpractice against teachers and schools. Do we strengthen the crucially important relations and collaborations between school and home by creating plaintiffs and defen-dants? What changes will likely occur in classrooms if suits for educational malpractice are recognized?

Raising a Cautionary Flag: Educational Malpractice and the Profes-sional Teacher does not argue in favor of recognizing the tort of educational malpractice. Instead, we raise a cautionary flag about the consequences of a policy change that recognizes this tort of negligence.

NOTES

1. B. Sonny Bal, "An Introduction to Medical Malpractice," *Clinical Orthopae-dics and Related Research* 467 (February 2009): 339–347, https://www.ncbi.nlm.nih.gov/pmc/articles/PMC2628513/. Site visited August 19, 2021,

2. Laurie S. Jamieson, "Educational Malpractice: A Lesson in Professional Accountability," *Boston College Law Review* 32 (1991): 899–965, 905.

3. William L. Prosser & Page Keeton, *Prosser and Keeton on the Law of Torts* (St. Paul, MN: West Publishing, 1984, 5th ed.): 189.

4. See Todd A. DeMitchell & Mark A. Paige, *Threading the Evaluation Needle: The Documentation of Teacher Unprofessional Conduct* (Lanham, MD: Rowman & Littlefield, 2020): 33–44.

5. For an overview and discussion of the effects of hemodialysis, see Mayo Clinic, "Hemodialysis," https://www.mayoclinic.org/tests-procedures/hemodialysis/about/pac-20384824. Site visited July 17, 2021.

6. Author, "Hospital: Patient Gets Kidney Meant for Someone Else," *Associated Press* (July 13, 2021), https://apnews.com/article/health-59d39f83aa2aa41b95dd723f-04ec358d. Site visited July 17, 2021.

7. Medical malpractice suits often result in a settlement between the parties. For example, in another Ohio (University of Toledo Medical Center) kidney transplant case, twenty-four year-old Sarah Fudacz, who was in end-stage disease, was to receive a perfectly matched kidney from her brother. A nurse inadvertently threw the kidney out prior to the transplant. Three months later Ms. Fudacz received a kidney transplant after undergoing numerous rounds of dialysis and surgeries. The Medical Center paid for her transplant expenses, including travel to Colorado to receive the transplant. In addition, the Medical Center paid $650,000 to settle the suit. WTOL11, "Family settles lawsuit with UTMC over botched kidney transplant," https:// www.wtol.com/article/news/family-settles-lawsuit-with-utmc-over-botched-kidney-transplant/512-5df55369-51c9–4536-a5d6-e566cc9865e1 (May 29, 2014, updated July 2, 2018). Site visited July 17, 2021.

8. Jameson, *supra* note 2, 903.

9. Michael J. Polelle, "Who's on First, and What's a Professional," *University of San Francisco Law Review* 33 (1999): 205–230, 206.

10. *Blair v. Eblen*, 461 S.W.2d 370, 373 (Ky. 1970).

11. *Peter W. v. San Francisco Unified School District*, 60 Cal. App. 3d 814 (Ct. App. 1976).

12. Ibid.

13. See, Patricia Abbott, "*Sain v. Cedar Rapids Community School District:* Providing Special Protection for Student-Athletes," *Brigham Young University Education and Law Journal* 2002 (2002): 291–312, 291, who states that "long ago, legal scholars held a funeral service for the tort of educational malpractice"; Mark Dynarski in "Can Schools Commit Malpractice? It Depends," *Brookings* (July 26, 2018) wrote, "A recent scan covering the past 40 years found 80 cases alleging education malpractice, and only 1 was successful (that it was successful could be traced to particular wording in the Montana state constitution)," https://www.brookings.edu/research/can-schools-commit-malpractice-it-depends/. Site visited July 18, 2021.

14. Jameson, *supra* note 2, 964.

15. Terri A. DeMitchell & Todd A. DeMitchell, "A Crack in the Educational Malpractice Wall," *The School Administrator* (October 2007): 34–36.

16. Mui Kim Teh & Charles J. Russo, "Educational Negligence: Is It a Viable Form of Action?" in Karen Trimmer, Roselyn Dixon, & Yvonne S. Findlay (eds), *The Palgrave Handbook of Education Law for Schools* (Switzerland: Springer, 2018): 39–58.

17. Prosser & Keeton, *supra* note 3, 161 ("a carrier, an innkeeper, a blacksmith, or a surgeon, was regarded as holding oneself out to the public as one in whom confidence might be reposed, and hence as assuming an obligation to give proper service, for the breach of which, by any negligent conduct, he might be liable"). Ibid.

18. Defined in the First Edition of *Black's Dictionary of Law* (1891) as "Malpractice; unskillful management or treatment. Particularly applied to the neglect or unskillful management of a physician, surgeon, or apothecary." John Collis, *Educational Malpractice: Liability of Educators, School Administrators, and School Officials*, (Charlottesville, VA: The Michie Company, 1990): 30.

19. Henry Campbell Black, *Black's Law Dictionary* (St. Paul, MN: West Publishing Company, 1979, 5th ed.): 864. See also *Board of Examiners of Veterinary*

Medicine v. Mohr, 485 P.2d 235 (1971) ("any professional misconduct or any unreasonable lack of skill or fidelity in the performance of professional fiduciary duties; . . .
objectionable or wrong practice; . . . practice contrary to rule").

20. John J. Culhane, "Reinvigorating Educational Malpractice Claims: A Representational Focus," *Washington Law Review* 67 (1992): 349–414, 371. Professor
Culhane offered an interesting observation about the role of higher education professional preparation institutions, by writing, "While reasonable patients rely on their
doctors, in some cases reasonable doctors may, in turn, have relied on their schools
to provide them with the basic tools of "literacy" for their profession." Ibid., 412.
He cited *Moore v. Vanderloo*, 386 N.W.2d 108, 115 (Iowa, 1986) for support of his
proposition, writing, "Any malpractice case would have an educational malpractice
action within it. For example, a doctor or attorney sued for malpractice by a patient
or client might have an action over against his or her educational institution for failure to teach the doctor or attorney how to treat . . . the client's problem." Ibid. See
also *Swidryic v. Saint Michael's Medical Center*, 493 A.2d 641 (N.J. Super. Ct. Law
Div. 1985), in which a physician who had been sued for medical malpractice filed a
malpractice suit against his residency program.

21. In addition to malpractice suits, physicians are also held accountable through
peer review of their hospital privileges. Congress, in 1986, passed the Health Care
Quality Improvement Act to promote "effective professional peer review" (42 U.S.C.
§11101[3]). For an example of the termination of hospital privileges for a surgeon,
see *Kalan v. MedStar-Georgetown Med. Ctr., Incorporation*, 253 A.3d 123 (D.C.
2021).

22. James Reason, *Human Error* (New York: Cambridge University Press, 1990).

23. See DeMitchell & Paige, *supra* note 4, writing of the importance of documentation, "While the great majority of teachers are dedicated, accomplished professionals who serve the best interests of their students, some teachers are ineffective.
Therefore, whom to place in front of students in a classroom, how to assist that
teacher to reach higher levels of performance, when and how to identify deficiencies,
and when to dismiss are critical decisions." Ibid., 2.

24. Professors Hutt and Tang use the term "negligent academic instruction" to
describe educational malpractice. It narrows the focus to the essential professional act
of teachers. Ethan L. Hutt & Aaron Tang, "The New Education Malpractice Litigation," *Virginia Law Review* 99 (2013): 419–492, 430. School law professors Martha
M. McCarthy, Nelda H. Cambron-McCabe, & Suzanne E. Eckes, *Public School Law:
Teachers' and Student Rights* (Boston, MA: Pearson, 7th ed.) have also used the term
"instructional negligence" interchangeably with "educational malpractice" (p. 83). However, "educational malpractice" is the term usually used by commentators and courts.

25. See, e.g., *Miller v. Loyola University of New Orleans*, 829 So.2d 1057, 1061
(La. Ct. App. 2002) (noting "persuasive public policy argument against finding a
cause of action for educational malpractice that is endorsed by most states"); *Nalepa v.
Plymouth-Canton Community School District*, 525 N.W.2d 897, 904 (Mich. Ct. App.
1995) (even if the student's suicide "flowed from the alleged malpractice, for public
policy reasons, we would still decline to recognize a duty").

26. For an example of state codes of conduct and ethics, see New Hampshire
Department of Education's Code of Ethics for Educational Professionals and Code

of Conduct for Educational Professionals, https://www.education.nh.gov/sites/g/files/ehbemt326/files/inline-documents/code-of-ethics-code-of-conduct.pdf.

27. Myrna Cooper, "Whose Culture Is It Anyway?" in Ann Lieberman (ed.), *Building a Professional Culture in Schools* (New York: Teachers College Press, 1988): 52.

28. Hutt & Tang, *supra* note 24, 427. The authors assert that educational malpractice suits based on VAM statistics will have several salutary effects—(1) school districts may weed out low performers; (2) teachers who cannot improve voluntarily leave the profession rather than "risk the shame of being fired"; and underperforming teachers may "ratchet up their effort level in order to avoid termination." Ibid., 492. For an earlier law review which asserts that educational malpractice is a viable tort, see Johnny C. Parker, "Educational Malpractice: A Tort Is Born," *Cleveland State Law Review* 39 (1991): 301–31, 320. Law professor Parker wrote: "The consequences of miseducation are clearly identifiable and judicially remediable. Nonetheless, judicial unwillingness to recognize the tort of educational malpractice has provided the teaching profession with a governmental immunity of sorts."

29. Brian G. Gorman, Catherine J. Wynne, Christopher J. Morse, & James T. Todd, "Psychology and Law in the Classroom: How the Use of Clinical Fads in the Classroom May Awaken the Educational Malpractice Claim," *Brigham Young University Education & Law Journal* 2011 (2011): 29–50.

30. Richard M. Ingersoll, "Power, Accountability, and the Teacher Quality Problems," in Sean Kelly (ed.), *Assessing Teacher Quality: Understanding Teacher Effects on Instruction and Achievement* (New York: Teachers College Press, 2011): 97–108, 97.

31. Jennifer K. Rice, *Teacher Quality: Understanding the Effectiveness of Teacher Attribute* (Washington, DC: Economic Policy Institute, August 2003): 1.

32. It is important to note that the term "educational malpractice" is used in contexts other than lawsuits for negligence in instruction. Some authors will use the term in a broader context to denote their concern with educational practices and curriculum. This usage of educational malpractice will not be discussed in this book. An example includes two instructors in the biology program at the University of Minnesota who used the term to describe high school biology curriculum programs that included creationism. Responding to their data which demonstrated that high percentage of American biology teachers who were still teaching, compared to 1991, creationism, the authors concluded, "This educational malpractice denies students an appreciation of the nature of science, contributes to the ongoing popularity of creationism with the public, and cheats students out of an understanding of one of the greatest ideas in history." Randy Moore & Sehoya Cotner, "Educational Malpractice: The Impact of Including Creationism in High School Biology Courses," *Evolution: Education and Outreach* 2 (2009): 95–100, 99.

33. See Frank D. Aquila, "Educational Malpractice: A Tort En Ventre," *Cleveland State Law Review* 39 (1991): 323–355, 325 and 326.

34. *Peter W. v. San Francisco Unified School District*, 60 Cal. App. 3d 814 (Ct. App. 1976).

35. 957 F.2d 410 (7th Cir. 1992).

36. For a discussion of these reimbursement cases, see Richard Fossey & Todd. A. DeMitchell, "Case Commentary: Students, the COVID Pandemic, and Academic

Dislocation: Tuition Reimbursement Lawsuits in New England," *Education Law Update* (Education Law Association) 1(4) (2021): 15–17.

37. 957 F.2d 410, 416 (7th Cir. 1992).

38. The authors developed and administered the EMVS as judgmental or expert sample of school law professors and attorneys. Their study, "Educational Malpractice: A Tort Whose Time Has Come? An Exploratory Mixed Methods Study," was accepted for publication by the *University of Florida Journal of Law & Public Policy*. Its publication has been planned for volume 32 issue 2, spring 2022.

39. 64 F. Supp. 2d 945 (C.D. 1999).

40. For an excellent review on VAM that raises a cautionary flag, see Mark A. Paige, *Building a Better Teacher: Understanding Value-Added Models in the Law of Teacher Evaluation* (Lanham, MD: Rowman & Littlefield, 2016).

41. Simon Burgess, Shenila Rawal, & Eric S. Taylor, *Characterising Effective Teaching* (Bristol: Nuffield Foundation & the School of Economics, University of Bristol): 2, https://www.nuffieldfoundation.org/wp-content/uploads/2022/05/Burgess-Characterising-Effective-Teaching-Full-Report-April-2022.pdf. The rubric of standards and associated descriptions of "Effective" can be found on pages 48–49. The authors concluded:

> This report has examined the influence of teachers' instructional practices: the choices teachers make about how to teach, and the extent to which they successfully carry out those choices. Using data from peer classroom observations, we document meaningful relationships between teachers' observed practices and their students' test scores. While not necessarily causal relationships, those relationships can aid in our individual and collective efforts to improve schooling. (Ibid., 43)

Section I

PROFESSIONAL MALPRACTICE

A Tort of Negligence

Chapter 2

The Paradox of the Teacher as a Professional and Education as a Profession

> Because the foundation of an educated society relies on the teachers who daily interact with students from early childhood to young adulthood, it is important to understand what it means to be a professional teacher.[1]

A profession is distinguished from an occupation. "Historically, the conceptualization of the professional and of professionalism referred to the level of autonomy and internal regulation exercised by members of an occupation in providing services to society."[2] In Europe, in the eighteenth and nineteenth centuries, occupations were differentiated from professions by the level of required special knowledge, a formal code of conduct, and a mandate to carry out the services that support the legal order and promote the common culture.[3]

Professional work, by its very nature, is complex and nonroutine. It involves a standard of practice recognized and adhered to by the practitioners operating within the structure of an accepted code of ethics that is adopted in the best interests of the people that a professional serves. Professionals are accorded a special deference in society, which allows them a measure of autonomy of action. This deference given to professionals also holds them accountable through malpractice when a recipient of their services is injured through a lack of due care. However, the definition of a profession is contested; it has defied common agreement as to its meaning.[4]

WHAT IS A PROFESSION?

TEXTBOX 2.1

A vocation is not a profession because those in it choose to call it one. It must be recognized as such.

Todd A. DeMitchell, Terri A. DeMitchell, & Douglas Gagnon, "Teacher Effectiveness and Value-Added Modeling: Building a Pathway to Educational Malpractice?" *Brigham Young University Education and Law Journal* 2012 (2012): 257–301, 300.

Is there a difference between asserting that you are a professional and claiming that you arc a member of a profession? In our common vernacular we often hear individuals assert that they are professionals. We also hear people describe someone's work as being professional or remark that they were treated professionally. The terms professional and profession are often used with little clarity as to what constitutes a profession and what acts are indicative of the good standing in a particular profession. All too often the claim of being a professional is a rhetorical device to elevate and imbue one's position with the mantle of authority.

To better understand what it means to act as a professional and sift through the number of uses to assist with our discussion, we posit that there are three major uses of what it means to be and act as a professional. A short discussion of the three follows.

First, a professional is someone who gets paid for a specific job as opposed to an amateur. For example, an amateur athlete is different from a professional athlete. Aside from a greater skill set, professional athletes are paid for their efforts. The parent who volunteers in their child's classroom lays no claim to being a professional teacher. On the other hand, a classroom teacher is recognized as a professional who usually holds a state-issued teaching certificate and who receives a paycheck for services rendered. To describe someone as an amateur teacher would be to cast aspersions on that teacher's competence.

Second, the word professional is commonly used to describe the way work is performed. People who use the word professional in this way often cite the demeanor of the worker toward the recipient of the work or the high quality of the work. It is used often to refer to a client's satisfaction with the work and the worker. In these situations, the focus is on the work without being tethered to a particular occupation.

For example, the cab driver who takes someone to the airport might be described as professional in that the cabbie was polite, attentive to safety, and punctual. A house painter who does a good job and completes a project on time might be described as a worker who has completed a task in a professional manner.

Similarly, educators are expected to act professionally and to refrain from unprofessional behavior that might give rise to disciplinary action based on the failure to act in a professional manner. A teacher who uses profanity in the presence of students or behaves belligerently toward superiors or colleagues might be said to be acting unprofessionally.

A third construction of the term professional is its use to describe an individual who is a member of a learned profession. These were traditionally law, medicine, and divinity and were "essentially intellectual in character,"[5] as described in the influential 1915 Flexner Report on the preparation of physicians. These professions are highly regulated and guided by their members' professional associations: the American Medical Society, for example, or a state bar association. The associations control entry into the profession they regulate and generally operate autonomously to uphold the standard of practice in the profession while adhering to their established ethical standards in service of others.[6]

George Strauss identified three main categories for organizing organizations that include professionals.

1. *Professional Societies*, concerned with the advancement of knowledge and/or professional interests.
2. *Quasi-Unions*, associations with a professional base and job-oriented interests.
3. Unions, which concentrate on the economic situation of their members.[7]

This chapter focuses are on neither of the conceptions of professionals—the professional athlete versus the amateur athlete or the cab driver who treats you in a professional manner and gets you directly to your destination quickly and in one piece. Instead, this chapter will focus on people who are members of a learned profession, or as Strauss would say, a member of a *professional society*.

TEXTBOX 2.2

Thus, knowledge, autonomy, and service have been considered the hallmarks of a profession.

Mary Antony Blair, "Teacher Professionalism: What Educators Can Learn from Social Workers," *Mid-Western Educational Researcher* 26(2) (2014): 28–57, 28.

The Learned Profession

As stated earlier, a profession is distinguished from an occupation. "Only professionals are *expected* to act in the public interest, to create a calculus that balances self-and-civic interest."[8] The term profession has its etymological roots in Latin for profess (*professio*). The individual makes a public declaration to be an expert in some skill or field of knowledge. The word professional can also be traced back to Old French, which is defined as professing or declaring one's faith, such as taking religious vows.[9] The Apostles' Creed, for example, is a profession of faith adopted by the Roman Catholic Church and some Protestant denominations.

Professionalism is built around expert knowledge, usually gained through extensive education and training.[10] Professional work is complex and non-routine. It involves a standard of practice recognized and adhered to by the practitioners but applied in varying contexts. The standards are enforced by the professional organization, typically through an internal code of ethics.[11] Professionals exercise judgment within the accepted standards of practice and within the articulated ethics for professional conduct in the best interest of the client or others.[12]

"Professionals are obligated to do whatever is best for the client, not what is easiest, most expedient, or even what the client himself or herself might want."[13] Similarly, William J. Goode argued that one of the two core principles of professionalism is a "service orientation."[14] The second is a specialized body of knowledge gained through extended study.

Building on the concepts of service and a specialized body of knowledge, David Carr identifies five propositions of a profession. His list, which is based on a study of the literature, includes the following precepts: (1) professions provide an important public service; (2) they involve a theoretically as well as practically grounded expertise; (3) they have a distinct ethical dimension which calls for expression in a code of practice; (4) they require organization and regulation for purposes of recruitment and discipline; and (5) professional practitioners require a high degree of individual autonomy for effective practice.[15]

Similarly, Tamar Ruth Horowitz, in her study of professionalism and semi-professionalism in education, describes a profession as follows:

(a) A profession is based upon a systematic body of knowledge that is both theoretical and practical.
(b) The professional mediates between the body of knowledge and the individual.
(c) The professional performs an essential service to the community.
(d) The professional requires a long period of training.

(e) The professional enjoys a high degree of authority.
(f) The profession practices a specific code of ethics.
(g) The profession involves a high degree of commitment.
(h) The profession has intensive "in-service" training.[16]

Simply put, professionals exercise the standard of accepted practice acknowledged by their profession within the structure of an accepted code of ethics that is offered in the best interests of the client/patient/student. Their practice is based on a body of specialized knowledge gained during a period of extended study and is given within an acceptance of considerable autonomous authority for the practitioner.

THE EDUCATION PROFESSION: THE PARADOX

TEXTBOX 2.3

Teaching seems to have more than its share of status anomalies. It is honored and distained, praised as "dedicated service" and lampooned as "easy work. . . . [teaching] has occupied a special but shadowed social standing.

Dan C. Lortie, *Schoolteacher: A Sociological Study* (Chicago, IL: University of Chicago Press, 1975): 10.

Are teachers considered professionals in the sense that they belong to a learned and highly skilled profession—a profession that is given a great deal of autonomy like that accorded to the professions of law and medicine? Are teachers accorded not only the deference that comes with their status but also held accountable as other professionals are held accountable for the services that they provide? Tichenor and Tichenor raise this question, writing, "While teachers may be viewed differently than other professionals, the importance of effective teachers in societal change cannot be underestimated."[17]

The impact of teachers on the education of children is widely accepted. Teachers view themselves as professionals,[18] but the wider community may not hold the same view of their status; a classroom teacher is not always associated with being a professional. Researcher Frederick Hess provocatively stated:

So—heresy alert—I suspect that the very question we're asking tonight—how to professionalize teaching?—is likely to lead us astray. I'd like to consider the possibility that teaching isn't a profession at all. It's a craft.[19] Like being a plumber, electrician, or air traffic controller. Honorable work. And the people who do this work are pretty good at it. Because they've been *trained* for the job they're hired to do. [20]

The acceptance of teaching as a profession for purposes of exploring educational malpractice is important and problematic. As Tamar Ruth Horowitz writes, "In certain respects teaching may be defined as a 'profession', while in other respects it can be more appropriately defined as a 'semi-profession.'"[21] Etizoni's seminal work, *The Semi-Professions and Their Organization: Teachers, Nurses, Social Workers*,[22] which developed the concept of the semiprofession, identified its following characteristics:

(1) Semiprofessions are an integral part of the bureaucratic organization of which it is a part.
(2) Semiprofessionals communicate knowledge rather than applying it.
(3) The training required is short and specific.
(4) The degree of commitment of the semiprofessional is limited.
(5) The practitioners are typically female.[23]

Semiprofessions are often regarded as having a lower social status with a shorter period of preparation/training with a less developed body of knowledge that directs practice. Members of semiprofessions typically have less autonomy and are held accountable through their supervisors rather than through the profession. In a law review article, Patrick Halligan asserted that education is not a profession within the construct of malpractice—"it is not a learned profession."[24]

Law Professor Frank D. Aquila, echoing Amitai Etizoni, asserting that education is a semiprofession, writes:

> A fundamental problem in trying to apply an educational malpractice cause of action is that education, itself is not a profession, at least, not in the sense of medicine and law. Professionalism may be considered a continuum with true "professions" at one end and "professionals, in name only," at the other end of the continuum. . . . A semi-profession, such as teaching, can be placed in the middle of this continuum.[25]

The issue of whether education is a profession is central to the issue of claiming malpractice and proving malpractice. Etizoni notes that some semiprofessions are in the process of becoming professions through a process of "professionalization." He considers education to be one of these semiprofessions. The push for the professionalization of education has swept across the education landscape for several decades with varying degrees of success.

Noted education commentator John Goodlad, states that four conditions must be in place before teaching can be considered a viable profession: (1) a coherent body of knowledge and skills; (2) some form of "professional" control over admission to teacher-education programs, with autonomy to decide the appropriate knowledge, skills, and standards; (3) a level of homogeneity in teacher-education candidates; and (4) a clear demarcation between qualified and unqualified candidates and legitimate programs and illegitimate programs.[26]

Specific to education and professionalism, the National Board for Professional Teaching Standards has identified five core propositions: (1) teachers are committed to students and their learning; (2) teachers know the subjects they teach and how to teach those subjects to students; (3) teachers are responsible for managing and monitoring student learning; (4) teachers think systematically about their practice and learn from experience; and (5) teachers are members of the learning communities.[27] These five propositions are supported by the assumptions that professionalism is predicated upon the following:

> A body of specialized, expert knowledge together with a code of ethics emphasizing service to clients. The knowledge base typically provides substantial, but not complete, guidance for professional practice. Professionals possess expert knowledge, but often confront unique, problematic situations that do not lend themselves to formulaic solutions. Professionals must cultivate the ability to cope with the unexpected and act wisely in the face of uncertainty. . . . Professionals . . . pursue an ethic of service and . . . employ special knowledge and expertise in the interests of their clients.[28]

Echoing the National Board, Linda Darling-Hammond offered the following three principles of professionalism:

1. Knowledge is the basis for permission to practice and for decisions that are made with respect to the unique needs of clients.
2. The practitioner pledges his or her first concern of welfare to the client.
3. The profession assumes collective responsibility for the definition, transmittal, and enforcement of professional standards of practice and ethics.[29]

While teaching satisfies some but not all of the criteria for a profession,[30] there has been a push for professionalization, which includes the development of a systematic body of knowledge that leads to standards of practice based on developing research on best practices and extended preparation, including longer periods of internship/student teaching and graduate-level requirements, as well as heightened criteria for admission to education programs. This movement has implications for the potential development of malpractice in education as a means of accountability to the public for important services rendered.

THE TEACHERS' VOICE: PERCEPTIONS OF WHAT MEANS TO BE A PROFESSIONAL EDUCATOR

TEXTBOX 2.4

Professional educators are connected to their purpose and driven by their moral compass. They have servant hearts and believe deeply in serving others.

Elementary School Assistant Principal (Response to Educators' Descriptors Study of the Profession (2021).

David Schuman posits, "Teachers want to be respected, want to be thought of as professionals, yet are members of strong labor unions."[31] Union membership and professional status may add to the paradox. In the first of a two-part study of teachers' perceptions of the compatibility of their dual role as a professional and a union member, 99 percent of the respondents agreed or strongly agreed that teaching is a profession ($M = 4.91$ out of Likert scale of 1–5).[32] Professionalism holds a special place for teachers.

The following question in the study asked whether professionalism is compatible with union activity. A total of 66 percent of the responding teachers agreed or strongly agreed with the stem question. The authors concluded their quantitative study of teacher perceptions by observing that "teachers are professionals. How their professionalism meshes with union membership and bargained contracts is tangled."[33]

Their follow-up study delved into the respondents' responses to the two prompts: "Unions support professionalism in the following ways" and "Unions harm professionalism in the following ways."[34] Reponses to union support for professionalism were organized into three themes: Protection, Advocacy, and Support.[35] Responses to union harm of professionalism had four themes: Blind Protection, Work of the Union, Divisiveness, and the Union Label.[36] The study's authors concluded:

> The findings of our research underscore that the teachers' view of professionalism and unionism is tangled. Teachers want the perceived protection that an industrial union historically affords its members. They also want the prestige of being recognized as a professional.[37]

In a study of teachers' perceptions of their academic freedom,[38] education professors Fries, Connelly, and DeMitchell conducted focus group research with public school teachers.[39] The participants were given a scenario on academic freedom that served as a springboard for the discussion.

Higher education considers academic freedom to be a constitutionally based freedom. The teachers in this qualitative study did not adopt the default position that the U.S. Constitution is the foundation for their academic freedom. Instead, the first theme that emerged from the data was that professionalism is defined by academic freedom and not the Constitution.

The teacher participants consistently referred to professionalism when discussing the contours of their academic freedom. Professionalism to them was less of a right and more of a responsibility. The focus of academic freedom was "on the learning of the student whereas in higher education the concern is with the autonomy of the professor."[40] The focus group couched their analysis of academic freedom in terms of their professional relationship to the students—students stand at the center of academic freedom, not the Constitution. This supports the service-to-other construct of a profession.

Teachers' Perspectives on Professionalism (2004–2005)

As seen earlier, a profession has some unifying concepts that give it structure. We also saw that some commentators raise concerns about whether, or to what degree, teachers fit into the professional construct. The voice of the teacher is important; how individuals perceive their role is important in how they construct their actions. Do the perceptions of teachers fit within the traditional construct of a profession? Do those perceptions reflect their work as a semiprofession or does the profession of teaching need a reconceptualization to more accurately capture its work and ethics?

Hugh Sockett identified five major attributes of a professional teacher.[41] These include character, commitment to change and continuous improvement, subject matter knowledge, pedagogical knowledge and obligations, and working relationships beyond the classroom.[42] Sockett's book was based on research in three classrooms. It sought to link the professional role of teachers, the moral demands of teaching, and the practical arts of teaching.

Tichenor and Tichenor conducted a focus group study at four elementary schools a decade after Sockett's work.[43] They organized their findings into Sockett's five categories of professionalism. Tichenor and Tichenor found that the teachers' comments from their research were most consistent with Sockett's category of character. Their participant's responses for character comprised the longest list of characteristics. Subject matter knowledge and pedagogical knowledge were collapsed into one category, with pedagogical knowledge weighted more heavily, possibly because the sample population

Table 2.1   Tichenor and Tichenor's Category Descriptors

Tichenor and Tichenor
Focus Group Questions:
1. What does it mean to be a professional teacher?
2. How do teachers exhibit professionalism?

Character	Commitment to Change and Continuous Improvement	Subject Matter and Pedagogical Knowledge	Beyond the Classroom
• Composed • Conscientious • Creative • Resilient • Respect for students • Passion for teaching • Good morals* • Good ethics* • Goal-oriented • Set high standards for self and students • Dress appropriately	• Continues education • Seeks opportunities to grow • Participates in meaningful professional development • Seeks opportunities to grow • Reflective	• Have knowledge of the curriculum • Articulate in various strategies • Possess content knowledge	• Collaboration and cooperation with faculty, staff, administration, and community members • Effective communications • Role model inside and outside the classroom • Mentors other teachers when appropriate

Source: Mercedes S. Tichenor & John M. Tichenor, "Understanding Teachers' Perspectives on Professionalism," *The Professional Educator* XXVII (fall 2004 and spring 2005): 89–95, 92–94.
Note: * Both of these are consistent with codes of conduct and codes of ethics.

was elementary school teachers. Tichenor and Tichenor's findings fit into Sockett's typology.

A sample of the descriptors in their categories is listed in table 2.1 and will be compared with the authors' research conducted in the fall of 2021.[44] It is important to note that Sockett's and the Tichenor and Tichenor's research identified professional responsibilities beyond the classroom, which is typically not identified as part of professional responsibilities in descriptions of medical, legal, and other professions.

Educators' Descriptor Study of the Profession

The authors, in the fall of 2021, conducted a qualitative study of educator perceptions of the profession. A total of 282 educators were surveyed, and all individuals had either worked or were currently serving as teachers and administrators. The educators contacted by email comprise a convenience sample compiled by the first author. The research did not request demographic data because the data would not be disaggregated.

The respondents were asked to list five words "that you believe best describe what is a professional educator." Respondents were also given the opportunity to share comments about the professional educator. Forty-two responded (15 percent) by submitting five descriptors, for a total of 210 responses. Twenty-one added comments on the professional educator and three submitted comments that educators were not professionals.

The 210 responses were analyzed using an emergent inductive qualitative analysis of theme-building, in which all responses were read and preliminary themes were identified through an iterative winnowing process.[45] The working themes were distilled into final themes. The first reviewer/author shared the rough data with a second reviewer/author along with the distilled themes and placement of statements into the appropriate themes with nonresponsive statements removed, such as "exploited," "manipulated," and "no excuses."[46] There was agreement between the two reviewer/authors; thus, a third review for a tiebreaker was not necessary. The same process was used for the added comments.

It is important to note the limitations of this type of data analysis. For example, we were unable to "probe" or ask, "What is happening here?"[47] It was problematic to do member checks to support validity or to do theoretical sampling.[48] Furthermore, the one-shot aspect of the short-answer data precluded the "unfolding" of data from in-depth interviewing or multiple sequential interviews.

The 196 cataloged responses are organized into five themes (see table 2.2 for descriptors):

(1) *Personal Characteristics* ($N = 76$, 38.8 percent), with two subthemes applied to individuals and applied to work:

   a. This theme is similar to the Tichenor and Tichenor's study. Both studies identify the internal characteristics that the educator brings to the classroom/school. The set of descriptors are closely aligned with the exception of the descriptor "caring," which is the most selected descriptor in the authors' theme, but it did not surface in the Tichenor and Tichenor's study.

(2) *Work Competence* ($N = 46$, 23.5 percent):

   a. This theme is similar to the Tichenor and Tichenor's category of Subject Matter Knowledge and Pedagogical Knowledge. Both refer to a level of knowledge necessary for educators to perform their duties.

(3) *Advanced Education* (N = 33, 16.8 percent):

    a. This theme is similar to Commitment to Change and Continuous Improvement, in that both studies identify the importance of continual learning. The difference is that this study identifies a higher level of education/training leading to expertise and specialized knowledge.

(4) *Relationships* (N = 21, 10.7 percent):

    a. The Tichenor and Tichenor's study did not identify relationships as associated with the professional educator. Instead, it was wrapped into their Beyond the Classroom category. What stands out in the more recent study is the identification of communication and collaboration as critical elements of successful teaching. The interconnection of teachers in the daily rhythm of the school and the importance of prior learning experiences of students are some of the major characteristics that tend to set education apart from other professions. Integrated learning through an articulated curriculum, the sharing of student learning responsibilities, and the shared responsibility for developing and maintaining the culture of the school and not just the climate in individual classrooms were other themes identified in the recent study. While a teacher may close their classroom door for instruction, the interrelations with others at the school require the development and exercise of effective interpersonal skills.

(5) *Ethical Behavior* (N = 20, 10.2 percent):

    a. Both studies identify this set of dispositions as integral to the professional educator. The difference is that the Tichenor and Tichenor's study folded ethical behavior into their Character category.

The two studies conducted just less than two decades apart have a large overlap of descriptors as to what constitutes the profession of education. The studies used different qualitative research methods with different populations in different time periods but still found commonality regarding the perceptions of the descriptions of the professional educator. Together the two studies may represent a shared perception of what constitutes the education profession.

A second part of the educators' descriptor study offered the participants an unstructured opportunity to comment about the professional educator. Responses from twenty-one respondents, some with multiple comments, were analyzed using the same inductive qualitative methods as the five descriptors analysis. It did not use a deductive method.[49] Only one major theme emerged from the data: alignment with the five categories of descriptors.[50] However, before we start the analysis, we were struck by two sets of comments that raised issues but did not rise to the level of a theme.

Table 2.2   Educators' Descriptor Study of the Profession (2021)

Educators Thematic Responses to:
"List Five Words That You Believe Best Describe What a Professional Educator Is."
196 Responses

Personal Characteristics (N = 76)	Work Competence (N = 46)	Advanced Education (N = 33)	Relationships (N = 21)	Ethical Behavior (N = 20)

• Individual
  - Empathetic
  - Caring
  - Compassionate
  - Respectful
  - Credible
• Work
  - Hard-working
  - Responsive
  - Purposeful
  - Creative/
    Innovative
  - Reflective/
    Inquisitive
	• Knowledgeable
	• Experienced
	• Educated
	• Skilled
	• Qualified/
	  Licensed
		• Highly
		  Educated
		• Life-Long
		  Learner
		• Expertise/
		  Expert
		• Specialized
		  Knowledge
			• Collaborator
			• Communicator
			• Student-
			  Centered
				• Ethical
				• Dedicated
				• Integrity
				• Principled

First, an elementary school teacher wrote, "This question is difficult to answer." And a former teacher, private school assistant principal, and public school high school principal began his comments by writing,

> After 15 years working as a teacher and school administrator, I drew an absolute blank when asked to describe the Professional Educator. It is NOT because I questioned the professionalism of the discipline but more so in the articulation of the professional practice. (Emphasis in original) (Educators' Descriptors Study of the Profession [2021], hereafter Educators' Descriptors Study)

While it is reasonable that asking someone to define something often gives them pause to organize their thoughts,[51] these aforementioned comments raise an interesting question: while educators assert their status as a professional, what it means to be a professional may not only be contested territory, but it may also be that it is a concept not clearly understood by educators. A consensus of what are the earmarks of a professional educator may help with the preparation and practice of a professional educator. Agreed-upon definitions of concepts serve as an anchor for the application of the concept.

Two comments raised the question of whether the status of professional should be conferred upon the completion of extended education and the granting of the proper licensure/credential. Instead, these two comments raise the question of whether professional status is automatic upon the issuance of a teaching certificate or whether professional recognition must be earned through practice. The two comments follow.

> In my mind, you don't automatically become a professional due to being hired. You become a professional based on behavior, achievement, and mindset.
> I think what I am getting to is that being a professional is something you demonstrate and earn—not a title given to everyone because they have the same job. (Educators' Descriptors Study)

However, the question of whether the status of professional educator must be earned is a deviation from the general literature on professions.

This set of comments is similar to research on teacher perceptions of academic freedom. In that research, a group of public school and private school educators took part in a focus group to discuss a scenario on K–12 academic freedom.[52] The third theme emerging from this research, defining academic freedom in K–12 education, was "professionalism." Similar to the aforementioned comments, one focus-group participant stated, "I don't think that you get [academic freedom] right away. Even when you get the job, I think that you have to earn it."[53]

The authors wrote of this theme as follows:

> The teachers in this focus group did not describe academic freedom as a right, which is bestowed by virtue of employment or credentialing. They character-ized it more as something that is earned through the development of expertise.[54]

The following comments from the Educators' Descriptor Study added depth and context to the earlier-mentioned themes. Their placement may be the subject of discussion, with some blending of categories. However, each fit into the composite perceptions of the respondents.

Personal Characteristics

Being a professional means treating students, families and colleagues with respect, using our skill set to help students succeed/achieve, and helping parents or guardians to do their best for their children.
I know many educators that I would consider professionals—they are learn-ers, and respectful, they have a servant leadership attitude with colleagues and their students, and they are always doing what's in the best interest of their students and communities.

Work Competence

A professional educator is someone who is trained and qualified to promote learning in a structured environment by adhering to practices that promote growth and curiosity to enhance the natural learning abilities of student(s).

More than anything, especially in these times, I see professionalism in educators through their ability to rise above daily negativity and trials to create
a positive and safe world for children.

A professional educator is one that is perceived by a reasonable community
as a leader that has the unique skills and dispositions to enhance the knowledge and competency, relating to a specific subject/topic, of others that are
under their responsibility.

Advanced Education

Key for me is specialized knowledge and skill, research-based, peer reviewed,
collaborative, licensed by an external agency with an expectation to stay
current in the field of specialization.

Relationships

Deep, empathetic understanding of these challenges, coupled with receptive
and expressive communication skills that extend to student, parent, and
collaborative exchanges with peers are required to navigate through complex and often contentious territory.

Ethical Behavior

A professional educator is willing to meet needs beyond the end of the school
day and is eager to comply with accommodations necessary for student
access and equity.

It is not surprising that the majority of the added comments aligned with the
descriptor themes, even though they were separate questions. The value of these
data is not the discovery of new themes of the profession of education. Rather
these comments add texture and depth and push against the silo approach to
what constitutes a profession. Themes and aspects of what constitutes a learned
society underscore the interactions and blending of its core concepts. A learned
society is more than a checklist, even as useful as checklists are.

The last portion of the Educators' Descriptor Study research gave participants the option of stating that education is not a profession and adding any
comments they wished to make. Three participants responded "Yes" to the
statement "I do not believe that educators are considered to be professionals."
The following are their comments.

Teachers are not paid like other professions and they often do not have professional independence nor the ability to exercise their best professional judgment.[55]
    While my answer to question A is that educators are not considered profes-
sionals, that answer is based primarily on the attitudes of others outside of

education who, regardless of how they may talk about educators, do not treat teachers as though they truly consider them to be professionals. This opinion is based upon my reading of the literature on teacher compensation, which consistently espouses the notions that educators work by the hour. It is also based on my experiences of how non-educators approach teachers when they are dissatisfied with an outcome (grades, discipline matters, etc.).[56]

The last commentator in the study responded that educators are not considered professionals by non-educators due to collective bargaining agreements that do not reflect the real work of educators, salary schedules that do not differentiate mediocre from outstanding, evaluation systems, lack of accountability, and "the inability of educators to articulate their practice through the lens of substantive research and action research within their own classroom is a significant barrier." (See the earlier discussion on the tension between union membership and membership in a profession.)

There is a consensus among the educator participants in the above-discussed studies that education is a profession. However, the commentators assert that education is not a profession in the mold of the traditional construction of a learned society. We conclude this chapter with a discussion of our template for the core elements of a profession. Next, we will discuss the context of education and its fit within the template.

A LEARNED SOCIETY TEMPLATE

The descriptive studies and the descriptions of the profession discussed earlier, it can be argued, provide a consensus upon which it is possible to draw a template of a learned society (profession). The proposed template has four major core phases, one building on the other. These phases are also structured by influences. A short beginning discussion of the phases and a discussion of the influences follow. It is not meant as an in-depth application of the template to education or to other professions whose members are considered to be part of a learned society. The phases are discussed in order.

Phase 1: Extensive Knowledge Attainment

Professionals are expected to have mastered a specialized knowledge base before beginning their careers? The knowledge base is more than a survey of information. It is an in-depth exploration based on accepted theories (Influence), over time, of the information and knowledge that informs and directs practice. It extends over initial entry into the profession to include ongoing professional development activities.

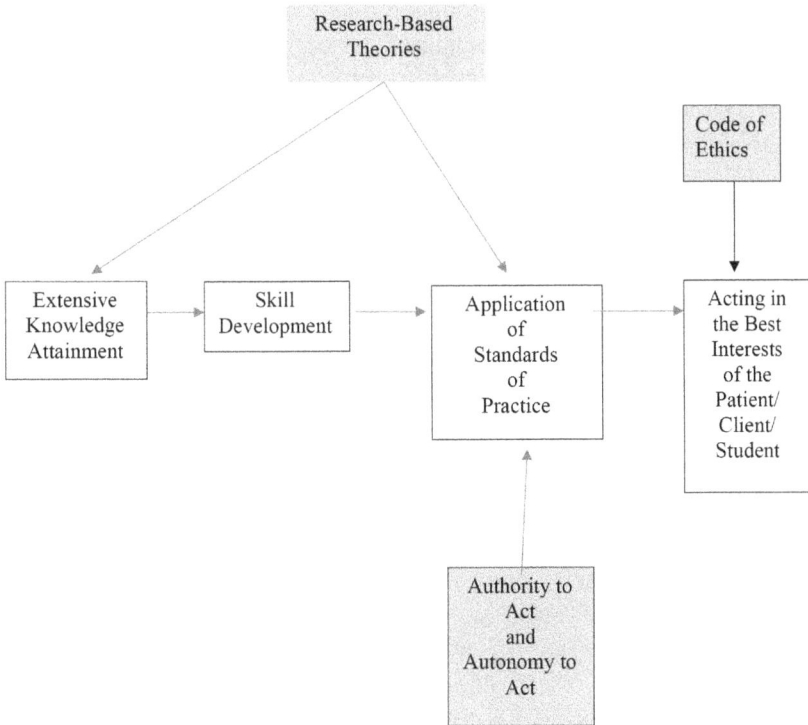

Figure 2.1   The Profession: A Four-Phase and Influences Template for a Learned Society

Law graduates, for example, must pass a bar examination to become licensed attorneys. These exams are administered by the various state bar associations, which operate independently from law schools. Some states have particularly rigorous bar exams, with high failure rates. In California, for example, 29 percent of first-time test-takers failed the bar exam in July 21, 2021. Among people who previously failed the exam and were taking it again, almost four out of five exam-takers failed.[57] Thus, law graduates who fail their state's bar exam are barred from practicing law even if they successfully complete their studies and obtain their JD degrees.

Medicine and law both require students to obtain both an undergraduate degree and doctoral-level education—the MD degree for medicine and the JD for law. In these professions, the professional organization defines the knowledge necessary for practice and ensures that the students complete their professional programs through rigid objective testing.

Phase 2: Skill Development

The knowledge base that professional-school students learn in their academic programs generally leads to mastery of theoretical knowledge. A law student will have learned the basic concepts of contract law and tort law. An MD graduate will have mastered specialized knowledge of diseases.

After graduation, fledging professionals are placed in some kind of practice-based internship. MD graduates complete their training in hospital-based internships, which can be followed by a residency program in the MD graduate's chosen specialty—internal medicine, for example, or psychiatry.

Law school graduates may complete a short internship in law school, but they are expected to master their professional skills in the world of practice. Most go to work in law firms, district attorneys' offices, or other public law agencies, where they practice under the guidance of a skilled practitioner.

Phase 3: Application of Standards of Practice

Professions develop standards of practice based on the knowledge base (Phase 1) and the theories (Influence) that define the profession. These constitute the expectations of practice that guide the prudent professional's actions. It is the way that things should be done, based on the research and definition of best practices approved by the profession. Failure to follow these standards of practice is generally regarded as negligence and can lead to a malpractice lawsuit.

For example, a lawyer who fails to file a lawsuit before the statute of limitation expires is guilty of legal malpractice and can be held liable for his client's damages. A doctor who removes the wrong organ during surgery is likewise guilty of medical malpractice can be sued for the injuries that were caused through negligence.

Professionals who are grossly negligent can lose their licenses to practice and are basically kicked out of the profession. In particularly egregious circumstances, they can be prosecuted for criminal negligence.

Phase 4: Acting in the Best Interests of the Patient/Client/Student

This last phase is the culmination of extensive and intensive studies, the development of skills through practice, internships, and residencies, in which the standards of practice are implemented in the best interests of the recipient. This phase keeps both the patient and the client at the center of the actions of the professional. Examples include the Hippocratic Oath, "First do no harm" (to the patient) and student-centered instruction.

Influences: Research-Based Theories, Authority and Autonomy to Act, and Codes of Ethics

Three of the phases (1, 3, and 4) are influenced by factors that provide context. The influence factors are theories, authority and autonomy for actions by the professional, and codes of ethics. Each influence will be discussed next.

Research-based theories are central to organizing data and information. They are essential in developing explanations of phenomena and forming a basis for action. A theory of how something works influences how the work will be conducted or how it is understood. It is a connection to existing knowledge. Theories are used in Phase 1. The prevalent theories are taught along with the knowledge to support the theory.

Theories are used in Phase 3 to assist the professional to act in more informed and efficient ways. Because professional work is complex and often confronts novel situations, theories are used to help the professional make sense of the issue.

As indicated by Phase 3, professional work almost always requires action. But a hallmark of professional action is the authority to act, granted by virtue of membership in the profession. The profession is recognized as a legitimate public actor who acts for the benefit of the public. "An occupation [is] recognized as a profession in part because people believe that its members jointly possess arcane knowledge on matters of vital public concern."[58]

The autonomy to act is granted to professionals due to their recognized expertise exercised to advance a public good. Their autonomy to act is an integral part of the profession. Professions are relatively free from outside oversight but held accountable by their profession with the license to practice and through malpractice suits. However, autonomy does not mean complete immunity from oversight.

Physicians who wish to practice in a hospital must first apply for hospital privileges to perform specified medical procedures at the hospital.[59] Permission to perform specific types of procedures, such as transplants, is reviewed by committees of peers. Attorneys admitted to the Bar are granted permission to practice law in specific jurisdictions.[60] State Bar membership is granted by the relevant state bar association, based on a finding that the applicant has mastered the basic rules of law that are in place in that particular state.

For example, several states in the West (California and Texas) have adopted legal principles from Spanish law, and some of these principles are different from the law in states that were shaped by the British common law. Likewise, some Louisiana law is based on the Napoleonic code, which is unique among the fifty state jurisdictions.

In all cases, the permission to practice a particular profession in a specific jurisdiction is governed by professionals (medical boards and the state bar associations). Laypersons are not decision makers or gatekeepers for the professions.

The professions are distinguished from other vocations in another way. A true profession requires its members to abide by a written ethics code promulgated to protect the best interests of the recipient of the services.[61] All professions have a code of ethics that guides the practice of their members.[62] "Professional codes of ethics represent a consensus of the normative values, beliefs, and concerns about appropriate behavior."[63] The code of ethics supports the commitment to serve the public and serves as a balance to professional autonomy. Skills and knowledge are often the leading criteria for admission to practice.

However, morality also influences a professional person's right to practice. For example, the Council on Ethical and Judicial Affairs of the American Medical Association requires physicians to act in an ethical manner defined by a "body of ethical statements developed primarily for the benefit of the patient."[64] Similarly, the American Bar Association has rules for professional conduct.[65]

Four phases and three influences help to define the chapter's question: "What is a profession?" But what of education, how does it fit into the template? Education and the template will be briefly explored.

EDUCATION AND THE TEMPLATE: EARLY THOUGHTS

TEXTBOX 2.5

The quality of teachers and teaching is undoubtedly among the most important factors shaping the learning and growth of students.

Richard M. Ingersoll, "Power, Accountability, and the Teacher Quality Problems," in Sean Kelly (ed.), *Assessing Teacher Quality: Understanding Teacher Effects on Instruction and Achievement* (New York: Teachers College Press, 2011): 97.

The Education Context: A Snapshot

Although the various professions perform a wide variety of services, they are generally understood to provide those services to benefit not only their clients or patients but the larger society as well. Health, an ordered society bounded by law, and the human spirit are unquestionably critical benefits to society as a whole.

Education lays claim to being a profession because the services educators provide benefit not only their students but also the society as a whole. Indeed, all the learned societies are built on a foundation of education. The earlier proclamations from the U.S. Supreme Court capture the importance of education to the citizenry. While there is congruence between the professions, there are important points of divergence.

Nevertheless, there are differences between the traditional learned societies and education. To what degree should those differences serve as the basis for determining whether education is a profession similar to law and medicine? Do those differences justify separating education from the learned societies? Labor and employment relations professor Robert Bruno, commenting on teacher professionalism wrote, "This means that a teacher's classroom experiences, and the teacher-student relationship, is what ultimately creates the boundaries for what it means to be a professional."[66]

Early studies on the professions focused on the traditional professions: societies of medicine, law, and theology. Consequently, the descriptions reflect the work of the individual professional person with an individual patient, client, or parishioner.

Most of the work performed by people in these three professions is done by the individual professional, often involving interactions of short duration but occasionally of more protracted duration in a highly focused situation, such as surgery. Often there is collaboration with peers on a consulting basis. The service is delivered with a high degree of autonomy for the practitioner and deference is given by the recipient of the service. Thus, it makes sense that the descriptors of what constitutes a particular profession inform the foundation of the codes of conduct and ethics for that professional group.

However, the work of teachers does not fit the descriptions discussed earlier. Teachers have prolonged, focused contact with their students (six-and-one-half hours a day, five days a week, 180 days a year). Probably no other professional group has such extended times with their client/patient. In general, educators interact with groups of students, not individuals, although these groups may vary greatly in size from a physical education class and music classes to small, advanced placement classes and special education classes.

Whereas most professionals typically practice with one individual at a time, giving full attention to that individual, teachers have a group of students in which the knowledge gained the and skills being transmitted must be applied in a group setting. This is an integral aspect of the context for schooling.

- Education is a cumulative phenomenon. Current learning is predicated upon prior learning. Teachers must adjust instruction to the readiness of students. If a student or a group of students do not have a firm foundation for the curricular goal, the teacher must adjust his or her instruction.
- Teachers are not only responsible for the effective organization of the curriculum and instructional delivery, but they are also responsible for creating and sustaining an environment conducive to student learning. A disciplined classroom is necessary for the focus of instruction and student activities. Those who have never been responsible for the behavior of a group

of students may not be aware of the challenge, the complexity, and stress involved in developing and maintaining a classroom environment that is conducive to learning. Most professionals are typically not concerned about maintaining control of their patients or clients.

• While professionals typically are considered role models, teachers are legally required to be exemplars for their students. A noted educational historian asserted in 1939 that the conduct of teachers has always been a matter of concern.[67] For example, another education historian stated in 1936 that the parents and community with great sincerity believed that a teacher should serve "the community through an upright exemplary life and whose influence will give their children the characters they themselves aspired to and failed to gain."[68]

The United States Supreme Court captured the mandatory role model expectation, by writing:

A teacher serves as a role model for [his/her] students, exerting a subtle but important influence over their values and perceptions. Thus, through both the presentation of course materials and the example he sets, a teacher has an opportunity to influence the attitudes of students toward government, the political process, and a citizen's social responsibilities. This influence is crucial to the continued good health of a democracy.[69]

In short, educators are held to be exemplars. This obligation "rests on the belief that students, at least in part, acquire their social attitudes and behaviors copying those of their teachers."[70] An Illinois Court of Appeals summed up the position of exemplar, writing, "We are aware of the special position occupied by a teacher in our society. As a consequence of that elevated stature, a teacher's actions are subject to much greater scrutiny than that given to the activities of the average person."[71]

In addition, and important to educational malpractice, Alice J. Klein writes, probably in opposition to Patrick D. Halligan (see note 24), "Although definitions of a profession often exclude education, courts have described educators as professionals, and public policy considerations support this proposition."[72]

Expectations for Teacher Performance

Teachers occupy a critical position in education. They stand at the crossroads of education, directing students to freeways or byways of educational attainment. The importance of their role in the education of the nation's youth is unquestioned. However, for our exploration of teachers for purposes of their competence for expectations of professional practice, we will look at research on teacher effectiveness. Specifically, we have selected the work of Stronge, Ward, and Grant[73] to review as an example of research on teacher effectiveness.

Stronge et al. examined classroom practices of effective versus less effective teachers based on the net gains in student-achievement scores in reading and mathematics. They found four dimensions of teacher efficiency. They caution that the dimensions are not silos and that there is some overlap.

- Instructional Delivery (this demonstrates the complexity of instruction)

  - Instructional Differentiation (including direct instruction, discovery learning, and individualized instruction);
  - Instructional Focus on Learning (spending more time on instruction than classroom management;
  - Instructional Clarity (teacher verbal ability has been linked with student achievement);
  - Instructional Complexity;
  - Expectations for Student Learning;
  - Use of Technology; and
  - Questioning.

- Student Assessment
- Learning Environment

  - Classroom Management;
  - Classroom Organization; and
  - Behavioral Expectations.

- Personal Qualities

  - Caring, Positive Relationships with Students;
  - Fairness and Respect;
  - Encouragement of Responsibility; and
  - Enthusiasm.[74]

The descriptors in table 2.2 dimension Personal Qualities fit into the educator's descriptor study theme of personal characteristics. Other descriptors fit into the Strong et al. findings, such a dedicated, hard-working, and student-centered.

Barak Rosenshine has also developed research-based principles of instruction.[75] While Professor Rosenshine's ten research-based principles are very helpful, they are part of a number of competing findings such as those we saw with the review of the Stronge research. There is not a set of standards that have the widespread acknowledgment of the expected standards that are taught in the nation's schools of education and form the core teaching expectations for practice in the nation's classrooms.

THE PHASES APPLIED TO EDUCATION

Phase 1: Extensive Knowledge Attainment

For K–12 educators, the requirement to acquire an advanced degree beyond the bachelor's degree, while encouraged, primarily through salary schedules that provide for pay raises for teachers with advanced degrees, graduate are typically not mandatory for credential recertification. Massacusetts is an example of an exception to the B.A. only required rule. Although many higher education institutions offer teaching credentials at the graduate level, the dominant required level of education for a teaching credential is a bachelor's degree and completion of a state-approved educator preparation program.

There are no states that require a master's degree for initial certification but several require that teachers complete their master's degree within a specified time from signing their first contract. But some educator specializations require a master's degree, such as school counselors and administrators.

Confounding the situation of extensive knowledge attainment is the nationwide practice of granting emergency credentials and using alternative certification routes. At times of teacher shortages, such as during the COVID-19 pandemic, standards for certification for entry into public school classrooms as a teacher, alternative certification routes become busy.

Professions have a robust research/literature that informs their practice. This is especially true for medicine, in which other fields contribute to their knowledge base. There is also a robust grant structure, starting with the federal government and augmented by foundations and the healthcare industry.

The legal profession is also informed by research, primarily legal periodicals that are sponsored by law schools. According to the University of Michigan Law School Library, there are over 1,500 law journals, including scholarly law journals, bar journals, and law-oriented newsletters.[76]

In recent years, education has increased its focus on building its research base. The American Educational Research Association (AERA) is the premier education-research organization and hosts an annual meeting attended by thousands of scholars and practitioners in the field of education. In 2017, AERA hosted more than 2,500 research-oriented sessions.[77]

Phase 2: Skill Development

Teachers also learn such critical practices as lesson planning, evaluation techniques, curriculum alignment with instruction, and questioning strategies.

Their practical training includes classroom-based experiences and student teaching of varying lengths. A few preparation programs, such as the University of New Hampshire's, require a year-long internship embedded in a classroom during the entire school day.

Phase 3: Application of Standards of Practice

The perception that the field of education lacks recognized standards of practice is a major reason that judges have dismissed educational malpractice lawsuits out of hand. This issue will be discussed in the next chapter. The central question is whether there are recognized standards of teaching practice that are taught and enforced in the schools.

The issue of what to teach is found in various curriculum standards developed by professional associations, state frameworks, and school district policies. The Common Core State Initiative is an example of student-learning goals, defining the skills and understandings that students must demonstrate.[78] What content should be taught is typically hammered out in the crucible of the political process. The controversy over critical race theory and the K–12 curriculum that arose in 2021 is an example of the public struggle over what knowledge is of the greatest worth and deserves a place in the school curriculum.

Instruction is the critical element of professional practice. The Stronge et al. research discussed earlier lists instructional delivery as its first dimension of effectiveness. While there is a duty to teach, the courts have not identified a clear authority as to what constitutes effective instructional practice, or what professors Hutt and Tang call the practice demonstrated by the "reasonably prudent educator."[79]

It is paradoxical, then, that teachers can be dismissed for incompetence but cannot be sued by the recipient of the teacher's ineffectiveness for malpractice.[80] Moreover, very few teachers are fired for ineffective teaching. A nationwide review of teacher-dismissal cases would undoubtedly show that tenured teachers are rarely fired for any reason, and the few who are fired are usually terminated for immoral conduct that generally has little, to do with their instructional practice.

Phase 4: Acting in the Best Interests of the Patient/Client/ Student

It is expected that educators will teach, interact with students, and create classroom climates that value students. A teacher participant in the Educators' Descriptors Study of the Profession (2021) stated, "I know many educators that I would consider professionals—they are learners, and respectful, they have a servant leadership attitude with colleagues and their students, and

they are always doing what's in the best interest of their students and community." Another respondent wrote, "Professional educators are connected
to their purpose and driven by their moral compass. They have servant hearts
and believe deeply in serving others."

Influences Applied to Education

Research-Based Theories

There is no dearth of research-based theories in education. They influence
Phase 1, Extensive Knowledge Attainment, but do they impact Phase 2,
Application of Standards of Practice. Do classroom teachers use educational
theories to influence and direct their practice? In other words, is research and
theories part of the classroom lexicon and practice?

Shana Hurley in a *Yale Law & Policy Review* analysis of the Right to Read
laws asserts that the scientific consensus on reading instruction is not "deeply
embedded" in classrooms.[81] She writes, "Even though reading scientists have
learned how to prevent children from experiencing a lifetime of functional
illiteracy, their findings are not making their way into classrooms."[82]

In fact, perennial reports on the dismal levels of student achievement in
reading and mathematics are evidence of a broader phenomenon—the dis-
connect between educational research and the reality of the American classroom.[83] There are more than 1,200 schools and departments of education in
American colleges and universities,[84] and most of them engage in some level
of research on teaching and learning, pedagogy, and school administration.
It would be difficult to make the argument that these entities have markedly
improved the quality of education in the United States over the past quarter
century, particularly in the schools of the inner cities.

Authority and the Autonomy to Act

Teachers have the authority to act by virtue of their employment. This is also
true for doctors, dentists, attorneys, and district attorneys. Like other professionals, teachers' employment status confers a certain amount of authority for
their practice. But they are also constrained by organizational policies and practices and by the individual policies and goals of the institutions that hired them.

Teachers' autonomy to act is nuanced. While they are employed to teach the
adopted curriculum and supervise their students, they have a certain degree of
autonomy in deciding how to teach the curriculum. When teachers close the
classroom door, their autonomy to act increases from other school settings.

Lortie described teachers' view of their classroom in the following manner:

> We found that they want a degree of boundedness around their classrooms;
> they cathect them, not the organization at large. They want more potentially

productive time with students. They depict other adults as intrusive and hindering, and they yearn for more resources as they try to influence their students. Others, they feel, should support them in their work with students—should uphold rather than denigrate their standing.[85]

In other words, teachers seek to reinforce their autonomy over the classroom, not over the school or over the profession. They are centered in their classroom and their students.

Code of Ethics

Possibly the most widely recognized educational code of ethics is the National Education Association Code of Ethics for Educators, which was adopted in 1975.[86] The code is categorized into a Preamble; Principle I, Commitment to the Student; and Principle II, Commitment to the Profession. The Preamble states in part, "The Code of Ethics of the Education Profession indicates the aspiration of all educators and provides standards by which to judge conduct."

Principle I, Commitment to Students, provides a clear set of expectations that protects students. It defines the contours of the teacher-student relationship. It also may provide a rubric for disciplinary action for unprofessional conduct.

Likewise, Principle II, Commitment to the Profession, obligates educators to uphold the high standards of the teaching profession. This principle admonishes educators not to misrepresent their own credentials or assist unqualified people to obtain the status of a professional teacher.

CONCLUDING COMMENTS

TEXTBOX 2.6

Educators Must Roar and Not Squeak

Such is the prestige of the Nobel award and of this place where I stand that I am impelled, not to squeak like a grateful and apologetic mouse, but to roar like a lion out of pride in my profession and in the great and good men [and women] who have practiced it through the ages

John Steinbeck's speech at the Nobel Banquet at the City Hall in Stockholm,, *The Noble Prize* (December 10, 1962), https://www.nobelprize.org/prizes/ literature/1962/steinbeck/25229-john-steinbeck-banquet-speech-1962/.*

*Our thanks to Louise White, English Teacher, for sharing this quote with us.

This chapter explored the question of what is a profession. We developed a four-phase template with three influence factors to explain what constitutes a profession in the context of learned societies. We believe that the template accurately captures the contours of a profession, and hopefully, will help other researchers focus their study on the field of education as a profession. It is too early to draw conclusions; however, the template provides a focal point for exploration and further research.

Consequently, we cannot state to what degree education fits the phases and influences. Context of service impacts the practice, and the context of educational practice is clearly different from most traditional professions. For example, the exercise of authority and autonomy to act are manifestly differently from the legal or medical practitioner. Educational practice is influenced by the inescapable groupness of teaching. While most professionals also bring their expertise to bear on one individual at a time, the individual recipient of educational services is nested in the group.

This chapter explored what is a profession and the fit with the special context of educators. The next chapter moves from a sociological lens to a legal lens and discusses the tort of negligence.

NOTES

1. Mercedes S. Tichenor & John M. Tichenor, "Understanding Teachers' Perspectives on Professionalism," *The Professional Educator* XXVII (fall 2004 and spring 2005): 89–95, 94.

2. OECD, *Supporting Teacher Professionalism: Insights from TALIS 2013* (Paris: TALIS, OECD, 2016): 28.

3. Ibid.

4. Abdul Rashid Mohmed, "Teachers' Professionalism: Prejudices, Problems, and Promises," *Semantic Scholar* (May 1, 2011), https://cice.hiroshima-u.ac.jp/wp-content/uploads/2014/03/4-3-8.pdf. See also Nihan Demirkasmoglu, "Defining 'Teacher Professionalism' from Different Perspectives," *Procedia: Social and Behavioral Sciences* 9 (2010): 2047–2051, writing, "The concept has been a controversial one in different occupation groups with a long history especially in sociological ground and still it is the subject of many scholarly debates" (p. 2047).

5. Abraham Flexner, *Is Social Work a Profession? Proceedings of the National Conference of Charities and Corrections* (Chicago, IL: Hildmann Printing Company, 1915): 154.

6. Mary Antony Blair, "Teacher Professionalism: What Educators Can Learn from Social Workers," *Mid-Western Educational Researcher* 26(2) (2014): 28–57.

7. George Strauss. "Professionalism and Occupational Associations," *Industrial Relations* 2 (1963): 27. Cited in Gail Ann Schlachter, "Professionalism and Unionism," *Library Trends* 25 (1976): 451–473, 451.

8. Charles T. Kerchner & Douglas E. Mitchell, *The Changing Idea of a Teachers' Union* (Philadelphia, PA: Falmer Press, 1988); 227 (emphasis in original).

9. Author, etymonline.com, https://www.etymonline.com/word/professional; Author, *Oxford English Dictionary* (June 2007, 3rd ed.), https://www.oed.com/viewdictionaryentry/Entry/152052.

10. Eliot Freidson, *Profession of Medicine* (Chicago, IL: University of Chicago Press, 1988).

11. Bernard Barber, "Some Problems in the Sociology of Professions." *Daedalus* 92 (1963): 669–688.

12. For example, The American Psychological Association's Ethical Principles of Psychologists and Code of Conduct sets "forth enforceable rules of conduct as psychologists" (American Psychological Association, "Ethical Principles of Psychologists and Code of Conduct: 2010 Amendments," http://www.apa.org/ethics/code/index.aspx); American Medical Association's Preamble to their Principles of Medical Ethics states, "The following Principles adopted by the American Medical Association are not laws, but standards of conduct which define the essentials of honorable behavior for the physician" (*AMA Code of Medical Ethics*, http://www.ama-assn.org/ama/pub/physician-resources/medical-ethics/code-medical-ethics/principles-medical-ethics.page?); and according to the American Bar Association, "It is professional misconduct for a lawyer to: (a) violate or attempt to violate the Rules of Professional Conduct, knowingly assist or induce another to do so, or do so through the acts of another" (Model Rules of Professional Conduct Maintaining the Integrity of The Profession, Rule 8.4 Misconduct http://www.abanet.org/cpr/mrpc/rule_8_4.html).

For an application of professional standards to instruction in higher education, see Todd A. DeMitchell, David J. Hebert, & Loan T. Phan, "The University Curriculum and the Constitution: Personal Beliefs and Professional Ethics in Graduate School Counseling Programs," *The Journal of College and University Law* 39 (2013): 303–345. The authors conclude, "Personal values are important, but in the public square where who can provide specific professional services is regulated by licensure, the college or university must be able to establish its curriculum to support the ethics of the profession." Ibid., 344.

13. Linda Darling-Hammond, "Accountability for Professional Practice," *Teachers College Record* 91 (1989): 59–80, 67.

14. William J. Goode, "Encroachment, Charlatanism, and the Emerging Profession: Psychology, Medicine, and Sociology," *American Sociological Review* 25 (1960): 902–914, 903.

15. David Carr, *Professionalism and Ethics in Teaching* (London: Routledge, 2000).

16. Tamar Ruth Horowitz, "Professionalism and Semi-Professionalism among Immigrant Teachers from the U.S.S.R. and North America," *Comparative Education* 21 (1985): 297–307, 297.

17. Tichenor & Tichenor, *supra* note 1, 89.

18. Todd A. DeMitchell & Casey D. Cobb, "Teachers: Their Union and Their Profession. A Tangled Relationship," *Education Law Reporter* 212 (2006): 1–20.

19. For a discussion of craft and other options of organizing education (labor, craft, art, professionals) for purposes of public sector collective laws, see Todd A. DeMitchell, *Teachers and Their Unions: Labor Relations in Uncertain Times* (Lanham, MD: Rowman & Littlefield, 2020): 61–63. Public sector bargaining laws selected labor—the industrial union—as the model thus impacting public education and the work of its educators.

20. Frederick Hess, "What Exactly Is Teacher Professionalism, Anyway?" *Education Next* (October 9, 2018) (emphasis in original), https://www.educationnext.org/what-exactly-is-teacher-professionalism-anyway-reading-pondiscio/.

21. Horowitz, *supra* note 16, 297.

22. Amitai Etzioni (ed.), *The Semi-Professions and Their Organization. Teachers, Nurses, Social Workers* (New York: Free Press, 1969).

23. Ibid.

24. Patrick D. Halligan, "The Function of Schools, the Status of Teachers and the Claims of the Handicapped: An inquiry into Special Education Malpractice," *Missouri Law Review* 45 (1980): 667–707, 676 and 677.

25. Frank D. Aquila, "Educational Malpractice: A Tort En Ventre," *Cleveland State Law Review* 39 (1991): 323–355, 354.

26. John I. Goodlad, "The Occupation of Teaching in Schools," in John I. Goodlad, & Kenneth Sirotnik (eds), *The Moral Dimensions of Teaching* (San Francisco, CA: Jossey Bass Publication, 1990): 3–34.

27. National Board of Professional Teaching Standards, "What Teachers Should Know and Be Able to Do: The Five Core Propositions of the National Board," www.nbts.org/about/coreprops.cfm#introfcp, 3–4.

28. Ibid., 6.

29. Darling-Hammond. *supra* note 13, 67.

30. Sonia Guerriero & Karolina Deligiannidi, "The Teaching Profession and Its Knowledge Base," in Sonia Guerro (ed.), *Pedagogical Knowledge and the Changing Nature of the Teaching Profession* (Paris: Centre for Educational Research and Innovation. OECD, February 21, 2017), https://www.oecd-ilibrary.org/education/pedagogical-knowledge-and-the-changing-nature-of-the-teaching-profession_9789264270695-en.

31. David Schuman, *American Schools, American Teachers: Issues and Perspectives* (Boston, MA: Pearson, 2004): 89. Todd A. DeMitchell wrote of this paradox, "Both roles of union member whose interests are being served by a union and a professional who serves the needs of others are legitimate and both may be contradictory at times." Todd A. DeMitchell, *Teachers and Their Unions: Labor Relations in Uncertain Times* (Lanham, MD: Rowman & Littlefield, 2020): 93.

32. Todd A. DeMitchell & Casey D. Cobb, "Teachers: Their Union and Their Profession. A Tangled Relationship," *Education Law Reporter* 212 (2006): 1–20, 11.

33. Ibid., 20.

34. Todd A. DeMitchell & Case D. Cobb, "Teacher as Union Member and Teacher as Professional: The Voice of the Teacher," *Education Law Reporter* 220 (2007): 25–38.

35. Ibid., 32–34.

36. Ibid., 34–36.

37. Ibid., 37.

38. Todd A. DeMitchell & Vincent J. Connelly, "Academic Freedom and the Public School Teacher: An Exploratory Study of Perceptions, Policy and the Law," *Brigham Young University Education and Law Journal* 2007 (2007): 83–117.

39. Kim Fries, Vincent J. Connelly, & Todd A. DeMitchell. "Academic Freedom in the Public K–12 Classroom: Professional Responsibility or Constitutional Right? A Conversation with Teachers," *Education Law Reporter* 227 (2008): 505–524.

40. Ibid., 517.

41. Hugh Sockett, *The Moral Base for Teacher Professionalism* (New York: Teachers College Press, 1993).

42. This last category, while often part of the expectations of the responsibilities of teachers, is typically not associated with the characteristics of other professions. Sockett asserts that teacher professionalism requires that responsibilities extend beyond the classroom. He writes, "Public education needs teachers who are able not only to shine in the four categories mentioned within the class- room but also to undertake the demands of partnership with other professionals, of collaborative leadership, and of a wider role within the school." Ibid., 8.

43. Tichenor & Tichenor, *supra* note 1.

44. Ibid., 92–94.

45. Andrea J. Bingham & Patricia Witkowsky, "Deductive and Inductive Approaches to Qualitative Analysis," in Charles Banover, Peter Mihas, & Johnny Saldana (eds), *Analyzing and Interpreting Qualitative Data after the Interview* (London: Sage Publishing, 2021): 133–146.

46. Several of these comments are reminiscent of Dan Lortie's seminal research on teachers. In his study of teachers in Five Towns, he writes, "They picture themselves as constrained, undersupplied, and underappreciated." Dan C. Lortie, *Schoolteacher: A Sociological Study* (Chicago, IL: University of Chicago Press, 1975): 185.

47. Barney G. Glaser, *Theoretical Sensitivity* (Mill Valley, CA: Sociology Press, 1978).

48. Anselm L. Strauss, *Qualitative Analysis for Social Scientists* (Cambridge, UK: Cambridge University Press, 2010).

49. Bingham & Witkowsky, *supra* note 45.

50. This analysis used the same technique of a modified grounded theory approach used in the descriptor analysis segment, focusing on coding and not using the techniques of memo-making and theoretical sampling, which are not possible in this data collection method. The approach consisted of data collection, open coding of all data, axial coding for the creation of conceptual families, and selective coding of formalizing the codes—the five themes; see, Kathy Charmaz, *Constructing Grounded Theory* (London: Sage, 2006); Juliet Corbin & Anselm L. Strauss, *Basics of Qualitative Research: Grounded Theory Procedures and Techniques* (London: Sage Publishing, 2008, 3rd ed.). These data were not approached from a confirmatory stance.

51. For example, a former teacher and assistant superintendent of curriculum and instruction began her comments writing, "Identifying five words to summarize a professional educator was a tall order."

52. Fries et al., *supra* note 39.

53. Ibid., 521.

54. Ibid., 520–521.

55. This respondent, a school counselor and non-profit curriculum director, also discussed educators who do not meet the requirements of the professional educator. She writes, "In addition, some teachers do not feel they need to work beyond a certain time of day regardless of the need and do not feel they need to follow IEP nor 504 plans, for examples." Teachers' Descriptors of Professionalism (2021).

56. The middle-school assistant principal further states, "Personally, I believe that the best teachers (like the best doctors, businesspeople, lawyers, etc.) are professionals. I also believe that some teachers, and some members of all professions, are unprofessional." This comment is similar to the earlier discussion, regarding how the status of professional educator is earned. Ibid.

57. State Bar of California State Bar of California Releases Results of July 2021 Bar Exam, November 12, 2021, https://www.calbar.ca.gov/About-Us/News/News-Releases/state-bar-of-california-releases-results-of-july-2021-bar-exam.

58. Lortie, *supra* note 46, 80.

59. For example, an oncologist who wishes to see and treat patients for leukemia must apply for hospital privileges to practice medical oncology, with a separate application to perform stem cell and bone marrow transplants (see University of Michigan Hospitals and Health Centers, Delineation of Privileges of Internal Medicine, Division of Hematology/Oncology, Oncology, https://www.med.umich.edu/mss/pdf/Oncology.pdf).

60. For example author Richard Fossey was admitted to the Alaska and Texas bars and author Terri A. DeMitchell was admitted to the California Bar and the U.S. District Court for the Southern District of California.

61. For a comparison of several codes of ethics, including education, see Lynn Hammonds, "Embracing the Model Code of Ethics for Educators across Multiple Jurisdictions: An Exploratory Multiple Case Study," Unpublished doctoral dissertation (EdD), University of Hawai'i, Manoa (July 2020): 10–19. The author summarized the similarities of codes of ethics for physicians, attorneys, accountants, and educators:

1. A call for professional competence.
2. Responsibility for the welfare of individuals in their care.
3. The setting of professional boundaries between the professional and those they serve.
4. The requirement for confidentiality to protect personal information.
5. A responsibility to the greater community that the professional serves.

Ibid., 18.

62. Author, *Professional Ethics, Center for the Study of Ethics in the Professions* (Chicago, IL: Illinois Institute of Technology, 2008), http://ethics.iit.edu/teaching/professional-ethics.

63. Regina Umpstead, Kevin Brady, Elizabeth Lugg, Joann Klinker, & David Thompson, "Educator Ethics: A Comparison of Teacher Professional Responsibility Laws in Four States," *Journal of Law & Education* 42 (2013): 183–225, 186. Furthermore, they wrote, "Professional codes of ethics in education concern how

educators *ought* to conduct themselves within the profession of education" (emphasis in original). Ibid., 188

64. American Medical Association, "AMA Code of Medical Ethics, Preamble" (Revised June 2001), https://www.ama-assn.org/sites/ama-assn.org/files/corp/media-browser/principles-of-medical-ethics.pdf. There are nine principles.

65. American Bar Association, "*Model* Rules of Professional Conduct: Preamble & Scope" (2020), https://www.americanbar.org/groups/professional_responsibility/publications/model_rules_of_professional_conduct/model_rules_of_professional_conduct_preamble_scope/. See also Rules of the Supreme Court of New Hampshire, Rule 42 Admission to the Bar; Committee on Character and Fitness (5)(a): "All persons who desire to be admitted to practice law shall be required to establish their moral character and fitness to the satisfaction of the Standing Committee on Character and Fitness of the Supreme Court of New Hampshire in advance of such admission," http://www.courts.state.nh.us/rules/scr/scr-42.htm.

66. Robert Bruno, "When Did the U.S. Stop Seeing Teachers as Professionals?" *Harvard Business Review* (June 20, 2018), https://hbr.org/2018/06/when-did-the-u-s-stop-seeing-teachers-as-professionals.

67. Willard S. Elsbree, *The American Teacher: Evolution of a Profession in a Democracy* (New York: American Book Company, 1939).

68. Howard K. Beale, *Are American Teachers Free? An Analysis of Restraints upon the Freedom of Teaching in American Schools* (New York: Scribner's Sons, 1936): 407.

69. *Ambach v. Norwick*, 441 U.S. 68, 78–79 (1979). See also *Tingley v. Vaughn*, 17 Ill. App. 347, 351 (1885) ("if suspicion of vice or immorality be once entertained against a teacher, his influence for good is gone. The parents become distrustful, the pupils contemptuous and school discipline essential to success is at an end").

70. Clifford P. Hooker, "Terminating Teachers and Revoking Their Licensure for Conduct beyond the Schoolhouse Gate," *Education Law Reporter* 96 (1994): 2.

71. *Chicago Board of Education v. Payne*, 430 N.E.2d 310, 315 (Ill. App. Ct. 1981). See, also, the Supreme Court of Pennsylvania writing in *Horosko v. Mount Pleasant Township*, 6 A.2d 866, 868 (Pa. 1939), "It has always been the recognized duty of the teacher to conduct himself in such a way as to command the respect and good will of the community, though one result of the choice of a teacher's vocation may be to deprive him of the freedom of action enjoyed by persons in other vocations."

72. Alice J. Klein, "Educational Malpractice: Can the Judiciary Remedy the Growing Problem of Functional Illiteracy," *Suffolk University Law Review* 13 (1979): 27–62, 41.

73. James H. Stronge, Thomas J. Ward, & Leslie W. Grant, "What Makes Good Teachers Good? A Cross-Case Analysis of the Connection between Teacher Effectiveness and Student Achievement," *Journal of Teacher Education* 62(4) (2011): 339–355.

74. Ibid.

75. Barak Rosenshine, "Principles of Instruction: Research-Based Strategies That All Teachers Should Know," *American Educator* (2012): 12–39.

76. Submitting Papers to Law Journals: Journal Rankings, University of Michigan Law Library, https://libguides.law.umich.edu/journal_submissions/rankings.

77. Author, "Facts about the AERA Annual Meeting," American Educational Research Association, https://www.aera.net/Events-Meetings/Annual-Meeting/Facts-About-the-AERA-Annual-Meeting.

78. Author, "Preparing America's Students for Success," Common Core State Standards Initiative (2022), http://www.corestandards.org.

79. Ethan Hutt & Aaron Tang, "The New Education Malpractice Litigation," *Virginia Law Review* 99(3) (2013): 419–492, 427.

80. See Todd A. DeMitchell & Mark A. Paige, *Threading the Evaluation Needle: The Documentation of Teacher Unprofessional Conduct* (Lanham, MD: Rowman & Littlefield, 2020), for a discussion of incompetence, which is listed as one of the "Five Deadly Eyes" for dismissal, pages 33–44.

81. Shana Hurley, "The Remediless Reading Right," *Yale Law & Policy Review* 40 (2021): 276–335, 278 and 279.

82. Ibid., 277.

83. Lauren Camera, "Across the Board, Scores Drop in Math and Reading for U.S. Students," *U.S. News & World Report* (October 30, 2019), https://www.usnews.com/news/education-news/articles/2019-10-30/across-the-board-scores-drop-in-math-and-reading-for-us-students.

84. Arthur Levine, "Educating Researchers, Education Schools Project" (2007): 6, https://files.eric.ed.gov/fulltext/ED504132.pdf.

85. Lortie, *supra* note 46, 201.

86. Author, "Code of Ethics for Educators, National Education Association" (September 14, 2020), https://www.nea.org/resource-library/code-ethics-educators.

Chapter 3

Malpractice

A Tort of Negligence

> Negligence is a breach of one's legal duty to protect others from unreasonable risks of harm. The failure to act or the commission of an improper act, which results in injury or loss to another person, can constitute negligence. To establish negligence, an injury must be avoidable by the exercise of reasonable care.[1]

The creed of the medical profession is, "First, do no harm." It is designed to provide a North Star for medical practitioners as a guide, a core belief, for their service to their patients. While not adopted by educators, it may also describe the obligation professional educators owe to their students, as discussed in chapter 2. This chapter reviews tort liability, which is the legal basis for educational malpractice.

PROFESSIONAL MALPRACTICE

TEXTBOX 3.1

Long ago, legal scholars held a funeral service for the tort of educational malpractice. From time to time, academics exhume the tort in law review articles for a post-mortem analysis of what courts view as its fatal flaws and to beat their chests in collective lamentation.

Patricia Abbott, "*Sain v. Cedar Rapids Community School District:* Providing. Special Protection for Student-Athletes," *Brigham Young University Education & Law Journal* 2002 (2002): 291–312, 291.

Professionals who engage in professional misconduct or who lack appropriate skill, resulting in injury, may be liable for malpractice. Malpractice is often distinguished from other wrongs committed by professionals, in that it deals with the quality of the services rendered to the client.[2] Professionals are held accountable through malpractice "for failure to perform in accordance with skills that define their jobs."[3]

Professionals are expected to utilize a standard of care recognized by their profession as appropriate, based on the training received and the commonly held set of practices associated with the service rendered.[4] Failure to exercise the accepted standard of care may form the basis for malpractice if the negligent delivery of the service is legal cause for an injury suffered due to the lack of an appropriate standard of care.[5]

Generally, the key to establishing a malpractice case is determining whether the professional performed in accordance with the standard of care observed by members of the profession.[6] In other words, the standard of care is used to measure the competence of the professional.

"Malpractice" is defined as:

Professional misconduct or unreasonable lack of skill. Doctors, lawyers, and accountants usually apply the term to such conduct. [It is the] failure of one rendering professional services to exercise the degree of skill and learning commonly applied under all the circumstances of the community by the average prudent reputable member of the profession with the result of injury, loss or damage to the recipient of those services or to those entitled to rely upon them. It is any professional misconduct, unreasonable lack of skill or fidelity in professional or fiduciary duties, evil practice, or illegal or immoral conduct.[7]

Bad outcomes in medicine do not establish a *prima facie* case for malpractice. The death of the patient is not the measure of malpractice; the delivery of the standard of care concerning the operation is instead dispositive. In other words, a malpractice suit will not prevail if the patient dies in spite of the fact that the physician did everything expected in the delivery of medical care. However, for instance, a surgeon who uses unsterilized instruments or leaves a sponge in the patient, these negligent acts fall outside the generally accepted practices of a surgeon and can form the basis for a malpractice claim. For example, during a relatively routine surgery for carpal tunnel, the anesthesia tube perforated the patient's esophagus requiring lifesaving surgery to correct the perforation and was placed in a coma for an extended period of time.[8]

As stated earlier, not all injuries or bad outcomes result in compensation for the harm. For example, in a case in which a child was born and soon succumbed to Tay-Sachs disease, the parents brought suit against the physician.

They asserted that, had they been advised that their daughter had the disease, they would have sought an abortion. The court denied them legal relief. The court wrote:

> There can be no doubt that the plaintiffs have suffered and the temptation is great to offer them some form of relief. Ideally, there should be a remedy for every wrong. This is not the function of the law, however, for every injury has ramifying consequences, like the ripplings of the waters, without end. The problem of the law is to limit the legal consequences of wrongs to a controllable degree.[9]

"Proving legal malpractice generally means showing that the client would have won their underlying case if not for their attorney's actions."[10] Common kinds of legal malpractice include:

- failure to meet a filing or service deadline,
- failure to sue within the statute of limitations,
- failure to perform a conflicts check,
- failure to apply the law correctly to a client's situation,
- abuse of a client's trust account, such as commingling trust account funds with an attorney's personal funds, and
- failure to return telephone calls or otherwise communicate with a client.

Malpractice actions have been traditionally brought under contract law, or tort law.[11] The trend, however, is to bring such actions in tort. With some exceptions, this is true even if the relationship between the plaintiff and the professional is established by a contract. Most malpractice cases are brought under the theory of negligence, which will be discussed later, but first we will briefly review the first two theories.

A duty of care arises between a physician and a patient if there is a contract for professional services. Therefore, if a physician and a patient agree that in exchange for a fee, the physician will treat the patient, an express contract will be created. In most instances, however, a physician and the patient do not enter into such formal negotiations. Instead, a patient simply enters the physician's office and receives treatment. In *Lyons v. Grethen*, the court found that when a physician makes an appointment with a new patient to treat a specific condition, a duty is created.[12]

Courts recognize that an implied contract is created if a physician treats a patient with the expectation of compensation. This is true regardless of who pays for the treatment.[13]

For example, in *Hiser v. Randolph*,[14] a physician refused to treat a patient who arrived at a hospital emergency room in a semiconscious state due to an acute diabetic condition. Forty minutes elapsed before another doctor treated the patient. This delay resulted in the death of the patient the next day.

The court found that the doctor's contract with the hospital created a duty to the patient, unless some reasonable justification could be shown for not rendering care. Thus, in this case, the contractual duty between the physician and the hospital created a duty on the part of the physician, despite the fact that the patient was not even treated by the physician.

Furthermore, physicians can be held liable under the theory of vicarious liability for the negligent acts of their employees if the acts occurred within the scope of employment. Therefore, if a nurse negligently injures a patient while giving the patient an injection, the physician can be held liable.

A breach of contract for an allegation of educational malpractice in public K–12 education is more of a rarity than a mainstream action. Because contracts require a legal detriment bargained for in exchange, this criterion may likely be met in private education through the payment of the private school's tuition in exchange for a specified type of education. But public education does not involve the same direct exchange.[15]

However, educational malpractice and breach of contract issues arose during the campus shutdowns in the spring of 2020. Students throughout the country sued their respective universities after classroom instruction was canceled due to the COVID-19 pandemic and switched to an online format. Students alleged that this unilateral move to remote learning deprived them of the full benefit of their contractual bargain. For example, the plaintiffs in *Oyoque v. DePaul University* alleged that their remote classes "are a shadow of the classes that students experienced on-campus prior to the campus closures."[16]

Statutes may also create a duty.[17] Some states require hospitals with emergency facilities to render emergency care.[18] Even without express statutes, some courts have found that licensing statutes and health regulations require that emergency care facilities treat emergency patients, thus creating a legal duty.[19] While compliance with a statute may be used as evidence that the defendant used due care, it may be alleged that the defendant was negligent because he or she did not do more than what was required by the statute.[20]

TORTS OF NEGLIGENCE

A tort is a civil wrong for which the courts will provide a remedy for the injury suffered, usually in the form of damages assessed against the defendant. The law of torts is concerned with the allocation of losses arising out of human activities. The word is derived from the Latin word *tortus*, which means twisted.[21] In common usage, it is a synonym for wrong. "The purpose of the law of torts is to adjust these losses, and to afford compensation for injuries sustained by one person as the result of the conduct of another."[22] Essentially, compensatory damages in a tort of negligence seeks to "make whole" the injured.

TEXTBOX 3.2

Probably no area of school law arouses more anxiety, confusion, and misunderstanding than the possibility of being sued for student injury.

David Schimmel, Suzanne Eckes, & Matthew Militello, *Principals Teaching the Law: 10 Legal Lessons our Teachers Must Know* (Thousand Oaks, CA: Corwin Press 2010): 13.

Tort liability embraces the concept that all persons have a duty "to exercise due care in [their] own actions so as not to create an unreasonable risk of injury to others."[23] Torts are simply a means for holding individuals responsible for their actions (intentional or negligent) or for their failure to act when they should, which results in an injury. It is primarily judge-made-law (arising out of court cases) and is grounded in the concept of fault.

A tort is a civil wrong, other than breach of contract, for which the court will provide a remedy in the form of an action for damages. If someone suffers a harm or loss due to the improper conduct of another, a tort may have been committed. A tort is an action brought by an individual. It is not a criminal action, although, actions that give rise to the tort, such as assault and battery, may also constitute a crime.

The most common tort is negligence. This tort is characterized by conduct that falls below an acceptable standard of care and results in an injury. Often the standard of care is defined as acting as a reasonable person would act under the same or similar circumstances.

TEXTBOX 3.3

Negligence is generally the omission or failure to do something that a reasonable person would do, or the doing of something that a reasonable person would not do.

David J. Sperry, Philip T. K. Daniel, Dixie Snow Huefner, & E. Gordon Gee, *Education Law and the Public Schools: A Compendium* (Norwood, MA: Christopher-Gordon Publishers, Incorporation, 1998, 2nd ed.): 1068.

TEXTBOX 3.4

School officials have a common law duty to anticipate foreseeable dangers and to take necessary precautions to protect students entrusted in their care.

Martha M. McCarthy, Nelda H. Cambron-McCabe, & Suzanne E. Eckes, *Public School Law: Teachers' and Students Rights* (Boston, MA: Pearson, 2014, 7th ed.): 419.

As individuals, we can be held accountable for our acts or our failure to act under certain circumstances. The same is true of school districts.[24] The public expects schools to provide a safe haven during school hours, protect their children, and provide their children with a proper learning environment.[25]

Schools owe a duty of care to their students under tort principles.[26] However, not all injuries to students result in a finding of liability. School districts are not an insurer of safety for school children.[27] Sometimes injuries to students occur that do not result in legal liability for a school district. As Judge Wachtler wrote in a concurring opinion on educational malpractice, "It is a basic principle that the law does not provide a remedy for every injury."[28]

Sometimes injuries to students occur which do not result in legal liability for a school district. For example, a student playing dodgeball stepped backward and tripped over another student's foot resulting in an injury. The "incident occurred so quickly that even the most intense supervision would not have averted the accident."[29]

Similarly, a female sixth-grade student was injured practicing a cheerleading stunt, which resulted in surgery, a hospital stay, a cast being placed on her arm, and three scars. She brought a lawsuit in which she alleged that the coaches allowed her to practice an "inherently dangerous" stunt that she was not prepared to perform, that there was no "close adult supervision," and that thin floor mats were used.[30] The plaintiff lost on summary judgment and appealed.

An Illinois appellate court affirmed the lower court's summary judgment, writing, "The District took sufficient safety precautions to protect [the Plaintiff] from injury and the fact that she was injured despite its effort does not equate to a finding of willful and wanton conduct."[31]

Tort law seeks to balance a plaintiff's claim of damages due to a suffered harm against the defendant's freedom of action. "Thus, in tort litigation, it is possible that even if it is appropriate to provide compensation to a specific plaintiff, the plaintiff will be denied compensation if it is determined that there may be negative social consequences associated with such decision." [32]

Such consequences are referred to as public policy concerns. This exception to a finding of liability is central to our discussion of educational malpractice cases, which will be discussed in the next chapter.

TEXTBOX 3.5

Elements of a Tort for Negligence in Educational Settings

Duty Owed—Did the educator owe the student a duty to anticipate foreseeable dangers and to take reasonable precautions to protect the student entrusted in his or her care from such dangers? This standard of care is measured against a reasonable person (educator) standard. Did the educator act as a reasonable and prudent educator would have acted under the same or similar circumstances?

Breach of Duty—Did the educator fail to exercise an appropriate standard of care, given the age of the students, the environment, and the type of instructional activity? Did the educator act as reasonable and prudent educator would act in the same or similar circumstances? Did the educator's action, or failure to act, create an unnecessary risk of harm?

Causation—Actual and Proximate—Did the educator's action or inaction cause the injury?

A. Cause-in-Fact—Was there a sequential and continuous connection between the educator's action or inaction and the resultant injury and was that negligence a substantial cause of the harm? "But for" the defendant's action or inaction, the plaintiff would not have suffered an injury.

B. Proximate Cause—Was it foreseeable that the educator's action or inaction would cause the injury? Was the injured person a foreseeable plaintiff?

Actual Injury—The plaintiff must have sustained a sufficient injury in order for the court to provide a remedy.

OBLIGATIONS OF AN EDUCATOR

Adequate Supervision
Proper Instructions
Properly Maintained Equipment
Provide Warnings Regarding Known Hazards

Torts are usually divided into three categories: (1) negligence, (2) intentional torts,[33] and (3) strict liability.[34] Tort actions regarding malpractice are brought under the theory of negligence if the acts of the professional that allegedly inflicted harm were not intended to cause harm. If the professional intended the allegedly harmful conduct, the malpractice action is brought under a theory of intentional torts. Since most harmful acts by professionals are unintentional, the most common theory for malpractice asserted against a professional is negligence.

In order to prevail in a tort for negligence, the plaintiff must prove the four elements of a tort, namely: (1) that there was a duty owed by the defendant to the plaintiff, a duty to conform to a specific standard of conduct; (2) that the duty was breached by the defendant, that is failure to conform to the standard required; (3) that the defendant's conduct was the actual and proximate cause of plaintiff's injury; and (4) that the actual damage to plaintiff resulted.[35] These four elements of a tort take on special meaning in the context of schools. We will review each prong of the *prima facie* case.

A DUTY OWED

Generally, a person has no affirmative duty to aid or protect another. However, there are situations when duty may be owed to another. Whether a defendant owes a duty to a plaintiff is a question of whether or not the defendant is under a legal obligation to act or not to act for the benefit of the plaintiff.

A public school educator's relationship with his or her student is one of those relationships in which one party (the educator) owes a duty to the other party (the student). In addition, a school board, like any landowner, "has an obligation to use reasonable care to maintain its property in a physically safe condition."[36]

"A child while in school is deprived of the protection of his parents or guardians. Therefore, the actor who takes custody is properly required to give him the protection which the custody or the way it is taken has deprived him."[37] "The duty owed derives from the simple fact that a school, in assuming physical custody and control over its students, effectively takes the place of parents and guardians."[38]

Since teachers stand *in loco parentis* (custodial and tutelary responsibilities),[39] they must take affirmative actions in the face of foreseeable risks to protect students. "Foreseeability generally requires proof of actual or constructive notice to the school of prior similar conduct which caused the injury."[40] "Duty requires the exercise of care for protection against *unreasonable* risks of harm."[41]

Factors relevant in determining whether a duty exists include the fore-seeability of injury,[42] the likelihood of injury, the magnitude of the burden of guarding against the injury, the consequences of placing that burden on the defendant, and the possible seriousness of the injury.[43] Whether a specific duty exists is a question of law to be determined by the court; a duty is not created by its mere allegation asserted by a plaintiff.[44] But do educators owe a duty of due care to their students? The answer is unequivocally yes.

There is no one set of standards for defining the duty that is owed by educators. Tort liability (with the exception of constitutional torts, which will not be discussed) is determined by the laws of the individual states, and the various states define the duty of care owed by educators in different ways.

For example, the uniform standard of care owed to students in California is that degree of care "which a person of ordinary prudence, charged with [comparable] duties, would exercise under the same circumstances."[45] The editors of the *University of Pennsylvania Law Review* wrote that teachers have been held to the "standard of a 'reasonable and prudent person acting under like circumstances.' "[46]

New Hampshire Educators owe their students a duty of reasonable supervision because schools share a special relationship with students entrusted to their care.[47] In Mississippi, "educators have the duty of exercising ordinary care, . . . or of acting as a reasonable person would act under similar circumstances."[48] In Kansas, the duty is "to properly supervise students and to take reasonable steps to protect students' safety."[49]

In all fifty states, students are compelled to attend school. This compulsion helps to form the common law duty as well as statutory duty, supported by case law, to anticipate foreseeable dangers and to take necessary precautions to protect students. Educators owe students a duty to "exercise such care of them as a parent of ordinary prudence would observe in comparable circumstances. The duty owed derives from the simple fact that a school, in assuming physical custody and control over its students, effectively takes the place of parents and guardians."[50] Mandatory schooling forces parents to rely on schools to protect their children during school activities.[51]

For example, a suit was brought against a school district for injuries sustained when a first grader tripped over a crack in the playground while playing tag. The court found for the defendant school district, stating that the school exercised "the same degree of care and supervision of [the child] that a reasonably prudent parent would employ in the given circumstances."[52]

Similarly, a teacher was on hall duty when a plaintiff seventh grader was running in the hall. He did not stop running when the teacher told him to stop running. As the student ran past the teacher, the teacher stuck out his leg and tripped the student. The student sued for negligent supervision and won. The court stated that the standard of care is that kind of supervision which a parent of ordinary prudence would undertake in comparable circumstances. Finding the teacher liable, the court asserted that a parent of ordinary prudence would not have tried to stop a child from running by sticking out his leg in the student's path.[53]

Schools do not owe a duty to their students in all situations. An example of when a school does not owe a duty to students is found in the state of Washington. An appellate court held that the school officials did not have a duty to supervise students participating in a senior "release" day.[54] School personnel had knowledge of the event but they neither planned nor attended the event. It was not a school-sponsored event, even though it involved students at the school.

Similarly, once a student leaves the control of the school, the duty typically ends, unless the student is on a school-sponsored trip or a school-associated activity.[55] For example, in *Raymond v. Iberia Parish School Board*, Anisha, an eight-year-old schoolgirl, experienced an asthma attack at school. The school initiated its procedures, including the use of her inhaler which was kept in the office. Her emergency contacts were notified. The aunt arrived and took the child to the grandmother's house. While there, Anisha collapsed. She was rushed to a hospital where she suffered a severe and permanent disabling brain injury.

A lawsuit was brought alleging negligence on the part of the school. The trial court granted summary judgment and the plaintiff appealed. The issue was whether the school owed a duty to Anisha. The question of duty is a question of law for the court to decide. The Louisiana Court of Appeals held, "The basis of the trial court's ruling was simply that the School Board's duty ended when Anisha was no longer under its care and control. We agree that this was the proper basis to dispose of the motion [to dismiss].[56]

An example of egregious conduct perpetrated by a teacher against one of his students is found in New York. A high school social studies teacher was convicted of the statutory rape of a fifteen-year-old student. The sexual contact took place off school grounds "beyond the scope of Barsky's employment as a teacher and when the plaintiff was not within the school's control."[57] The court reasoned that the school did not have custody of the female student at the time of the assaults. "Without custody of the child, the school has no duty; without a duty there can be no liability."[58]

While schools typically owe a duty to students who are under their supervision, they are not insurers of their students' safety.[59] For example, in *Brownell*, a student was shot while standing in front of the school just after school hours by a nonstudent gang member.[60] The court held that schools couldn't insure the safety of students, particularly after or before school hours and off school premises.[61] Similarly, a student was seriously injured when he ran back to the highway to retrieve papers he had dropped after exiting the school bus. The Idaho court held that the school owed no duty to the student at the time of the accident. It had fulfilled its duty by seeing him to the driveway of his house.[62]

Obligations of an Educator

The duty that educators owe students is often described as a professional obligation. These obligations typically involve three activities: (1) adequate supervision; (2) proper instructions; and (3) properly maintained buildings, grounds, and equipment. The fourth obligation of an educator spans all three obligations—to provide warnings regarding known or reasonably foreseeable hazards.[63]

Adequate Supervision

Allegations of failure to provide adequate supervision for students are perhaps the most common negligence claim.[64] The gym, playground, and athletics activities account for 49 percent of the places where negligent supervision is reported.[65] "Constant and unremitting vigilance and supervision are not required. What is always required, however, is the care that a reasonable and prudent person would take in the circumstances."[66]

This duty to adequately supervise does not mean that supervision must be continuous and controlling of all movements and activities of students. "There is just no way that a teacher can give personal attention to every student all of the time."[67] Sudden, spontaneous, and unanticipated acts cannot be guarded against by a reasonable person. Educators are not insurers of students' safety and cannot be held liable for "every thoughtless or careless act by which one pupil may injure another."[68] A New York Supreme Court, Appellate Division stated, "Perfection in supervision is not required."[69]

The level of supervision required varies with the circumstances surrounding the supervision. Such factors as the age and maturity of the students, the prior knowledge about the students and or situation, and the nature of the specific activity are all important considerations. For example, working with first graders in the classroom or outside the classroom generally requires a higher level of supervision than that provided to high school students. In at least one jurisdiction, the courts have held that the playground is "a place where close supervision of the children is all but mandatory."[70]

Similarly, if high school students are using a trampoline, then the degree of supervision owed to the students increases dramatically because the risk of foreseeable harm has increased. Obviously, the chemistry lab; the woodshop;

and many athletic activities, such as swimming and gymnastics, call for a greater degree of vigilance and more specific supervision on the part of the educator than regular classroom instruction. Thus, the reasonable educator will adjust the degree of supervision to meet the foreseeability of danger not only for the entire activity but for portions of an activity calling for more direct supervision.

TEXTBOX 3.6

[W]here one creates, deals in, handles, or distributes an inherently dangerous object or substance . . . an extraordinary degree of care is required of those responsible. . . . The duty is particularly heavy where children are exposed to a dangerous condition which they may not appreciate.

Here, a dangerous instrument was placed in the hands of children without any special degree of care, supervision, or direction. Alcohol, a highly flammable substance, was left in their control to be used in connection with a *faulty* alcohol burner which had continually given trouble. That the situation was fraught with danger is proven by the results.

The duty incumbent upon [the teacher] under these dangerous circumstances was to either positively warn these girls not to attempt to light the burner if it went out or to personally supervise their use of the equipment or provide adequate adult supervision in his absence. He did none of these things.

Station v. Travelers Insurance Company, 292 So.2d 289, 291–292 (La. Ct. App. 1974) (emphasis in original).

Proper Instructions

Proper instructions are necessary to reduce the risk of injury when a student undertakes an activity, especially a dangerous activity. A chemistry lab is a prime location where inadequate instructions or failure to warn a student of known or foreseeable dangers has led to successful claims of negligence. For example, a teacher was held liable for failing to warn and instruct students about the use of methanol around a flame.[71]

To just give an instruction once is probably not enough if there is an ongoing foreseeable risk of injury. For example, a successful claim was brought against a field hockey coach who told his players at the beginning of the season to wear their mouth protectors. A sixteen-year-old student was struck in the mouth with a hockey stick. She was not wearing her mouth protector. The coach failed to remind the students to wear their mouth protectors and failed to check to see that the players had their mouth protectors in, which can be readily seen by a quick scan of a player's face. The coach had observed the student for thirty minutes during which time she did not wear her protector but took no action.[72]

A physical education teacher directed two students to fight each other as part of an improvised lesson. Neither student had received any instructions in boxing. One student was superior to the other in size, strength, and athletic ability. After giving the students gloves for the fight, the teacher sat in the stands and watched the fight, never intervening or giving directions even when it was apparent that the smaller student was getting pummeled. During the second round, the smaller student was killed. The teacher was held liable for inadequate supervision and lack of proper instructions.[73]

However, when students receive proper instructions and fail to follow them, the teacher may not be held liable. For example, a shop teacher gave appropriate and detailed instructions on the use of power saws. A student did not follow the instructions and lost several fingers. The teacher was found not liable for the student's injuries.[74]

However, in a 1935 case, a student sued for severe injuries sustained when the assignment he was working on exploded. He was working on a dangerous experiment (mixing explosives to make gunpowder). The student was only told to follow the directions in the textbook but he did not. He sued the school alleging negligent instruction of the dangerous experiment. The Court of Appeals reversed the lower court, writing:

> It is not unreasonable that it is the duty of a teacher of chemistry, in the exercise of ordinary care, to instruct students regarding the selection, mingling, and use of ingredients with which dangerous experiments are to be accomplished, rather than to merely hand them a text-book with general instructions to follow the text. . . . It may also be a proper question for the determination of the jury as to whether the delivery of a text-book to an inexperienced pupil with mere instructions to follow the text, in the performance of a dangerous experiment in chemistry, is a sufficient exercise of care.[75]

Properly Maintain Buildings, Grounds, and Equipment

Courts will routinely award monetary damages to students who are injured by unsafe conditions that school authorities knew or should have known about and failed to take necessary precautions to reduce the risk of injury. "All school personnel share a common responsibility to keep school facilities reasonably safe."[76] However, not all injuries at school result in a finding of negligence. The issue of notice or constructive notice of a dangerous condition is important.

A fifth-grade student slipped and fell in front of his locker as a result of accumulated water on the floor. In order to sustain a slip and fall action against the school district, the plaintiff had to prove that the school district knew that water had accumulated on the floor or that the "defect must be visible and apparent and it must exist for a sufficient time prior to the accident to permit defendant's employees to discover and remedy it."[77]

There was no evidence to show that the principal or members of the faculty or staff had knowledge of any water accumulation and therefore no liability was found. At the trial, school employees specifically stated that they did not see any water in front of the student's locker nor was there a history of a problem of water accumulation in that spot from either rain or snow. However, when a student put his arm through a broken window and was injured, the defendant school district lost because it had allowed the broken window to go unfixed for four months.[78]

In another instance, school district leaders in a Tennessee school were made aware that kitchen workers were receiving electrical shocks "strong enough to 'shock the water . . . out of you.' "[79] The defendant school district made four attempts to fix the problems but apparently decided to wait to fully rectify the situation until a large renovation project planned for the near future was begun. Unfortunately, the cafeteria manager received a debilitating shock prior to the major renovation. The plaintiff won at the appellate court level. The school district had been put on notice of a dangerous condition and it failed to remedy the problem.

Provide Warnings Regarding Known or Reasonably Foreseeable Hazards

This obligation encompasses the three prior obligations. Basically, if an educator has knowledge of a hazard that can likely cause injury, the educator must take appropriate steps to reduce the risk of injury. For example, if a dangerous situation exists due to construction near the school, it has an obligation to notify parents of the increased risk of harm.

However, courts will pose the question whether the defendant educator knew or should have known about the dangerous condition. Ignorance or turning a blind eye to a potential problem is a poor strategy. For example, a student was injured by a snowball and brought a suit for negligent supervision. The court held that the "educators knew or should have known, of hard frozen snow or ice in the school yard that caused the child's injury."[80] However, a duty to warn is not found in all situations.[81]

In a Connecticut case, the failure to warn of known or reasonably-should-have-known dangers had major consequences for a student and her private school.[82] Cari Munn, a fifteen-year-old student at a private Connecticut school went on a school-sponsored summer trip to Tianjin, China. While on a field trip to a rural area, Cara was bitten by a disease-carrying tick and contracted encephalitis, which left her permanently disabled and severely impacted her life and future. She brought a suit for negligence. After a lengthy appellate process starting in 2015, the Second Circuit Court of Appeals affirmed the judgment in 2018, including the amount of money damages ($41.5 million) Cara won.[83]

Cara and her fellow students headed to China, without knowing they would visit a forested, nonurban area that might contain ticks. Munn and her parents received no warnings about how to prevent insect-borne diseases during the trip. On June 23, 2007, the Hotchkiss students went on a weekend excursion that included a visit to the Great Wall and a hike to the top of Mount Panshan. No one warned the students to apply bug spray before they trekked up the mountain or to wear proper clothing and shoes. Instead, they wore shorts, T-shirts or tank tops and some wore sandals.

Ten days after the hike Cara became sick and disoriented. By the time her parents got to China, she was partially paralyzed and unable to speak. Although her condition improved, she was permanently disabled and never regained the capacity to speak. Her brain function was compromised, and she suffered from diminished executive function, which made it difficult for her to construct multistep solutions to everyday problems.

The jury found Hotchkiss negligent for "failing to warn [Cara] of the risk of insect-borne illnesses" and failing to ensure that she "used protective measures to prevent insect-borne infection."[84] Neither Cara nor her parents were warned about travel to a forested area that might contain disease-carrying ticks and insects. In the jury's opinion, Hotchkiss was "solely negligent" for Cara's injuries.[85] "But for Hotchkiss's negligence," the jury concluded, "she would have applied bug spray that would properly repel insects, and as a result prevent her from contracting insect-borne diseases like [encephalitis]."[86] The judge found that Cara's injuries were foreseeable.

In finding Hotchkiss liable to Cara Munn for negligence, a Connecticut jury reaffirmed a basic principle of tort law that has been articulated across the United States, which is that schools have a duty to warn or to protect students from foreseeable dangers.

A Duty of Care for Professionals

Professionals must conform to the duty of care defined by their profession. Generally, the reasonable person standard applies, but if the defendant renders services in a recognized trade or profession, he or she is held at a minimum to the standard of care customarily exercised by members of that profession or trade, whether he or she actually possesses the requisite skills. If the professional does in fact have a higher degree of skill than that customarily possessed by other professionals in the same field, the professional is held to the standard of care that a reasonable person with superior knowledge or skill would exercise. Thus, professionals are held to a higher standard than others engaged in the same profession.

Physicians are obligated to provide a standard of care to their patients typically based on professional norms.[87] The standard of care or the duty owed by the physician to the patient is grounded in the customary practices of the medical profession. The customary practice is normally described as the customary practice in the same or similar community.[88] The standard, however, is not unitary or monolithic. There is a respectable minority rule that "serves as an accommodation for the exercise of clinical judgment."[89]

The standard of care is typically articulated through expert witness testimony. In a medical malpractice case, a patient brought a suit for injuries sustained in a laparoscopic-assisted sigmoid colectomy that resulted in the need for postoperative surgery to repair a damaged ureter. The Appellate Court affirmed the lower court's ruling for the defendant. Addressing the duty owed, the Court of Appeals wrote, "plaintiff's expert opined that defendants deviated from the standard of care without detailing what procedures or actions should have been undertaken and whether those procedures or actions were required under the applicable standard of care."[90]

An attorney who represents and advises a client impliedly creates a duty that the attorney possesses the necessary skill to handle the matters that may result.[91] Failure to possess the necessary skills or knowledge or to exercise the standard of care will result in liability.[92] Chief Judge Alvey in an 1889 decision wrote that clients of an attorney has a right to expect the attorney to exercise "ordinary care and diligence in the execution of the business intrusted [*sic*] to him, and to a fair average degree of professional skill and knowledge."[93] Neglecting to employ these skills and knowledge responsible for the loss or damage.

An example of legal malpractice is found in *Smith v. Lewis*, where an attorney who did not specialize in the area of family law represented a woman in a divorce case. Before advising her of her rights, the attorney failed to research the issue of the community-property nature of her husband's military pension. The courts found this omission to be malpractice.[94]

Certain actions are considered on their face to lack reasonable care, such as missing a time line which results in the loss of a claim[95] or settling a case contrary to the express instructions of the client.[96] They are therefore breaches of duty.

The above examples illustrate that courts readily find a duty of care has arisen when the case involves professionals such as physicians and lawyers. Similarly, courts have found that educators owe a duty to their students, but generally not one associated with professional malpractice.

BREACH OF DUTY

A breach of duty occurs when the defendant's conduct falls below that required by the standard of care owed to the plaintiff. An important consideration is how the educator discharged or failed to discharge his or her duty. For example, an educator who fails to act properly when there is duty to act has acted with misfeasance. Second, an educator who fails to act when required to act has breached his or her duty through nonfeasance. And, last, an educator who acts unlawfully and wrongfully breaches a duty.

Breach of duty is the application of the facts to the reasonable person standard that demonstrates breach. For example, a shop teacher owes his or her students a duty to provide proper instructions before allowing them to use a welding torch. A student is injured when she uses the welding torch improperly as directed by the teacher. The teacher's failure to provide the required instructions establishes a breach of duty.

Breach of duty may also be shown by evidence of a statutory violation. For example, a bus driver breached the law when he failed to use his stop sign and lights, which resulted in an injury to a student. His violation of the law constituted a breach of duty.[97]

In some instances, an educator must have knowledge of the dangerous condition in order to be held responsible. For example, in a New York case, a student was hit in the eye with a stick thrown by another student during lunch recess. The horseplay between the two students that lead to the injury lasted approximately one minute.

A New York Appellate Court held that the third-party act of throwing the stick could not have been reasonably anticipated, thus there was no breach.[98] "An injury caused by the impulsive, unanticipated act of a fellow student ordinarily will not give rise to a finding of negligence absent proof of prior conduct that would have put a reasonable person on notice to protect against the injury causing act."[99] In these situations, the courts find that the standard of knew or should have known does not apply because it would be unreasonable for the educator to have anticipated the act.

On occasion, an individual who owes a duty to the injured party injures a person and a specific finding of breach is not possible. In those unique situations the doctrine of *res ipsa loquitur* ("the thing speaks for itself), although rare, allows a plaintiff to demonstrate breach without a specific factual finding of breach. In certain cases, breach of duty can be inferred from the facts. In *Byrne v. Boadle*,[100] breach was established when a barrel rolled out of a warehouse's second-story window and hit a passerby. The court concluded that barrels do not roll out of windows on their own. Therefore, some unspecified negligent act caused the barrel to roll out the window.

This doctrine "spares the plaintiff the requirement of proving specific acts of negligence in cases where the plaintiff asserts . . . injury, the cause of which cannot be fully explained, and the injury is of a type that would not ordinarily result if the defendant were not negligent."[101] *Res ipsa loquitur* is applied in medical malpractice but largely unused in attorney malpractice.[102] However, these types of breach cases appear in education.[103]

The Texas Supreme Court defined *res ipsa loquitur* in medical malpractice as applying when the "unaided laymen must be able to determine that negligence must have occurred from their common knowledge, and not solely through the aid of an expert."[104] Examples of medical malpractice applying *res ipsa loquitur* include leaving a sponge inside a patient when closing after a surgery[105] and operating on the wrong part of the patient's body.[106]

Res ipsa loquitur is used in medical malpractice when: (1) the patient suffers an injury that is not an expected complication of medical care; (2) the injury does not normally occur, unless someone has been negligent; and (3) the defendant was responsible for the patient's well-being at the time of the injury.[107]

The Reasonable Person Standard

The courts apply a uniform and objective standard of care called the "reasonable person." The reasonable person is a mythical person who is always prudent and careful—not to be identified with any ordinary individual who might occasionally do unreasonable things. The application of the reasonable person standard involves comparing the conduct of the defendant with "what the reasonable person would do 'under the same or similar circumstances.' "[108] This hypothetical reasonable person has

1. the same physical characteristics as the defendant;
2. normal intelligence, problem-solving ability, and temperament;
3. normal perception and memory with a minimum level of information and experience common to the community; and
4. such superior skill and knowledge as the defendant has or purports to have.[109]

In a New York case, a coach was held to the standard of the reasonably prudent coach and not the reasonably prudent parent.[110] This appears to establish a higher standard of reasonableness for educators who have acquired special knowledge and skills. "Teachers, being college graduates and state licensed, are expected to act like reasonable persons with similar education."[111] Consistent with our discussion in chapter 2 on professionalism, an education law professor wrote, "In an effort to determine whether the defendant acted as a reasonable person, courts also consider whether the defendant had claimed to have had any superior knowledge or skills."[112]

Medical Breach of Duty

For physicians, the standard of care that is owed to a patient can be established by state statute or by professional standards. Breach means that a physician, dentist, or surgeon failed to react or act in accordance with medical standards to a patient's illness or injury, or that an act he or she took was indeed negligent, and the outcome resulted in additional harm to the patient.[113]

Medical News Today identified examples of cases of medical error or negligence that could lead to a breach of the duty of care owed to patients. They include

- misdiagnosis or failure to diagnose;
- unnecessary or incorrect surgery;
- premature discharge;
- failure to order appropriate tests or to act on results;
- not following up;
- prescribing the wrong dosage or the wrong medication;
- leaving things inside the patient's body after surgery;
- operating on the wrong part of the body;
- the patient has persistent pain after surgery;
- potentially fatal infections acquired in the hospital; and
- pressure ulcers or bedsores.[114]

A 2013 international study of malpractice articles published by *BMJ* (formerly the *British Medical Journal*) found that the most common "medical misadventure" is failure or delayed diagnosis of disease, including cancer, myocardial infarction in adults, and meningitis in children. Medication error was the second most common medical error.[115] An open letter to the U.S. Centers for Disease Control and Prevention based on a study by researchers at Johns Hopkins found that medical error was the third-leading cause of death behind heart disease and cancer.[116]

In determining whether a physician has breached the requisite standard of care, several factors are examined. These factors include the state of professional knowledge at the time of the act, the omission by the physician, and established modes of practice. The professional knowledge requirement recognizes that medical service is a progressive science and therefore, treatment rendered must be evaluated considering the knowledge at the time in question. In addition, physicians are not held liable for mistakes in judgment where the proper action is open to debate.[117]

However, it is important to note that attorneys, like physicians, are not always held liable for errors in judgment. If an attorney acts reasonably and in the best interest of the client, then he or she will not be held liable for errors in judgment.[118] Sound tactical decisions that do not result in obtaining a client's desired outcome are not actionable.

An example of this carve-out of the duty owed for the providers of professional services was recognized by the Minnesota Supreme Court in the 1978 case of *City of Mounds View v. Walijarvi*. The court identified architects, doctors, engineers, attorneys, and others for the application of a standard that does not demand success with every decision or action. The underlying rationale for this rule is based on the "inexact sciences" they are called upon to exercise in the face of "random factors" that must be anticipated but for which there is not an exact measurement. Consequently, "the indeterminate nature of these factors makes it impossible for professional service people to gauge them with complete accuracy."[119]

"Because of the inescapable possibility of error which inheres in these services, the law has traditionally required, not perfect results, but rather the exercise of that skill and judgment which can be reasonably expected from similarly situated professionals."[120] Should educational malpractice be accepted by the courts as a viable cause of action for students, would it make sense that this defense would also be available to the educator who selects one reading approach over another when a particular student does not gain a specific-level outcome?

CAUSATION: THE THIRD ELEMENT OF A TORT

Once a duty owed by the defendant to the plaintiff has been established, and the facts demonstrate that the plaintiff breached the duty owed by failing to act as a reasonable person, the plaintiff must next show that the act or failure to act was the cause of the injury. Causation has two elements: cause-in-fact and proximate cause (legal cause).

Cause-in-fact

Cause-in-fact is often called the but-for test, which states, but for the defendant's conduct, the injury would not have occurred. The second part of cause-in-fact is the substantial factor test. Under this test, the defendant's conduct is the cause-in-fact if it is substantial enough to lead reasonable persons to conclude that there existed an unbroken chain between the act and the injury. The term cause-in-fact "embraces all things which have so far contributed to the result that without them it would not have occurred."[121]

"To make a *prima facie* showing of [cause-in-fact], the plaintiff must show the defendant's negligent conduct more probably than not was a cause of the injury."[122] "The defendant's negligence need not be the sole cause of the plaintiff's injury, but simply a cause or a contributing cause."[123] If the plaintiff's negligence is not a substantial factor in producing the harm, then there is no liability.

Even if the defendant's act or omission met the standards of the but-for and the substantial factor tests, the defendant's actions may not be the proximate or legal cause of the plaintiff's injury. The doctrine of proximate cause limits the liability of defendants.

Proximate Cause

Proximate cause, or legal cause as it has sometimes been called, has been linked to duty, in that a reasonable person has a duty to protect an individual from foreseeable harm. It is the foreseeability of harm that links duty and causation. Proximate cause has its roots in a landmark 1928 case, *Palsgraf v. Long Island Railroad Company*.[124]

In this case, a passenger was running to catch a train. Two porters tried to help the man board the train. While assisting the passenger, the package he was carrying became dislodged and fell upon the rails where it exploded; he was a fireworks salesperson. The concussion from the blast overturned some scales many feet away which fell on another passenger, injuring her. It was found that the explosion and resulting injury would not have occurred but-for the actions of the railroad company employees.

Judge Cardozo, speaking for the majority, held that there was no liability because there was no negligence. Negligence, he argued, was a matter of relation found between the parties, which must be founded upon the foreseeability of harm. In other words, the conduct of an actor creates a zone of danger. Individuals within that zone of danger become foreseeable plaintiffs. If it is foreseeable that a particular action, or omission to act, can cause harm to a specific individual, then proximate cause is established. The link between proximate cause and duty is that a duty is only owed to individuals who are foreseeably within the zone of danger.

This concept is elucidated by quickly reviewing the dissenting opinion in *Palsgraf* written by Judge Andrews. The dissenting view held that everyone owes to the world at large the duty to refrain from unreasonable acts which threaten the safety of others. The duty is to protect society from unnecessary danger and not specific individuals alone. According to Andrews's view, once a cause-in-fact has been demonstrated, the defendant can be liable to any plaintiff who suffers harm no matter how attenuated the injury is from the original action.

Foreseeability is the key to establishing proximate cause. The more dangerous the act, the larger the zone of danger, and the greater the likelihood of increased numbers of foreseeable plaintiffs. A teacher who does not go to a recess duty where there are hundred primary-age students playing on the monkey bars, swings, and jungle gyms conceivably has hundred foreseeable plaintiffs. It is within the realm of human experience that students left unsupervised in an area where play equipment is available can be injured.

Even though the teacher cannot ensure the safety of the students, a reasonable teacher would not leave the students unsupervised in the playground area. It could be argued that the presence of the teacher providing proper supervision by being vigilant would deter most dangerous acts. Similarly, it is foreseeable that leaving the guard off a power saw could cause injury to a student using the saw.

However, if a student is struck with a fist by another student and the school officials had no knowledge of the student's propensity to do violence, the attack is not foreseeable and school authorities are not liable for the injury that occurs.[125] Obviously, once it is known that a particular student has a propensity to act in a dangerous manner, then that knowledge serves as foreseeability, thus requiring a standard of care regarding that particular student.

Associated with this obligation is the notice that an educator receives when a student exhibits a tendency toward action that increases the likelihood of harm to self and/or others. An example is a student who is prone to violence in the classroom. It is foreseeable that the student may strike other students under certain conditions. The reasonable teacher takes reasonable precautions in light of that knowledge.

An example of the fit between cause-in-fact and the proximate cause foreseeability element is found in *Cedar Falls v. Cedar Falls School District*.[126] In September 1995, the City of Cedar Falls held its annual safety program for kindergarten students. During the program, several of the students went over to an unattended golf cart with the key in the ignition. One of the students apparently stepped on the accelerator, releasing the brake. The cart surged forward pinning a kindergarten student against the side of an ambulance.

The student later died from his injuries. Applying the cause-in-fact analysis, the court asserted that a jury could find that the accident would not have occurred "but for" the negligence in supervising the students. "The cart would not have started had the children been prevented from playing on it."[127] Furthermore, the court applied the proximate cause analysis to the facts and concluded that "because it was foreseeable the children would be curious and interested in the golf cart, the jury could conclude their conduct fell within the original risk created by the District's actions."[128]

The Professions and Causation

A physician cannot be held liable, even if negligent, if the negligent actions did not cause the injury plaintiff claims to have suffered. For example, a physician who negligently prescribed a decongestant for a patient with heart disease could not be held liable for the patient's subsequent heart attack without proof that the medication contributed to the patient's death.[129] Furthermore, the defendant's negligence must be the proximate cause of the plaintiff's injuries. In other words, the injury must be a foreseeable result of the physician's action or inaction or it must be proven that but for the fact that the physician prescribed the decongestant, the patient would not have died.

With respect to attorneys, the issues of causation and ascertaining damages can be complicated, and often these issues are intertwined. One of the most common claims against an attorney is the failure to comply with time requirements. Such an error on the part of an attorney can result in the loss of the legal action by the plaintiff, thus precipitating a legal malpractice claim against the tardy attorney. While such an error as failing to file an action within the time limitations seemingly should be considered malpractice, it may not be. The requisite element of causation must be present. Therefore, it must first be determined that, but for the defendant's negligent actions, the plaintiff would not have been injured. The plaintiff must then show injury.

SUFFICIENT INJURY: THE LAST ELEMENT

Injury is not presumed; the plaintiff must show actual injury or harm. In cases where an injury has occurred due to the negligence of another, the plaintiff has a duty to mitigate his or her damages. For example, a student who meets the first three elements of the tort of negligence but only sustains an abrasion that heals quickly may not meet this test. The sufficiency of the injury is often not reported because if the injury was slight the case may have been settled out of court or a motion to dismiss may have been granted. Most discussions of injury involve the severity of the injury. If negligence is proved, then the severity of the injury is used to calculate the monetary award.

DEFENSES TO A FINDING OF NEGLIGENCE

Once the plaintiff has established the *prima facie* case of negligence by proving duty owed, breach, causation, and sufficient injury, the defendant has the opportunity to assert a defense. There are several defenses available to the defendants to rebut charges of negligence.

Accidents/Acts of God

First, not all bad things that happen to individuals are a result of someone's negligence. Accidents do happen, although in our litigious society whenever an injury occurs there is a vigorous search to find someone liable. The simple truth is that sometimes accidents do happen and no amount of reasonable action on the part of another could prevent them. Often, when this defense is asserted, the act that gave rise to the injury is ascribed as an act of God, something unforeseen and outside of the control of the participants.

Immunity

Even when plaintiffs prevail, the court does not always make them whole. For example, immunity is one of the defenses to a tort. Immunity is derived from the ancient idea that "the King can do no wrong."[130] In *Russell v. The Men of Devon*, an eighteenth-century decision by an English court, a wagon owner sued the men of Devon County who were responsible for maintaining the roads when his wagon broke down as a result of a bridge being in disrepair.[131] Finding for the defendant, Lord Ashhurst and his fellow judges wrote in pertinent part: "But there is another general principle of law which is more applicable to this case, that it is better that an individual should sustain an injury than that the public should suffer an inconvenience."[132]

American courts adopted the English doctrine of sovereign immunity until the early twentieth century, when courts began to recognize that private individuals who are injured by a governmental action should be entitled to compensation. In *Molitor v. Kaneland*,[133] the Supreme Court of Illinois ruled in favor of the plaintiff who was injured after getting off a school bus. The court asserted that sovereign immunity was no longer tenable because it rested on a "rotten foundation."

ASSUMPTION OF THE RISK

The third defense is assumption of the risk. Generally, this defense asserts that an individual who voluntarily assumes the risk of an activity cannot recover for injuries associated with that activity. It assumes that he or she knew of and appreciated the risks associated with that activity and still volunteered to participate. In effect, an assumption of risk transfers the foreseeability of harm to the plaintiff.[134] A common application of assumption of the risk is fond when spectators attend ball games. A spectator assumes the risk normally associated with attending a ball game and therefore cannot sue a batter who hits a foul ball that strikes and injuries the spectator.

In school settings, assumption of risk is most often associated with extra-curricular sports.[135] "Participants are held to assume normal risks by their actual or implied consents to play the game."[136] For example, a student's ankle was fractured sliding into a base. The coach was not liable for the injury because such a risk is an inherent part of the game, and the risk was known to the plaintiff and assumed by the plaintiff.[137]

In another case, a high school custodian allowed a number of high school students to play basketball in the school's gymnasium during the semester break. During the game two students collided while scrambling for a rebound. One of the students suffered a fractured spine. A lawsuit for negligence was brought against the school district. The Idaho Supreme Court held that the plaintiff student had assumed the risk of normal physical contact associated with playing basketball. In addition, the court found that the absence of super-vision was not the proximate cause of the injury. The court asserted that had a coach or teacher been supervising the game, the collision and resulting injury would not have been prevented. The student lost.[138]

Another losing case for a plaintiff student involved a member of the seventh-grade volleyball team. The athlete was struck in the back of the head during a volleyball practice. While there was some dispute as to whether the injury occurred after the coach signaled the end of the practice or during the practice, the court upheld the grant of summary judgment dismissing the negligent supervision claim. The court held, "Players who voluntarily join in extracurricular interscholastic sports assume the risks to which their roles expose them but not risks which are unreasonably increased or concealed."[139] The risks associated with playing volleyball were not unreasonably increased when the student athlete walked off the court, whether play was ended or not.

The key to assumption of risk is the knowing of the risk that is being assumed and its foreseeable consequences. For example, a young student who does not understand the danger of an act typically is not considered to have assumed the risk of the act. The typical test for this defense for children is whether a particular child, considering his or her age, background, and inher-ent intelligence indulges in the gross disregard of his or her own safety in the face of known, understood, and perceived danger.[140] Assumption of risk associated with participation of an activity does not relieve a school district of its obligation to use reasonable care in light of foreseeable harm.

Contributory Negligence

Contributory negligence occurs when the plaintiff's actions or omissions are negligent and contribute to his or her own injury by falling below the standard expected for his or her own protection. The early application of contributory negligence barred the plaintiff from recovery even if the defendant was also partially at fault and negligent. Over the years, contributory negligence has been modified and weakened. "As a result, in most jurisdictions today, a slight degree of fault will not prevent a plaintiff from prevailing."[141]

"However, since a child is not expected to act with the same standard of care as an adult, teachers have more difficulty in showing contributory negligence than they would if the plaintiff was an adult."[142] The actions of the plaintiff student must be reasonable for a child of similar age, maturity, intelligence, and experience. Students are usually not considered to be contributorily negligent, unless they understood and appreciated the danger posed by the activity.

For example, a six-year-old child ran into the street and the side of a car while returning to school. Because of his age, the court found that the six-year-old did "not share in the fault for his injury because he acted in a manner that could have been expected of a child of his age."[143] But, a high school senior who was an accomplished diver and swimmer was solely responsible for her injuries when she attempted to execute a shallow dive.[144]

In another case, a father attended a basketball tournament held at the local high school to watch his twelve-year-old son play. There were three sets of bleachers set up for the three basketball games. The father changed bleachers each time his son changed courts. At the third bleacher he took a seat on the highest row, he leaned back after sitting there for ten minutes, crossed his leg, leaned back and fell to the floor. The third set of bleachers did not have a back support. He sued the school district for the injuries that he sustained in the fall.

The trial court found that the father was contributorily negligent and that his conduct proximately caused the injury. On appeal, the Indiana Court of Appeals remanded the case to decide whether the plaintiff knew or should have known that there was no back behind the last tier of seats. At the trial the plaintiff stated that he did not think about whether he was seated on the final row.[145] Judge Baker dissented, arguing that the plaintiff "may not have known that the bleachers did not have a back support is of no moment, inasmuch as any reasonably prudent person would have checked before leaning backward."[146]

The courts have held that the creation of a physician-patient relationship requires that the duty established be reciprocal. Thus, the patient is required to use the care a person would ordinarily use in similar circumstances and if he or she does not, then the patient cannot hold the physician liable for harm. Specifically, a patient is required to provide adequate information to the physician, follow the instructions given by the physician and submit to the treatment the physician orders. If failure to do so enhances the injury, the patient will not be able to recover damages for his contribution to the injury.

For example, in an action against a physician for the improper diagnosis of appendicitis, the court held the plaintiff contributorily negligent for failing to disclose pertinent information to the physician and for failing to seek further medical help when her condition worsened.[147] In another case, a patient was determined to be contributorily negligent when her physician told her to return in six months after a lump was found in her breast and she waited fifteen months, resulting in a loss of survival expectancy.[148]

Comparative Negligence

As stated earlier, in traditional contributory negligence cases, once the defense has been established, the plaintiff is barred from any recovery. However, in many states contributory negligence has been replaced or modified with comparative negligence. Comparative negligence apportions liability, and thus it is less harsh than the all-or-nothing aspect of contributory negligence. Contributory negligence is measured by percentages. "Any damages recovered from the defendant will be diminished by the proportion of the plaintiff's fault or negligence."[149]

For example, a student was injured while jumping on a trampoline right before the start of the physical education class in November when the coach had not yet entered the gymnasium. The coaches gave a verbal warning not to jump on the trampoline without a coach being present at the beginning of the school year but did not restate the warning. The student who jumped on the trampoline before class had heard the warning and had not jumped on the trampoline prior to the day he was injured. The jury found that the student was 45 percent negligent and the school was 55 percent negligent. The school district paid the defendant $55,000 of the total $100,000 judgment.

A jury in Kansas found a school district 90 percent negligent and two students at fault for 10 percent of their injuries. The two high school students walked rapidly toward a closed hallway door at their high school. The two boys reached the door at the same time and reached for the crossbar to open the door. One of the student's hands slipped shattering the plate glass in the door. The glass was not safety glass and it shattered severely injuring the two students.[150]

Educational malpractice suits for negligence follow the patterns discussed earlier. First, the *prima facie* case of duty, breach, causation, and injury must be established by the plaintiff. Once these elements are established, the defendant can raise one of the affirmative defenses discussed earlier. However, the defendant will most likely submit a motion to dismiss based on public policy considerations that support dismissal on the basis of a failure to state a cognizable claim.

TEXTBOX 3.7

Last-Clear-Chance Doctrine

The last-clear-chance doctrine is used in tort cases involving shared responsibility for the accidental injury and is associated with contributory negligence. Essentially, the doctrine considers which party, defendant or plaintiff, had the last opportunity to avoid the accident that caused the harm. It has been used to ease the harsh effects of contributory negligence by allowing a plaintiff to potential recover some damages as opposed to no damages.

Author, "Last Clear Chance," *Legal Information Institute, Cornell Law School* (July 2020), https://www.law.cornell.edu/wex/last_clear_chance.

Comparative negligence essentially replaced the need for the last-clear chance doctrine by allowing the plaintiff to recover some damages even though the plaintiff was partially responsible for the injury

Katherine Bitses, "The Doctrine of 'The Last Clear Chance'" *St. John's Law Review* 19 (November 1944): 33–38, 34.

The next section will discuss the early education malpractice cases. It will explore the application of the tort defenses and discuss the application of public policy.

NOTES

1. Martha M. McCarthy, Nelda H. Cambron-McCabe, & Suzanne E. Eckes, *Public School Law: Teachers' and Students Rights* (Boston, MA: Pearson, 2014, 7th ed.): 441.
2. Ronald E. Mallen, "Recognizing and Defending Legal Malpractice," *South Carolina Law Review* 20 (1979): 203–211, 205. Mallen asserts that legal malpractice is "deficiency in the quality of services," and that an attorney's liability for malpractice is "comparable to that of other professionals." Ibid.
3. John G. Culhane, "Reinvigorating Educational Malpractice Claims: A Representational Focus," *Washington Law Review* 67 (1992): 349–414, 372.
4. For example, "a physician owes a patient (1) [the] duty to possess the requisite knowledge and skill such as is possessed by the average member of the medical profession, (2) [the] duty to exercise ordinary and reasonable care in the application of such knowledge and skill, and (3) [the] duty to use best judgment in such

application," *American Jurisprudence*, Physicians and Surgeons, Etc. 311 (1981, 2nd ed.).

5. A negligent act may form the basis for professional malpractice. Malpractice typically is not an intentional act. Nonetheless, in a closely watched case, a nurse administered the wrong neuromuscular blocking agent, which was often used in surgery, causing paralysis as opposed to the proper drug, which was a sedating agent for an anxious patient undergoing a diagnostic scan. The patient suffered brain damage and died. The nurse subsequently lost her nursing license and in a highly unusual move was indicted and arrested for impaired adult abuse and reckless homicide. Shawn Kennedy "Case of Nurse Charged with Homicide for Medication Error Raises Concerns," *AJN Off the Charts* (Blog of the American Journal of Nursing) (February 19, 2019), https://ajnoffthecharts.com/case-of-nurse-charged-with-homicide-for-medication-error-raises-concerns/.

6. See *Hall v. Hilburn*, 466 S.2d 856 (Miss. 1985), for a discussion of the parameters of the medical standard.

7. *Black's Law Dictionary* (St. Paul, MN: West Publishing Company, 1979, 5th ed.): 864. See also *Board of Examiners of Veterinary Medicine v. Mohr*, 485 P.2d 235, 239 (Okla. 1971) ("any professional misconduct or any unreasonable lack of skill or fidelity in the performance of professional or fiduciary duties; . . . objectionable, or wrong practice; . . . practice contrary to rules).

8. *Broward Hospital District v. Kalitan*, 219 So. 3d 49 (Fla. 2017).

9. *Howard v. Lecher*, 366 N.E.2d 64, 66 (N.Y. App. Div. 1977) (internal quotation marks removed).

10. Author, "Legal Malpractice" *Justia* (October 2021), https://www.justia.com/injury/legal-malpractice/.

11. John Collis, *Educational Malpractice: Liability of Educators, School Administrators, and School Officials* (Charlottesville, VA: The Michie Company, 1990): 64.

12. 218 Va. 630, 239 S.E.2d 103 (1977).

13. Culhane, *supra* note 3, 372.

14. 126 Ariz. 608, 617 P.2d 774 (1980).

15. See Frank D. Aquila, "Educational Malpractice: A Tort En Ventre" *Cleveland State Law Review* 39 (1991): 323–355, 336 and 337. Writing, "Because public education is provided free of cost, students themselves do not directly pay money in exchange for receiving public education." Ibid., 377. Aquila provided an interesting discussion of the application of students as third-party beneficiary of the employment contract between the school district and the teacher.

16. *Oyoque v. DePaul University*, 520 F. Supp. 3d 1058, 1062–1063 (N.D. Ill. 2021). The Appellate Court rejected the University's assertion that the claim of breach of contract was a repackaged educational malpractice claim. The court, however, did affirm that educational malpractice suits are non-cognizable in Illinois. The court summed the argument, writing, "The complaint does not challenge the adequacy of a promised educational service, and the resolution of the plaintiffs' claims would not require 'second-guessing the professional judgment of the University faculty on academic matters'." Ibid., 1063.

17. However, in *Helling v. Carey*, 83 Wisc. 2d 514, 519 P.2d 981 (1974), the court found that compliance with a statute did not exculpate the defendant. In this case, an ophthalmologist did not regularly screen patients for glaucoma who were under forty, since professional standards at the time did not require screening at that age. The defendant, who was treated by the physician and under forty, contracted glaucoma resulting in visual impairment. The court allowed the plaintiff to recover in this case, holding that the ease and safety of the pressure test, coupled with the seriousness of the disease, made it negligent not to administer the test.

18. Cal. Health & Safety Code §1317 (West 2002).

19. *Guerrero v. Cooper Queen Hospital*, 537 P.2d 1329 (Ariz. 1975).

20. See *Christou v. Arlington Park-Washington Racetrack Corporation*, 432 N.E.2d 920 (Ill. App. Ct. 1982).

21. W. Page Keeton, Dan B. Dobbs, Robert E. Keeton, & David G. Owen, *Prosser and Keeton on the Law of Torts* (St. Paul, MN: West Publishing Company, 1984, 5th ed.): 2. ("The metaphor is apparent: a tort is a conduct which is twisted, or crooked, not straight.")

22. Ibid., 6.

23. *American Jurisprudence*, 2nd ed. 57 (2004), §75.

24. Tort liability applies to both public and private schools. For example, a second-grade student was severely burned when her teacher lit a votive candle and left the candle on her desk and the student got too close to it catching her bluebird costume on fire. *Smith v. Archbishop of St. Louis*, 632 S.W.2d 516 (1982).

25. Cary Silverman, "School Violence: Is It Time to Hold School Districts Liable for Inadequate Safety Measures?" *Education Law Reporter* 145 (2000), 535–555, 553.

26. "It is well-settled that a cause of action exists for a school's or a teacher's failure to supervise adequately conduct on school grounds that threatens students with physical injury." Robert H. Jerry II, "Recovery in Tort for Educational Malpractice: Problems of Theory and Policy," *University of Kansas Law Review* 29 (1981): 195–212, 208.

27. *Maldonado v. Tuckahoe Union Free School District*, 817 N.Y.S.2d 376 (A.D. 2 Dept. 2006).

28. *Donohue v. Copiague Union School District*, 418 N.Y.S.2d 375, 379 (Wachtler, J, concurring).

29. *Knighter v. William Floyd Union Free School District*, 857 N.Y.S.2d 726, 727 (A.D. 2 Dept. 2008).

30. *Biancorosso v. School District No.30C*, 151 N.E.3d 662, 664–665 (Ill. App. Ct. 2019) (emphases in original).

31. Ibid., 666.

32. Todd A. DeMitchell & Terri A. DeMitchell, "Statutes and Standards: Has the Door to Educational Malpractice Been Opened?" *Brigham Young University* 2003(2) (2003): 485–518, 491.

33. It is a volitional act as opposed to a negligent act. The most common intentional torts are assault, battery, false imprisonment, infliction of mental distress, trespass to land or chattel, and conversion. "Negligence differs from an intentional tort in that negligent acts are neither expected nor intended, whereas an intentional tort can

be both anticipated and intended" (Kern Alexander & M. David Alexander, *American Public School Law* (Belmont, CA: West Thomson Learning, 2001, 5th ed.): 555.

34. Strict liability occurs when an injury results from the creation of an unusual hazard such as the storage and transportation of explosives or the possession of large dangerous animals. It is liability without fault. A trampoline was not held to be an abnormally dangerous instrumentality, and thus a school district was not held strictly liable for the severe injury to a sixth-grade student who used it (*Fallon v. Indian Trail School*, 500 N.E.2d 101 (Ill. App. Ct. 1986). For a discussion of strict liability as applied to the sexual abuse of students, see, Todd A. DeMitchell & Richard Fossey, "Strict Liability under Title IX for Employee Sexual Abuse of Students: *Leija v. Canutillo Independent School District*," *International Journal of Educational Reform* 5 (1996): 107–114.

35. Todd A. DeMitchell, *Negligence: What Principals Need to Know about Avoiding Liability* (Lanham, MD: Rowman & Littlefield Education, 2007): 24.

36. *Jonathan A. v. Board of Education of the City of New York*, 779 N.Y.S.2d 3, 6 (A.D. 1 Dept. 2004).

37. *Restatement (Second) of Torts* §320 comment (b) at 131.

38. *Mirand v. City of New York*, 614 N.Y.S.2d 372, 375 (Ct. App. 1994).

39. *Vernonia School District 47J v. Acton*, 115 S.Ct. 2386 (1995).

40. Karen M. Richards, "Is Danger Lurking in Our Schools? The Duty to Adequately Supervise Students," *NYSBA Municipal Lawyer* 26(4) (2012): 9–14, 9, https://system.suny.edu/media/suny/content-assets/documents/generalcounsel/pubs/Richards_SuperviseStudents.pdf.

41. *Collette v. Tolleson Unified School District, No. 214*, 54 P.3d 828, 835 (Ariz. App. Div. 1 2002).

42. An example of the plaintiff's responsibility under the foreseeability's standard asks whether it knew or should have known of an individual's propensity to engage in such acts is found in a 2021 New York case, *Knazak v. Hamburg Central School District*, 152 N.Y.S.3d 199 (A.D. Dept. 2021). A student was sexually molested by another student while they were alone in a classroom. In New York, schools "are under a duty to adequately supervise the students in their charge, and they will be held liable for foreseeable injuries proximately related to the absence of adequate supervision," ibid., 201. The plaintiff brought a lawsuit against the school district for negligent supervision. The court denied the school district's motion to dismiss and the school district appealed. The Appellate Court held that even though the student had an "extensive and troubling disciplinary history," he was not disciplined for aggressive behavior directed at others nor was he disciplined for sexually inappropriate behavior or threats of physical or sexual violence. Ibid., 202. The court summed the case holding that without prior evidence of any prior similar conduct, the school district had no actual knowledge of a propensity for sexual assault, the claim for negligent supervision fails. One of the judges dissented, writing, "I conclude that here a jury needed little more than its own common experience to conclude that [the] defendant had sufficient notice of a dangerous situation and could have reasonably anticipated the misconduct in this case." Ibid., 203.

43. *Diaz v. Krob*, 636 N.E.2d 1231 (Ill. App. Ct. 1994).

44. *Rock v. State*, 681 A.2d 901 (R.I. 1996).

45. *Bellman v. San Francisco High School District*, 11 Cal.2d 576, 582 (Cal. 1938).

46. Editors, "Note, Educational Malpractice" *University of Pennsylvania Law Review* 124 (1976): 755–805, 772.

47. *Marquay v. Eno*, 662 A.2d 272 (N.H. 1995).

48. *Levandoski v. Jackson County School District*, 328 So.2d 339, 342 (Miss. 1976).

49. *Dunn v. Unified School District No. 367*, 40 P.3d 315, 326 (Kan. Ct. App. 2002).

50. *Mirand v. City of New York*, 614 N.Y.S.2d 372, 375 (Ct. App. 1994).

51. *Wyke v. Polk County School Board*, 129 F.3d 560 (11th Cir. 1997).

52. *Santanna v. City of New York*, 722 N.Y.S.2d 545, 555 (A.D. 1 Dept. 2001).

53. *Gonzalez v. City of New York*, 730 N.Y.S.2d 154 (A.D. 2 Dept. 2001).

54. *Rhea v. Grandview School District*, 694 P.2d 666 (Wash. Ct. App. 1985).

55. *Hurlburt v. Noxon*, 565 N.Y.S.2d 683 (N.Y. Sup. Ct. 1990).

56. *Raymond v. Iberia Parish School Board*, 323 So.3d 447, 450 (La. Ct. App. 2021). "In this case, the determinative facts are not in dispute. Anisha's injuries occurred long after she was in the care and custody of her aunt and grandmother who were authorized to care for her in the absence of her mother." Ibid., 449.

57. *C.M. v. City of New York*, 800 N.Y.S.2d 898, 900 (Sup. 2005).

58. Ibid. Even though the sexual assault would not have occurred absent the employee's power over the student by virtue of his employment, the school was not found to be vicariously liable for the injury. The court also found that the school district had not negligently supervised the teacher because it did not have notice of inappropriate behavior.

59. See *Dunn v. Unified School District No. 367*, 40 P.3d 315, 328 (Kan. App. 2002) (there is no question that a school has a duty to provide a suitable environment conducive to the general health, safety, and welfare of each student. Even though a school has such a duty, it cannot be an insurer against all accidents).

60. *Brownell v. Los Angeles Unified School District*, 5 Cal. Rptr. 2d 756 (Cal. Ct. App. 1992).

61. This is generally true, unless the school assumes a responsibility that the students have come to rely upon for their safety. A good example is providing supervision for students who arrive one hour early for school when the student handbook states that the school will assume responsibility for proper supervision one-half hour before the start of school. If students and parents have come to rely upon that additional supervision because the school has undertaken to provide it, the school must discharge that duty in a reasonable manner. See *Johnson v. Ouachita Parish Police Jury*, 377 So.2d 397 (La. Ct. App. 1979), in which it was held that a school district was under no legal duty to provide a school safety patrol, but once it assumed the duty it must act reasonably to meet the duty.

62. *Summers v. Cambridge Joint School District No. 432*, 88 P.3d 772 (Idaho 2004).

63. McCarthy et al., *supra* note 1, 419.

64. In a nationwide study by LRP, negligent supervision accounted for 43 percent of the school negligence suits resulting in awards. Rachael Kaiman (ed.), *School Negligence and Safety Claims: An Inside Look at Limiting Your School's Exposure* (Palm Beach Gardens, FL: LRP Media Group, 2003): 3.

65. Karen-Ann Broe & Nancy W. Brown (2004) *Preventing Catastrophic Student Injuries,* Paper Presentation, Education Law Association, Tucson, Arizona, 19.

66. Michael Imber & Tyll van Gell, *Education Law* (Mahwah, NJ: Lawrence Erlbaum Associates, Publishers, 2000, 2d ed.): 458.

67. *Banks v. Terrebone Parish School Board*, 339 So.2d 1295, 1295 (La. Ct. App.1976).

68. *Danna v. Sewanhaka Central High School*, 662 N.Y.S.2d 71, 73 (A.D. 2 Dept. 1997).

69. *Simonides v. Eastchester Union Free School District*, 31 N.Y.S.3d w210, 211 (A.D. 2 Det. 2016).

70. *Vonungren v. Morris Central School District*, 658 N.Y.S.2d 760, 761 (A.D.3 Dept. 1997).

71. *Bush v. Oscada Area Schools*, 250 N.W.2d 759 (Mic. Ct. App. 1977).

72. *Baker v. Briarcliff School District*, 613 N.Y.S.2d 660 (A.D. 2 Dept. 1994).

73. *LaValley v. Stanford*, 70 N.Y.S. 249 (1947).

74. *Izard v. Hickory City Schools Board of Education*, 315 S.E.2d 756 (N.C. Ct. App. `1984).

75. *Mastrangelo v. West Side Union High School District*, 42 P.2d 634, 636 (1935).

76. Fred Hartmeister, *Surviving as a Teacher: The Legal Dimension* (Chicago, IL: Precept Press, 1995): 187.

77. *Lottie v. Edwards-Knox Central School District*, 652 N.Y.S.2d 144, 145 (A.D. 3 Dept. 1997).

78. *Johnson v. Orleans Parish School Board*, 261 So.2d 699 (La. Ct. App. 1972).

79. *Keaton v. Hancock County Board of Education*, 119 S.W.3d 218, 220 (Tenn. Ct. App. 2003).

80. *Cioffi v. Board of Education of City of New York,* 278 N.Y.S.2d 249 (N.Y. App. Div. 1967).

81. For example, in a 2021 case, a student was hit by a motor vehicle while crossing a busy roadway to get to her bus stop. The Florida District Court of Appeals held that the school district did not have a duty to warn. It did not create the busy roadway, the busy roadway was not "inconspicuous," and the board did not have custody or control of the student while she was walking to her bus stop. *School Board of Palm Beach City v. Edwards*, 327 So.3d 1251 (Fla. App. 4 Dist. 2021).

82. For a discussion of this case, see Richard Fossey & Todd A. DeMitchell, "*Munn v. Hotchkiss School*: A Jury Awards $41 to a Student Who Contracted Encephalitis on a School-Sponsored Field Trip in Rural China," *Education Law Reporter* 382 (2020): 446–453. The jury found that Cara had not contributed to her injuries and awarded her $450,000 in past economic damages, $9,800.000 in future economic damages, and $31,500,000 in noneconomic damages. Ibid., 448, f.n. 15.

83. *Munn v. Hotchkiss School*, 724 F. Appx. 25 (2d Cir. 2018).

84. *Munn v. Hotchkiss School*, 24 F. Supp. 3d 155, 167 (D. Conn. 2014), *aff'd*, 724 F. Appx. 25 (2d Cir. 2018).

85. Ibid., 193.

86. Ibid., 176.

87. James F. Blumstein, "The Legal Liability Regime: How Well Is It Doing in Assuring Quality, Accounting for Costs, and Coping with an Evolving Reality in the Health Care Marketplace?" *Annals of Health Law* 11 (2002): 125–145, 130. The author raises the question about two paradigms as models for malpractice. He writes, "Fundamental to an understanding of a discussion of the legal liability regime is an awareness of competing visions of medical care—the professional model and an economic model." Ibid., 125.

88. *Ibid.*, 131.

89. *Ibid.*, 133.

90. *Golden v. Pavlov-Shapiro*, 31 N.Y.S.3d 699, 700 (A.D. 4 Dept. 2016).

91. *Citizens' Loan Fund and Saving Association v. Friedley,* 23 N.E. 1075 (Ind. 1890).

92. See, e.g., *Campbell v. Magana*, 8 Cal. Rptr. 32 (Cal. App. 1960) and *George v. Caton*, 600 P.2d 822 (N.M. App. 1979).

93. *Cochrane v. Little*, 71 Md. 323, 325 (1889).

94. 531 P.2d 589 (Idaho 1974).

95. *Cotton v. Travaline*, 432 A.2d 122 (N.J. Super. A.D. 1981).

96. *Rogers v. Robson*, 407 N.E.2d 47 (Ill. 1980).

97. See *Yurkovich v. Rose*, 847 P.2d 925 (Wash. Ct. App. 1993).

98. *Janukajtis v. Fallon*, 726 N.Y.S.2d 451 (A.D. 2 Dept. 2001). See also *Siegell v. Herricks Union Free School District*, 777 N.Y.S.2d 148 (A. D. 2 Dept. 2004), in which a student was shoved during a relay race. The court held that the offending student's history of disciplinary problems involving violence was insufficient to place the school on notice that he would injure someone. Absent that type of knowledge, the school district did not have a duty to prevent spontaneous and unforeseeable acts of students.

99. Ibid.

100. 159 Eng. Rep. 299 (1863).

101. *A.C. Ex Real Cooper v. Bellingham School*, 105 P.3d 400, 403 (Wash. App. Div. 1 2004).

102. See E. Robert Wallach & Daniel J. Kelly, "Attorney Malpractice in California: A Shaky Citadel," *Santa Clara Lawyer* 10 (1970): 257–273, 266.

103. *Res ipsa loquitur* was asserted when a metal-encased frame of glass fell on a student while she was seated in a mobile-classroom unit. Frames of glass do not normally fall out of their frames without some inferred negligence. *Douglas v. Board of Education*, 468 N.E.2d 473 (Ill. 1984).

104. *Farr v. Wright*, 833 S.W.2d 597, 600 (Tex. App.—Corpus Christi 1992, writ denied).

105. *Schorlemer v. Reyes*, 974 S.W.2d 141, 145 (Tex. App.—San Antonio 1998, writ denied).

106. *Manax v. Ballew*, 797 S.W.2d 71, 72–73 (Tex. App.—Waco 1990, writ denied).

107. The Public Health Law Map, "Res Ipsa Loquitur," *The LSU Medical and Public Health Law Site* (April 19, 2009), https://biotech.law.lsu.edu/map/ResIpsaLoquitur.html.

108. Keeton et al., *supra* note 21, 175.

109. McCarthy et al., *supra* note 1, 426.

110. *Benitez v. New York City Board of Education*, 543 N.Y.S.2d 29 (N.Y. 1989).

111. McCarthy et al., *supra* note 1, 427.

112. Ibid.

113. Author, "Breach of Medical Malpractice Law," *Newsome/Melton* (n.d.), https://www.medicalmalpracticehelp.com/glossary/breach-of-duty/.

114. Yvette Brazier, "What Is Medical Malpractice?" *Medical News Today* (April 5, 2017), https://www.medicalnewstoday.com/articles/248175.

115. E. Wallace, J. Lowry, S. M. Smith, & T. Fahey, "The Epidemiology of Malpractice Claims in Primary Care: A Systematic Review," *BMJ Open* (June 13, 2013), https://www.ncbi.nlm.nih.gov/pmc/articles/PMC3693415/.

116. Martin A. Makary, "Open Letter to the U.S. Centers for Disease Control and Prevention" (May 1, 2016), https://www.documentcloud.org/documents/2822345-Hopkins-CDC-letter.html.

117. *Creasey v. Hogan,* 637 P.2d 114 (Or. 1981) and *Becker v. Hidalgo,* 556 P.2d 35 (N.M. 1976).

118. *Roofers Local 30/30B v. Katz*, 398 Pa. Super. 564, 581 A.2d 607 (1990).

119. *City of Mounds View v. Walijarvi*, 263 N.W.2d 420, 424 (Minn. 1978).

120. Ibid. The court wrote, "Thus, doctors cannot promise that every operation will be successful; a lawyer can never be certain that a contract he drafts is without latent ambiguity; and an architect cannot be certain that a structural design will interact with natural forces as anticipated." Ibid.

121. Keeton et al., *supra* note 21, 265.

122. *Nisbet v. Bucher*, 949 S.W.2d 111, 115 (Mo. App. E.D. 1997).

123. Ibid.

124. *Palsgraf v. Long Island Railroad Company*, 162 N.E. 99 (N.Y. 1928).

125. *Emery v. Chapman*, 495 So.2d 371 (La. Ct. App. 1986).

126. 617 N.W.2d 11 (Iowa 2000).

127. Ibid., 17.

128. Ibid., 18.

129. *Fall v. White,* 449 N.E.2d 635 (Ind. App. 1983).

130. See E. Blythe Stason, "Governmental Tort Liability Symposium," *New York University Law Review* 29 (1954): 1321.

131. 2 T.R. 667, 100 Eng. Rep. 359 (1778).

132. Ibid., 673.

133. 163 N.E.2d 89 (Ill. 1959).

134. David J. Sperry, Philip T. K. Daniel, Dixie Snow Huefner, & E. Gordon Gee, *Education Law and the Public Schools: A Compendium* (Norwood, MA: Christopher-Gordon Publishers, 1998, 2nd ed.): 1088.

135. See *Kahn v. East Side Union High School District*, 75 P.3d 30 (2003), in which a swimmer broke her neck while practicing a racing dive. To overcome the assumption of risk defense, the activity would have to be totally outside the range of activities

ordinarily associated with the sport; *Serrell v. Connetquot Central School District,* 798 N.Y.S2d 493, 494 (A.D. 2 Dept. 2005) ("The injured plaintiff, an experienced high school football player, voluntarily assumed the risk of injury by participating in the varsity football practice in which he was injured").

136. Alexander & Alexander, *supra* note 33, 578.

137. *Kelly v. McCarrick,* 841 A.2d 869 (Md. Spec. App. 2004).

138. *Albers v. Independent School District #302 of Lewis City,* 487 P.2d 936 (Idaho 1971).

139. *Hochreiter v. Diocese of Buffalo,* 764 N.Y.S.2d 753, 754 (A.D. 4 Dept. 2003).

140. *Simmons v. Beauregard Parish School Board,* 315 So.2d 883 (La. Ct. App. 1975).

141. McCarthy et al., *supra* note 1, 432.

142. Alexander & Alexander, *supra* note 33, 570. "A child is by nature careless and often negligent, and knowing this a teacher should allow for an additional margin of safety. This is especially true with younger children." Ibid.

143. *Sutton v. Duplessis,* 584 So.2d 362 (La. Ct. App. 1991).

144. *Aronson v. Horace Mann-Barnard School,* 637 N.Y.S.2d 410 (App. Div. 1996).

145. *Funston v. School Town of Munster,* 822 N.E.2d 985 (Ind. App. 2005).

146. Ibid., 989.

147. *Carreker v. Harper,* 196 Ga. App. 658, 396 S.E.2d 587 (1990).

148. *Roers v. Engebretson,* 479 N.W.2d 422 (Minn. 1992).

149. Sperry et al., *supra* note 133, 1087.

150. *Dunn v. Unified School District No. 367,* 40 P.3d 315 (Kan. App. 2002).

Section II

EMERGING TORT ACTIONS

Chapter 4

The Early Educational
Malpractice Suits

A Failed Tort

Educational malpractice is a tort theory beloved of commentators, but not of courts.[1]

The early 1970s ushered in the beginning of the judicial exploration of the tort of educational malpractice. A 1972 article in the *Saturday Review* asserted that a tort lawsuit for inadequate instruction resulting in inadequate basic skills was a viable cause of action.[2] This was four years before the seminal educational malpractice case, *Peter W. v. San Francisco Unified School District*, was decided and the issue of educational malpractice was first adjudicated.[3] The *Peter W.* case was highlighted in chapter 1 "The Graduation Scenario." *Peter W.* and selected early cases that established the foundation for educational malpractice will be explored next.

PETER W. V. SAN FRANCISCO UNIFIED
SCHOOL DISTRICT

In *Peter W.*, the stage was set for all subsequent educational malpractice actions, by clearly denying recovery and firmly refusing to recognize educational malpractice as an actionable tort. In this case, a high school graduate sued the San Francisco Unified School District, the superintendent, and governing board, to recover for alleged negligence in instruction and intentional misrepresentation of the student's progress. The plaintiff claimed that these actions resulted in depriving him of basic academic skills. In other words, he asserted that he had not been adequately educated.

The plaintiff in this action was an eighteen-year-old male who had recently graduated from the San Francisco Unified School District after having been enrolled in the school system for a period of approximately twelve years. He claimed that, although he had graduated from high school, he possessed only a fifth-grade reading ability.

TEXTBOX 4.1

The novel-and troublesome-question on this appeal is whether a person who claims to have been inadequately educated, while a student in a public school system, may state a cause of action in tort against the public authorities who operate and administer the system.
We hold that he may not.

Peter W. v. San Francisco Unified School District, 60 Cal. App. 3rd 817 (Ct. App. 1976). (Emphasis added)

The plaintiff alleged in part that the four requisite elements for bringing an action in tort were present in his case. In his complaint, the plaintiff alleged that the defendant school district, which includes its agents and employees, had a duty to provide plaintiff with an adequate education and that the defendant breached that duty. In addition, the plaintiff alleged that this breach of duty was in fact the proximate cause of plaintiff's inability to read at grade level and that the plaintiff has been injured because of this inability.

At the outset, the court's opinion acknowledged that the parties to the action did not debate the adequacy of the plaintiff's claim with respect to negligent acts, proximate cause, and injury, therefore clearly recognizing most of the required elements in a tort suit. The court, however, had very serious reservations regarding the elements of the standard of care, causation, and injury. Therefore, the court determined that educators owe no duty of care to students, despite the fact that such a duty is readily recognized in suits against other professionals.

Peter W. offered three theories to support his contention that a duty of care existed: (1) by accepting the responsibility for teaching students, the school district assumed the duty to perform its instructional responsibilities with reasonable care; (2) teachers and students in the school district were in a special relationship that supports the teachers' duty to exercise reasonable care; and (3) the duty of teachers to exercise reasonable care in instruction and supervision of students has been recognized in California judicial decisions.

The court admitted that the facts impose upon the defendant a duty of care within the common meaning of the term. However, the court dismissed each of the theories raised by the plaintiff for want of relevant authority, establishing that the enrollment of the plaintiff in defendants' schools creates a legal duty that will sustain liability for negligence for their alleged breach. The court acknowledged that the concept of a duty of care as currently recognized is not immutable but cautioned that certain principles must be considered controlling. The most pertinent principle for purposes of this issue expounded by the court was that "judicial recognition of such duty in the defendant, with the consequence of his liability in negligence for its breach, is initially to be dictated or precluded by considerations of public policy."[4]

Despite the constraints placed on expanding the concept of duty, the court acknowledged that the California Supreme Court had or sanctioned new areas of tort liability when the wrongs and the injuries involved were both comprehensible and assessable within the existing legal framework. However, the court in *Peter W.* was unwilling to extend the concept of a duty of due care to the facts presented in this case due to the court's belief that there is no recognizable standard of care, cause, or injury in education:

> Unlike the activity of the highway or the marketplace, classroom methodology affords no readily acceptable standards of care, or cause, or injury. The science of pedagogy itself is fraught with different and conflicting theories of how or what a child should be taught, and any layman might—and commonly does—have his own emphatic views on the subject. The "injury" claimed here is the plaintiff's inability to read and write. Substantial professional authority attests that the achievement of literacy in the schools, or its failure, are influenced by a host of factors which affect the pupil subjectively, from outside the formal teaching process, and beyond the control of its ministers. They may be physical, neurological, emotional, cultural, environmental; they may be present but not perceived, recognized but not identified.[5]

Based on this reasoning, the court found that a duty of due care should not be created because of the multiple factors involved in education and because of an assumption on the part of the court that there is no recognized methodology with regard to education. The concern over not being able to establish a duty owed is compounded by the issue of causation. How to determine which of the "host of factors" is under the control of the teacher or of the school. The court held that the plaintiff's inability to establish a causal link between the alleged conduct and the resulting injury precluded his cause of action for educational malpractice.[6]

The last, and the most cited, reason for not recognizing educational malpractice is that a finding for the plaintiff student would violate public policy, an argument beyond the reach of the *prima facie* case of negligence. The court asserted that policy considerations "negate" an actionable duty of care based on the unique policy position that public education occupies. The court wrote, "Few of our institutions, if any, aroused the controversies, or incurred the public dissatisfaction, which have attended the operation of the public schools during the last few decades."[7]

The court in closing its opinion explained:

> To hold them to an actionable "duty of care," in the discharge of their academic functions, would expose them to the tort claims—real or imagined—of disaffected students and parents in countless numbers. They are already beset by social and financial problems which have gone to major litigation, but for which no permanent solution has yet appeared. The ultimate consequences, in terms of public time and money, would burden them—and society—beyond calculation.
>
> Upon consideration of the role imposed upon the public schools by law and the limitations imposed upon them by their publicly-supported budgets and of the just-cited "consequences to the community of imposing [upon them] a duty to exercise care with resulting liability for breach" we find no such "duty" in . . . plaintiff's complaint.[8]

Thus, the plaintiff's action failed because the court refused to find that a California school district owed a duty of care while instructing students. According to California law, educators must adequately supervise students,[9] but according to *Peter W.* they do not have a duty to adequately educate them as a matter of public policy. The policy argument is the most frequently asserted argument against educational malpractice. One legal commentator commented *Peter W.* and its following cases as a "talisman to ward off a storm of calamities" that would "inevitably descend upon the U.S. judicial system."[10]

DONOHUE V. COPIAGUE UNION FREE SCHOOL DISTRICT[11]

TEXTBOX 4.2

The failure to learn does not bespeak a failure to teach. It is not alleged that the plaintiff's classmates, who were exposed to the identical classroom instruction, also failed to learn.

Donohue v. Copiague Union Free School District, 64 A. D. 28, 39 (N.Y. A.D. 1978).

Three years after the case of *Peter W.* was heard in California, a similar action was brought by a high school student in New York. In *Donohue v. Copiague Union Free School District*, the plaintiff alleged that he had attended Copiague Senior High School from 1972 to 1976 and graduated without the rudimentary ability to read and write. Consequently, he had to seek tutoring to acquire the skills he did not gain in school. The plaintiff sought $5 million in damages.

He asserted that the defendant school district was under the obligation to teach the subjects and properly assess his capacity to learn and his progress toward qualifying for a Certificate of Graduation. Specifically, the student alleged that the defendant gave him passing grades and/or minimal or failing grades, failed to properly evaluate him, and failed to properly hire personnel experienced in these matters. Specific to his claim of educational malpractice, the complaint asserted a failure to

> teach the plaintiff in such a manner so that he could reasonably understand what was necessary under the circumstances so that he could cope with the various subjects which they tried to make the plaintiff understand; failed to properly supervise the plaintiff; failed to advise his parents of the difficulty and necessity to call in psychiatric care.[12]

The complaint asserted two causes of action. The first was educational malpractice and the second was the negligent breach of a constitutionally imposed duty to educate under New York law.

The New York intermediate appellate court rejected the second claim with very little discussion. However, the first cause of action, alleging educational malpractice, was analyzed in depth. The court found that such a cause of action was indeed plausible and stated that "the imagination need not be overly taxed to envision allegations of a legal duty of care flowing from educators."[13]

However, after determining that a cause of action in educational malpractice was indeed possible, the court opined that such claims should not be entertained for public policy reasons. The court found that the control and management of educational affairs in the state of New York was vested in the Board of Regents and the Commissioner of Education and that the courts should not interfere with the decision-making of that entity absent a gross violation of public policy. The court did not, however, elaborate on what type of violation might be considered gross, but clearly, a lack of due care while instructing students was not considered a gross violation of public policy.

Specifically, the court held as follows:

> To entertain a cause of action for "educational malpractice" would require the
> courts not merely to make judgments as to the validity of the broad educational
> policies—a course we have unalteringly eschewed in the past—but, more
> importantly, to sit in review of the day-to-day implementation of these poli-
> cies. Recognition in the courts of this cause of action would constitute blatant
> interference with the responsibility for the administration of the public school
> system lodged by Constitution and statute in school administrative agencies.[14]

Whereas the court in *Peter W.* found that no duty of care exists in the
educational setting, and therefore an action in malpractice is not possible, the
Donohue court found that the four elements of a tort do exist in educational
malpractice cases.[15] Specific to proximate cause, Judge Jasen wrote, "While
this element may be difficult, if not, impossible to prove in view of the many
collateral factors involved in the learning process, it perhaps assumes too
much to conclude that it could never be established."[16]

But Judge Wachtler, taking a different tack in a short concurring opinion,
asserted that the practical problems raised by this cause of action are for-
midable. "Factors such as the student's attitude, motivation, temperament,
past experience and home environment may well all play an essential and
immeasurable role in learning."[17] The judge concludes that the legal theory of
educational malpractice should not be recognized in the courts.

The admonishment of the Supreme Court, Appellate Division, in *Donohue*
denying relief under educational malpractice bears restating:

> This determination does not mean that educators are not ethically and legally
> responsible for providing a meaningful public education for the youth of our
> State. Quite the contrary, all teachers and other officials of our schools bear an
> important public trust and may be held to answer for the failure to faithfully
> perform their duties. It does mean, however, that they may not be sued for dam-
> ages by an individual student for an alleged failure to reach certain educational
> objectives.[18]

Thus, a California appellate court in *Peter W.* and a New York appellate
court in *Donohue* found that "the lack of agreed-upon standards for teaching
practice and public policy concerns regarding financial responsibility formed
the basis for the failure of lawsuits for educational malpractice."[19]

In *Peter W.* and *Donohue* the plaintiff students were unsuccessful in large
part because no duty of care as defined through a standard of practice was
recognized by the court. "No standardization of educational process, thus
no professional standard of care," wrote one educational malpractice commentator.[20] In short, the two courts ruled that educators could not be held

accountable in a tort of negligence for the services they render for both legal and policy reasons.

HOFFMAN V. BOARD OF EDUCATION OF CITY OF NEW YORK[21]

TEXTBOX 4.3

In *Hoffman v. Board of Education* (49 N.Y.2d 121) and *Donohue v. Copiague Union Free School Dist.* (47 N.Y.2d 440), we dismissed complaints for educational malpractice, holding that as a matter of public policy the courts would not second-guess the professional judgments of public school educators and administrators in selecting programs for particular students.

Torres v. Little Flower Children's Services, 64 N.Y.2d 119, 123 (N.Y. 1984).

Soon after the plaintiff, Daniel Hoffman, entered kindergarten in the New York City school system in 1956, he was tested by one of the school system's clinical psychologists who determined that he had an intelligence quotient (IQ) of 74. Consequently, he was placed in a class for Children with Retarded Mental Development. Because Hoffman had a severe speech defect that made communication difficult, the clinical psychologist recommended that the plaintiff be re-evaluated within a two-year period based on his concern "so that a more accurate estimation of his abilities can be made."[22]

Daniel was placed in a class for Children with Retarded Mental Development. In 1959 and 1960 he was given achievement tests, in which his score for reading readiness indicated a potential for learning to read that was higher than average, but his achievement scores indicated that he "possessed extremely limited reading and mathematical skills."[23] Daniel's IQ was not retested until 1968 when he was transferred to the Queens Occupational Training Center.

His IQ scores were 85 for verbal and 107 for performance for a full-scale score of 94. These scores indicated that Daniel was not "retarded." Consequently, he was no longer eligible to be enrolled in the Queens program and was dismissed for the fall 1969 semester.[24] Thereafter, an action was commenced against the Board of Education of the City of New York. The plaintiff alleged that the board was negligent in its original assessment of Daniel and their failure to retest within the two-year recommendation.

At trial, the jury awarded damages to the plaintiff in the amount of $750,000. The Appellate Division of the Supreme Court affirmed the judgment. "The court characterized defendants' failure to retest plaintiff as an affirmative act of negligence, actionable under New York law."[25] Thus, the court attempted to distinguish its case from *Donohue* and thereby allowing the *Hoffman* case to avoid the public policy restrictions of *Donohue*.

On appeal, the Court of Appeals disagreed, asserting:

> We had thought it well settled that the courts of this State may not substitute their judgment, or the judgment of a jury, for the professional judgment of educators and government officials actually engaged in the complex and often delicate process of educating the many thousands of children in our schools.[26]

The Court of Appeals reversed the Appellate Division's order and dismissed the complaint based on the precedent set by *Donohue*. The court's decision was grounded on the principle that courts should not interfere with the professional judgment of those legally entrusted with the responsibility for the administration of schools. The court was loath to second-guess the "propriety of each of the procedures used in the education of every student in our school system."[27]

The Court of Appeals concluded that the court system is not the proper forum to ascertain the proper placement of a student. Instead, the court believed that the proper forum for the resolution of these types of educational decisions is through administrative processes.

Justice Meyer submitted the only dissent. The Justice agreed with the Appellate Division's holding that the case does not involve educational malpractice. Instead, it involved "discernible affirmative negligence" for the board's failure to follow the recommendation to conduct a re-evaluation within two years. This failure is "readily identifiable as the proximate cause of plaintiff's damages."[28]

HUNTER V. BOARD OF EDUCATION OF MONTGOMERY COUNTY[29]

TEXTBOX 4.4

I do not agree with the majority, however, that individuals engaged in the educational process who, through professional malpractice, negligently injure a child entrusted to their educational care should not be held liable. In my view a cause of action against such individuals should exist for such negligent injuries.

Hunter v. Board of Education of Montgomery County, 292 Md. 481, 492 (1982) (Davidson, J., concurring and dissenting).

Majority Decision

This issue of educational malpractice was once again heard in 1981 and decided in 1982 in *Hunter v. Board of Education of Montgomery County*. In this suit, the parents of Ross Hunter filed a lawsuit against the Montgomery County Board of Education, the principal of Ross's school, a school employee who conducted the diagnostic testing on Ross when he was in second grade, and his sixth-grade teacher. The Circuit Court and the Court of Special Appeals concluded that Hunters' educational malpractice case could not be maintained, and the Maryland Court of Appeals heard the case on appeal.

The Hunters alleged that the school system negligently evaluated their son's learning abilities and caused him to repeat first-grade materials while he was in second grade. According to the Hunter family, this "misplacement" caused Ross to feel "embarrassment," which resulted in the development of "learning deficiencies" and caused him to experience "depletion of ego strength."[30]

The Appellate Court noted that educational malpractice suits had been unanimously rejected, citing the relevant cases, including the three cases discussed earlier: *Peter W.*, *Donohue*, and *Hoffman*. The court wrote that the cases were generally precluded by considerations of public policy, including:

> the absence of a workable rule of care against which the defendant's conduct may be measured, the inherent uncertainty in determining the cause and nature of any damages, and the extreme burden which would be imposed on the already strained resources of the public school system to say nothing of those of the judiciary.[31]

Citing *Peter W.* and *Donohue* as authority, Maryland's highest court found that a cause of action for damages for acts of negligence committed by educators is precluded by public policy and emphasized its concerns about the difficulty of measuring damages. The court substantially agreed with the reasoning employed by the courts in *Peter W.* and *Donohue* about awards of money damages. The Maryland Court of Appeals wrote that "an award of money damages . . . represents a singularly inappropriate remedy for asserted errors in the educational process."[32]

In addition, the majority in the *Hunter* decision expressed concerns about the difficulties in establishing legal cause and the inherent immeasurability of damages in educational negligence actions against school systems. "Moreover," the court opined, "to allow [the Hunters'] asserted negligence claims to proceed would in effect position the courts of this State as overseers of both the day-today operation of our educational process as well as the formulation of its governing policies. This responsibility we are loathe to impose on our courts."[33]

The court concluded that parents and students who feel aggrieved by the actions taken by public school educators are not without remedy. However, the complainants must seek administrative remedies, not judicial remedies.

Dissent

Judge Davidson concurred that the plaintiffs can maintain an action against the school district for intentional injuries. However, he dissented in part, asserting that plaintiffs should be able to maintain an action against educators when their professional practice negligently injures a student. The judge stated that educators are professionals having special training and state certification and hold themselves out as possessing certain skills and knowledge that non-educators do not possess. "As professionals, they owe a professional duty of care to children who receive their services and a standard of care based upon customary conduct is appropriate."[34] Negligent conduct on the part of a public educator consequently may harm a student.

The dissent broke with the majority as well as other courts. Judge Davidson writes, "Unlike my colleagues, I believe that public policy does not prohibit such claims [as malpractice] from being entertained."[35] Thus, the dissent discards the public policy argument for not finding educational malpractice suits as a viable tort for negligence. In addition, Judge Davidson also stated that there would not be unleashed a flood of litigation as a result of recognizing educational malpractice nor would educational malpractice "position the courts of this State as overseers of both the day-to-day operation of our educational process as well as the formulation of its governing policies."[36]

Judge Davidson's dissent not only distances his argument from the majority but from the developing law on educational malpractice at that time. He concludes:

> In recognizing a cause of action for educational malpractice, this Court would do nothing more than what courts have traditionally done from time immemorial—namely provide a remedy to a person harmed by the negligent act of another. Our children deserve nothing less.[37]

B.M. V. STATE[38]: THE SUPREME COURT OF MONTANA UPHOLDS AN EDUCATIONAL MALPRACTICE SUIT

TEXTBOX 4.5

The court's recognition of the cause of action in *B.M. v. State* concerned the misplacement of a student in special education, not the failure to educate a student in basic academic skills.

Michael A. Magone, "Educational malpractice—Does the Cause of Action Exist?" *Montana Law Review* 49(1) (1998): 140–146, 146.

Since the decision in *Hoffman*, several other special education cases have been brought unsuccessfully under the theory of negligence. Most of the allegations revolved around improper diagnosis, improper placement, and improper education. For example, cases have included allegations of mistesting and misclassification, resulting in the student not being provided with appropriate special education,[39] and negligent interpretation of tests or diagnosis, resulting in the improper placement of a student in a classroom for mentally retarded individuals.[40]

Interestingly, however, cases involving improper diagnosis that can be asserted as medical malpractice are successful. Again, the courts are showing a willingness to allow recovery for misdiagnosis in a medical setting but are not willing to allow recovery for misdiagnosis in an educational setting. In *Snow v. State*, recovery was afforded due to the fact that the improper diagnosis resulted in the improper placement of the student in a class for mentally retarded students.[41]

As seen earlier, similar actions by educators did not result in recovery for the aggrieved student. However, in this case, recovery was awarded due to the fact that the court found that the malpractice was medical and not educational because of the hospital-like setting.

The courts again crossed the boundary between educational and medical malpractice and awarded damages based on the distinction of the setting. In *Cantone v. Rosenblum*, a successful medical malpractice suit was brought against a center for the emotionally disturbed for failure to diagnose a hearing problem.[42] Therefore, while the actions taken by the individual charged with malpractice may be the same, the courts are allowing recovery in one setting, but not in the other.

The early case law on educational malpractice was essentially consistent. Malpractice suits on the basis of a failure to educate lost. A case in Montana, *B.M. v. State*, has been considered an exception to the trend.

B.M. was placed in foster care at age nine months. While in kindergarten, the minor child displayed learning difficulties. She was tested in January 1973, with the consent of the foster father. Her test results showed that she had an IQ of 76 and was classified as eligible for educable mentally retarded even though the required score was 50 to 75.[43] Her program was approved to start in September 1973. The inclusion program consisted of four identified special education students, including the child involved in the lawsuit. The four students attended a regular first-grade class, with a special education teacher providing support within the classroom and could be pulled out to the resource room as needed.

The pull-out option after five weeks increased in frequency to counteract distraction. The pull-out portion of the day expanded to approximately 40 percent of the instructional day. While in the resource room, the students were taught the same material but at a slower pace. The foster parents were not informed of the change in the program. Upon learning of the program change, the foster parents removed their daughter from the program. The parents claimed that the behavior of their child spiraled downward. The foster mother brought a lawsuit.

The complaint alleged that the State was negligent in placing her in the program and that the misplacement violated her rights to due process and equal protection. On summary judgment after discovery, the District Court granted summary judgment to the State, ruling that the "State owes no legal duty of care to students negligently placed in special education programs." In addition, the Valley County District Court ruled that the school district had not violated the child's due process or equal protection rights. The plaintiffs appealed.

The Supreme Court of Montana, first setting aside the immunity defense advanced by the lower court, reviewed one of the major prongs from the emerging educational malpractice suits. It broke ranks with other state courts, holding that it had "no difficulty in finding a duty of care owed to special education students."[44] The Court cited Article X, § 1 of the 1972 Montana Constitution,[45] followed by a citation to the statutory language. This is critical to overcoming the arguments of the earlier courts.

The Court asserted that the "school authorities owed the child a duty of reasonable care in testing her and placing her in an appropriate special education program."[46] After this assertion the court stated that it would not ascertain whether this duty was breached and instead remanded it to the trial court. The claims of violations of due process and equal protection did not prevail. In a 4–3 decision, the case was remanded for further proceedings.

The Montana Supreme Court did not address the other concerns of causation, damages, and intrusion into the daily operations of the public schools articulated by other courts. It is interesting to note that the Court did not cite any of the leading cases on educational malpractice. However, the concurring opinion written by Chief Justice Haswell did cite *Peter W.* and *Donohue* but asserted that this was not a case of the educational malpractice genre involving negligent failure to educate in basic academic skills.

Interestingly, the court emphasized that it was not endorsing a cause of action for educational malpractice by writing that "no action lies for this type of claim for policy reasons".[47] The court tried to differentiate its holding from the growing body of cases and the Chief Justice in his concurrence tried to emphasize the difference in the issue before the court and the educational malpractice issues.

Justice Sheehy dissented with a concurrence by Justice Harrison[48] and Justice Weber.[49] The dissent phrased the issue as one of public policy and note the phrasing of the Chief Justice's concurrence, in which he framed the legal question in pertinent part as "whether the statutes defining the student's eligibility for the special education program."[50] The dissent applied *Donohue*, *Hoffman*, and *Peter W.*, as well as other malpractice cases, to the question of the role of public policy. The review supported Justice Sheehy's conclusion that the policy considerations before the court should be controlling and the District Court's summary judgment for the defendant should be affirmed.

THE EARLY CASES: A WRAP-UP

TEXTBOX. 4.6

The current educational malpractice case law demonstrates the general fear of the courts to become involved in virtually any non-tangible dimension of public education. This fear, however, has unfortunately left several true victims in the dust of its fleeting path. With the exception of Montana, the courts have generally applied an "educational malpractice" rubber stamp to these otherwise plausible claims under the guise of public policy.

Kimberly A. Wilkins, "Educational Malpractice: A Cause of Action in Need of a Call for Action," *Valparaiso University Law Review* 22(2) (1988): 427–360, 444.

These cases are not an exhaustive list of educational malpractice cases. Rather, they are a representative list of the early educational malpractice litigation in which students sought redress based on claims that they were negligently educated. Follow-on malpractice cases, to varying degrees, anchored their analysis on the bedrock of these cases except for *B.M. v. State*, a notable outlier.

The cases cited four hurdles to the viability of a lawsuit for educational malpractice. Three hurdles can be categorized as deficiencies in proving the necessary elements for a *prima facie* case of negligence. The fourth hurdle is public policy considerations.

First, to make out a *prima facie* case of negligence, the plaintiff must show that the defendant owed a duty of care to the plaintiff. Thus, in an educational malpractice case, a student must establish that the school system and its employees have a duty of care to educate the student in a reasonable manner.

Unfortunately for plaintiffs, the courts have refused to recognize an accepted standard of care that school districts and teachers must meet when teaching their students. There is no common standard of pedagogy or universally accepted theory of education that can be applied to establish a standard of care in education.

Second, a student bringing an educational malpractice claim must show causation. In other words, the student must prove that the defendant educators caused the student to be poorly educated.

Again, the courts have universally declined to attribute poor educational outcomes to the school district or the teachers where a plaintiff student was educated. The student's motivation, innate ability to learn, the socioeconomic status of the parents, and the parents' educational level may all have contributed to a poor educational outcome. In short, courts have been unwilling to rule that a student's low educational level can be attributed to the educators who were in charge of the student's learning program.

A third element necessary for establishing a *prima facie* case of educational malpractice is injury. Students bringing educational malpractice lawsuits against educators must show that they were damaged by poor educational practices. Court decisions demonstrate that judges are skeptical about their ability to put a dollar amount on any alleged damages that students claim to have experienced as the result of being negligently educated. Judges also recognize that damages, were they to be awarded, would impose onerous costs on school districts that lose educational malpractice suits. Thus, educational malpractice claims have failed due in part to judicial reluctance to assess damages.

Finally, the courts have articulated again and again that there are strong public policy considerations that weigh against recognizing a cause of action for educational malpractice. Essentially, the judiciary has concluded that the public good would not be well served if courts took on the job of determining whether the day-to-day decisions of classroom teachers and administrators constitute negligence.[51]

In this regard, courts have expressed deep concern about the likelihood that a cause of action for negligent education would open the proverbial floodgates of litigation and expose school districts to astronomical awards for money damages.[52] Thus, as noted in *Hunter*, this cause of action would place an extreme burden on the fiscal resources of the public schools.

Moreover, as a matter of public policy, the courts are reluctant to tread on the territory of the school and the classroom. Although all judges were once participants as students in the educational enterprise, they have no special expertise that qualifies them to intrude into the day-to-day operations of schools.

For example, one commentator on educational malpractice early lawsuits writes:

> One of the reasons cited by the courts for not recognizing a duty of care is the history of noninterference by the courts in educational matters. In *Hoffman* (1979) the court stated that it should not substitute its judgment or the judgment of a jury for the professional judgment of professional educators, except in instances of gross violations of public policy.[53]

The foundation for educational malpractice cases for K–12 education was laid above. Next, we explore educational malpractice in higher education.

NOTES

1. *Ross v. Creighton University*, 740 F. Supp. 1319, 1327 (N.D. Ill. 1990).

2. Gary Saretsky & James Mecklenburger, "See You In Court?" *Saturday Review* (October 14, 1972): 50. The article advanced legal arguments for a lawsuit that a class of sixth-grade students, many of who had not yet learned to read. Two years later, but two years before *Peter W.* was decided, but not filed, University of California, Berkeley, law professor Stephen D. Sugarman expanded on the possibility of money damages being awarded for nonlearners. Stephen D. Sugarman, "Accountability through the Courts," *The School Review* 82 (1974): 233–259.

3. 60 Cal. App. 3d 814 (Ct. App. 1976).

4. Ibid., 822.

5. Ibid., 824.

6. Ibid., 825.

7. Ibid.

8. Ibid.

9. California Education Code §44807.

10. Patricia Abbott, "*Sain v. Cedar Rapids Community School District*: Providing Special Protection for Student Athletes?" *Brigham Young University Education & Law Journal* (2002): 291–312, 294.

11. *Donahue v. Copiague Union Free School District*, 391 N.E.2d 1352 (N.Y. 1979).

12. Complaint, *Donahue v. Copiague Union Free School District,* filed on March 22, 1977, in the Supreme Court of the State of New York—Suffolk County _ Index number 77–1128, 4.

13. *Donahue v. Copiague Union Free School District,* 391 N.E.2d 1352, 1353 (N.Y. 1979).

14. Ibid., 1354.

15. Ibid., 1354, writing, "The fact that a complaint alleging 'educational malpractice' might on the pleadings state a cause of action within traditional notions of tort law does not, however, require that it be sustained. The heart of the matter is whether, assuming that such a cause of action may be stated, the courts should, as a matter of public policy, entertain such claims. We believe they should not."

16. Ibid., 1353–1354.

17. Ibid.

18. *Donohue v. Copiague Union Free School Dist*rict, 64 A.2d 29, 35 (N.Y. A.D. 1978).

19. Todd A. DeMitchell, Terri A. DeMitchell, & Douglas Gagnon, "Teacher Effectiveness and Value-Added Modeling: Building a Pathway to Educational Malpractice?" *Brigham Young University Education and Law Journal* 2012(2) (2012): 257–301, 279.

20. Richard Funston, "Educational Malpractice: A Cause in Search of a Theory," *San Diego Law Review* 18 (1981): 743–812, 774.

21. 49 N.Y 2d 121 (1979).

22. Ibid., 124.

23. Ibid.

24. Ibid.

25. Ibid., 126.

26. Ibid., 125–126. Responding to the lower court's characterization of the difference between the case before it and *Donohue*, the Appellate Court wrote, "The policy considerations which prompted our decision in *Donohue* apply with equal force to 'educational malpractice' actions based upon allegations of educational misfeasance and nonfeasance." Ibid., 126.

27. Ibid., 127.

28. Ibid. (Meyer, J. dissenting).

29. 292 Md. 481 (1982).

30. Ibid., 484. "The petitioners further claim that the individual educators, acting intentionally and maliciously, furnished false information to them concerning the student's learning disability, altered school records to cover up their actions, and demeaned the child." Ibid. However, this discussion only focuses on the negligence claim.

31. Ibid.

32. Ibid., 487.

33. Ibid., 488.

34. Ibid., 496 (Davidson, J., concurring and dissenting).

35. Ibid., 497 (Davidson, J., concurring and dissenting).

36. Ibid. (Davidson, J., concurring and dissenting).

37. Ibid., 497–498 (Davidson, J., concurring and dissenting).

38. 649 P.2d 425 (1982).

39. *Tubell v. Dade County Public Schools*, 419 So.2d 388 (Fla. 1982).

40. *Smith v. Alameda County Social Services Agency*, 153 Cal. Rptr. 712 (Ct. App. 1979); *Agostine v. School District of Philadelphia*, 527 A.2d 193 (Pa. Cmwlth. 1987); *DeRosa v. City of New York*, 517 N.Y.S.2d 754 (App. Div. 1987). See also negligent classification, placement, and teaching of dyslexic students (*D.S.W. v. Fairbanks No. Star Borough School District*, 628 P.2d 554 [Alaska. 1981]; negligent evaluation and placement of a learning-disabled student (*Doe v. Board of Education of Mont-gomery County*, 453 A.2d 814 [Md. 1982]); and negligent placement and education of a Spanish-speaking learning-disabled student (*Torres v. Little Flower Children's Services*, 485 N.Y.S.2d 15 [1984], *cert. denied*, 474 U.S. 864 [1985]).

41. 469 N.Y.S.2d 959 (App. Div. 1983), *aff'd mem.*, 488 N.Y.S.2d 987 (1984).

42. 587 N.Y.S.2d 743 (A.D. 2 Dept. 1992).

43. *B.M. v. State*, 649 P.2d 425, 426.

44. Ibid., 427.

45. Ibid.

46. Ibid.

47. Ibid., 428.

48. Ibid., 430, writing one sentence, "I concur with the foregoing dissent (Harrison, J. concurring in dissent).

49. Ibid., 430–431. Justice Weber (dissenting) wrote, "I concur in the foregoing dissent of Justice Sheehy. In view of the difference of opinion expressed by the members of this Court, and because of the potential for claims by disaffected students and parents in countless numbers, I suggest that the legislature properly may consider whether it desires to impose an appropriate limit in this type of litigation."

50. Ibid. 428 (Haswell, C.J. concurring).

51. *Black's Law Dictionary* 1041 (1979, 5th ed.). "Thus, certain classes of acts are said to be "against public policy," when the law refuses to enforce or recognize them, on the ground that they have a mischievous tendency, so as to be injurious to the interests of the state, apart from illegality or immorality."

52. For a critique of the flood-gate argument in *Hoffman*, see Robin E. Rosenberg, "*Hoffman v. Board of Education*," *Hofstra Law Review* 10(1) (1981): 279–309. The author asserts that, while the flood-of-litigation has some strength in cases like *Peter W.* and *Donohue*, it is "irrelevant in the unusual circumstances" of *Hoffman*. Ibid., 304–305. One of the arguments advanced against the flood-of-litigation is the policy of deterrence. This policy asserts that the burden of liability compels a change in behavior that creates "a higher standard of care among educators and benefit the educational needs of children." Ibid., 307.

53. Terri A. DeMitchell, "Educational Malpractice: Will School Reform Efforts Make It Possible," in Todd A. DeMitchell & Richard Fossey (eds), *The Limits of Law-Based School Reform: Vain Hopes and False Promises* (Lancaster, PA: Technomic Publishing Company Incorporation, 1997): 63–74, 72. The author further writes, "The courts in *Donohue* (1979) and *Hunter* (1982) added that the participation in school matters would interfere with the authority vested in school officials to oversee the schools." Ibid.

Chapter 5

Higher Education Malpractice and Breach of Contract in the Time of the Pandemic

COVID-19 has placed universities in a no-win position. If they implement remote instruction as a substitute for the in-person classes traditionally offered, complaints about the quality of instruction are inevitable. However, if they bring students back to campus, they face the risk that COVID-19 infections can escalate rapidly.[1]

Though the Court is sympathetic to all who have been aggrieved by the pandemic, not all grievances are redressable by courts of law.[2]

COVID-19 rolled over the United States in the spring of 2020. The entire nation, including colleges and universities, was unprepared for the speed and viciousness of the virus. Normal practices that students relied upon were disrupted; it can be argued that a *force majeure* of unforeseen circumstances prevented the fulfilling of expectations for college life by the irresistible force of the rampaging virus.[3]

In the face of a staggering number of COVID infections that threatened to swamp hospitals and healthcare facilities, virtually all universities closed their campuses in order to protect students, faculty, and staff. Most higher education institutions also closed dormitories and sent their students home. They also closed student health clinics, recreation centers, and student-activity facilities.

Students had paid tuition and fees for the spring 2020 semester, expecting to take classes on campus and to have access to auxiliary facilities that they supported with fees. But when the pandemic struck, classroom teaching became untenable, and colleges switched to offering instruction online.

For many students, these responses were not what they expected, and they questioned the quality of the online instruction they were receiving. As one University of Chicago student stated, "Sitting in my own home, and not in a gorgeous classroom paid for by rich donors and students' tuition—that's not what I was promised."[4]

Students across the nation brought suit against their universities (both public and private), demanding refunds.[5] While students asserted breach of contract for the forced change, universities often defended against these suits by arguing that students' claims amounted to nothing more than a charge of educational malpractice—a cause of action that had been roundly rejected not only in the K–12 education sector (as outlined in earlier chapters) but in the higher education sector as well.

Since a California appellate court's decision in *Peter W.*, suits for educational malpractice in the K-12 sector have almost all failed because courts generally ruled that these suits do not assert a cognizable claim of negligence. As discussed earlier, recognized appropriate instructional practices have not been articulated and adopted in the educational community, and thus it is difficult to define what pedagogical duty is owed by instructors to their students. Nor has there been a clear path for determining causation for any alleged educational harm.

And, perhaps most importantly, courts have rejected educational malpractice claims for policy reasons, including the fear that recognizing a cause of action for educational malpractice would open a floodgate of litigation. Courts repeatedly articulated a reluctance to intrude into the day-to-day school operations or to second-guess pedagogical decisions made by educators. Thus, educational malpractice claims have uniformly failed in K–12 litigation. But what about higher education malpractice suits?

Educational malpractice, a cause of action that has been emphatically rejected by the courts in K–12 schools, has appeared as part of the recent wave of student lawsuits brought against colleges and universities. This chapter will explore whether courts have rejected educational malpractice in the higher education sector as they have in the K–12 school setting.

The chapter will begin with a discussion of the seminal educational malpractice case involving a higher education institution: *Ross v. Creighton University*, decided by the Seventh Circuit Court of Appeals in 1992.[6] As we will see, the Seventh Circuit followed the lead of *Peter W.* and other judicial decisions in rejecting educational malpractice as a valid cause of action against a university. Basically, the Seventh Circuit adopted the philosophy of the lower court in *Ross*, which wrote that "educational malpractice is a tort theory beloved of commentators, but not of courts."[7]

MALPRACTICE IN HIGHER EDUCATION: *ROSS V. CREIGHTON UNIVERSITY* IS THE SEMINAL CASE

TEXTBOX 5.1

Beginning with the landmark case of *Peter W. v. San Francisco Unified School District* in 1976 and culminating with *Ross v. Creighton University* in 1992, educational malpractice in the US was born, raised, and buried. Indeed, considerable legal precedent now holds that no cognizable tort claim arises out of negligently failing to educate students in K-12 and higher education settings.

Dan Underwood, "Educational Malpractice in a New Light: Emerging Trends in Negligent Causes of Action in Higher Education," Stetson University Law and Higher Education Conference 1 (February 2002), https://www.stetson.edu/law/academics/highered/home/media/2002/Educational_Malpractice_and_Negligence.pdf.

Kevin Ross was recruited by Creighton University to play varsity basketball. He entered the university with significantly lower academic skills than the average first-year Creighton student.[8] He left the university short of the necessary credits required for graduation and only had the language skills of a fourth grader and the reading skills of a seventh grader.[9]

Ross brought suit against Creighton University for the failure to educate him, clearly an allegation of educational malpractice.[10] Like the plaintiff in *Peter W.*, he contended that he was not provided a meaningful education and that his prospects for post-college employment were negatively impacted as a result of the university's negligence.

Ross's lawsuit was a case of first impression in Illinois. The district court dismissed his cause of action for a failure to state a claim,[11] thus aligning with "the majority of courts that had refused to recognize a cause of action for educational malpractice."[12] On appeal, the Seventh Circuit articulated several policy concerns that other courts had identified as valid reasons for refusing to recognize the tort of educational malpractice.

First, the Seventh Circuit noted, there is no universally recognized standard of care to use as an evaluative tool for the actions of educators and the services that they provide to students. In other words, no theory of pedagogy has been generally accepted and uniformly implemented in the education community.[13]

Second, the appellate court observed, causation is difficult to establish in the context of educational malpractice. Even if it were established that Ross had not achieved a base level of education, it would be difficult to place the blame on any particular party.

While teachers are the most important variable in a student's formal education, there are other covariables that influence student educational outcomes, as the Seventh Circuit noted.[14] The *Ross* court identified several of these covariables including, "student attitude, motivation, temperament, past experiences, and home environment." All these variables "may all play an essential and immeasurable role in learning."[15] Thus, it might be impossible for a court to determine which individual educator failed to instruct a particular student in a non-negligent manner.

For example, a pre-*Ross* case foretold this problem of establishing causation, writing that some breach of contract claims against schools might require "the factfinder to enter the classroom and determine whether or not the judgments and conduct of professional educators were deficient."[16] According to a New York court, judges need to tread lightly when there is a claim of deficient education. Whether the claim is framed as breach of contract or educational malpractice, these allegations requires the judiciary to step outside its wheelhouse.

These considerations mirror the conclusions of *Peter W.* However, the *Ross* court added a special concern when a college or university is sued for educational malpractice. A judicial examination of teaching and learning at a higher education institution necessarily entangles the courts in the "university setting where it necessarily implicates considerations of academic freedom and autonomy."[17] This is an important consideration.

The *Ross* court also distinguished between an educational malpractice claim in a university setting and a claim for breach of contract. The court stated that a plaintiff who brings a breach of contract claim for failure to educate must do more than just allege that their education was not good enough. Rather, the plaintiff "must point to an identifiable contractual promise that the defendant failed to honor."[18]

The court offered the following distinction: a potential breach of contract complaint does not allege that the university failed to adequately perform the service, but rather the university failed to. The Seventh Circuit Court of Appeals applied this construction to Ross's complaint. The court read his complaint as more than a failure to provide him with a certain quality of service.

Rather, the court asserted that Ross alleged that the University knew he was academically unprepared to participate in the curriculum and made an explicit promise to provide him with certain specific services so that he could participate in Creighton's academic setting in a meaningful way. Therefore, the court's analysis was not whether Creighton University provided "deficient" academic services, instead "its inquiry would be limited to whether the University had provided any real access to its academic curriculum at all."[19]

The appellate court disagreed with the district court's ruling that Ross's breach of contract claim should be dismissed at the pleadings stage. The Seventh Circuit allowed Ross contract claim to proceed on narrow grounds, concluding: "[W]e believe that the district court can adjudicate Mr. Ross' specific and narrow claim that he was barred from *any* participation in and benefit from the University's academic program without second-guessing the professional judgment of the University faculty on academic matters."[20]

The Seventh Circuit remanded Ross's case to the lower court with a directive—the remand to examine whether Creighton University acted in good faith by delivering on its promise of additional academic assistance.

The Seventh Circuit's *Ross* decision is a seminal case in higher education law, because the Seventh Circuit essentially adopted the *Peter W.* decision's view that courts should not adjudicate tort claims based on assertions that a student was negligently educated. Thus, both K–12 schools and universities are judicially insulated against lawsuits for educational malpractice.

Miller v. Loyola University of New Orleans, a post-*Ross* case, illustrates a classic educational malpractice lawsuit. In this case, Leonce Miller, a law school student at the Loyola University of New Orleans, sued the university for failure to provide complete and adequate instruction for a course on the professional and ethical standards of the legal profession.[21] This case is instructive because the majority explored educational malpractice as outlined by *Ross* and the dissent's disagreement that the contract complaint should be rejected at this stage of the proceeding foreshadows the following discussion of COVID-19 reimbursement cases.

In general, the courts have rejected educational malpractice claims in the higher education sector for the same reasons that courts have rejected them in the K–12 sector for lack of a defined duty, the difficulty of demonstrating causation, and policy considerations.

However, college and university students can often assert a claim for recovery that is not available to K–12 students who attend public schools—breach of contract.[22] In fact, in the *Ross* case, the Seventh Circuit allowed Ross's breach of contract claim to go forward, even though it rejected his educational malpractice claim.

This distinction between breach of contract claims and educational malpractice can be seen in a line of cases that developed after the COVID pandemic appeared in the spring of 2020. In virtually all these cases—and there were more than 300 lawsuits filed—students sought tuition refunds when their classes were shifted from a classroom setting to an online format.

Students claimed that their online classes were inferior to face-to-face instruction and that their universities had not delivered what they promised, which was to put live teachers in the same room with their students.

In several of these cases, the universities attempted to get these tuition-refund lawsuits dismissed prior to trial on the grounds that students were merely arguing that they received inferior instruction. These claims, the universities argued, were educational malpractice claims, not breach-of-contract claims, and thus should be summarily dismissed.

In a surprising number of cases, however, courts rejected the universities' arguments. In the view of several judges, students' lawsuits for tuition refunds stated a valid claim that their institutions breached an explicit or implied promise to offer classroom instruction. In other words, students were arguing that they did not receive what they paid for. Therefore, these judges declined to dismiss students' tuition-refund claims based on their conclusions that the claims were grounded in contract law and not the law of negligence.

EDUCATIONAL MALPRACTICE IN THE TIME OF COVID-19. BREACH OF CONTRACT VERSUS MALPRACTICE: THE RAZOR'S EDGE

TEXTBOX 5.2

Even where plaintiffs do not expressly assert a malpractice claim, and instead assert breach of contract, negligence, or even possibly a constitutional claim, schools should review the underlying allegations to determine if they are really asserting a claim for inadequate educational services. If so, those claims are likely barred because, as one court put it, schools "must be allowed the flexibility to manage themselves and correct their own mistakes.

Lucero v. Curators of the University of Missouri, 400 S.W.3d 1, 8 (Mo. Ct. App. 2013).

The legal relationship between colleges and their students has evolved over the years. Until the mid-twentieth century, higher education institutions were generally considered to occupy the place of parents in their relationships with students and could exercise this parental role to discipline students and regulate their behavior. The legal term for this relationship is *in loco parentis*. Acting *in loco parentis*, colleges could expel students for any reason and sometimes for no reason at all.

In 1961, however, in *Dixon v. Alabama State Board of Education*,[23] the Fifth Circuit Court of Appeals ruled that students at a public college have a constitutional right to procedural due process and could not be suspended or expelled without being given notice of the charges against them and the right to be heard before a fair tribunal. Later, the Fifth Circuit recognized a student's constitutional right to privacy when living in a public university's residence hall and that police could not search the students' dorm rooms to advance criminal investigations without obtaining a warrant.[24]

Later, a string of court decisions ruled that colleges are not in an *in loco parentis* relationship with students and thus colleges could not be held liable when students injured themselves after abusing alcohol. As the Third Circuit of Appeals puts it in *Bradshaw v. Rawlings*, a 1979 decision, "Modern American college is not the insurer of the safety of its students."[25]

If a college is no longer understood to be in a parental relationship with its students, what is that relationship? Most courts have concluded that students and colleges are in a contractual relationship, with both students and colleges having defined rights and responsibilities.

TEXTBOX 5.3

The contractual relationship between student and university has undergone an evolutionary process through which it has become firmly established as a characterization of the relationship between institutions of higher learning and their students. . . . Contract theory has provided students a means to seek redress of their disagreements with colleges and universities. Courts have embraced the contractual relationship in an effort to frame the reciprocity of rights and obligations between student and institution.

Kerry Brian Melear, "Contracts with Students," in Richard Fossey & Suzanne Eckes (eds), *Contemporary Issues in Higher Education Law* (Cleveland, OH: Education Law Association, 2015, 3rd ed.): 305–332, 307.

Nevertheless, as a New York federal district court cautioned, contract principles "d[o] not provide judicial recourse for every disgruntled student."[26] And, for purposes of our discussion, a student cannot assert a breach of contract claim if it is really a veiled claim for educational malpractice.[27]

A breach of contract claim against a college or university must identify a specific promise that was made and breached. Broad claims of an ineffective or low-quality education have been dismissed as disguised educational malpractice claims that require a court to determine the soundness of a college's educational methods. This, the courts have refused to do.

Nevertheless, as a judge in a recent Vermont tuition-reimbursement case noted, "Because Plaintiff's claims do not challenge the quality of education he received, but rather allege that he was deprived of certain educational services for which he contracted for and paid, his claims are not barred by the educational malpractice doctrine."[28]

COVID-19 Tuition-Reimbursement Cases: Malpractice and Breach

Even before the COVID-19 pandemic, students brought lawsuits against colleges and universities to recover their tuition based on allegations of educational malpractice. John Collis[29] identifies *Trustees of Columbia University v. Jacobsen*[30] as one of the earliest court decisions involving a student's demand for a tuition refund based on the poor quality of instruction. In that case, the university initially brought a suit against Roy Jacobson, a former student, to recover the balance of the tuition Jacobsen allegedly owed.

Jacobsen counterclaimed, accusing Columbia of making misrepresentations in its catalogs and brochures. Specifically, Jacobsen asserted that the college stated that it would teach such attributes as "wisdom, truth, character, enlightenment, understanding, justice, liberty, honesty, courage, beauty, and similar virtues and qualities."[31]

A New Jersey appellate court identified the crux of Jacobsen's charges when it quoted him as saying, "I have really only one charge against Columbia: that it does not teach wisdom as it claims to do."[32] The court held for Columbia University on summary judgment, writing, "We agree with the trial judge that wisdom is not a subject which can be taught and that no rational person would accept such a claim made by any man or institution."[33]

Jacobsen's claim is similar to the claims advanced in the COVID-19 tuition suits. Students are alleging that they did not receive the education they were promised—in-person instruction. Beginning in the spring of 2020, students brought more than 300 lawsuits seeking to recover tuition and fees they paid in the expectation they would be taught in traditional college classrooms.

All these cases challenged the courts to overcome their reluctance to pass judgment on decisions made by college officials and to hear students' demands for a refund of their tuition. For example, a New York appellate court ruled more than fifty years ago that a student could not recover tuition even though his university canceled instruction for nineteen days due to riots and disorder. The court stated that colleges and universities have the authority to maintain order on their campuses. Therefore, a lower court "erred in substituting its judgment for that of the university administrators."[34]

However, a notable pre-COVID case arose when a student sued to recover tuition paid for a doctoral program that closed at Vanderbilt University. Although the court acknowledged that the judiciary "must abstain from substituting its judgment for that of the university faculty on such matters as degree requirements and academic dismissals of students,"[35] it clearly entered into the decision-making sphere of the university. In language that came close to endorsing the theory of educational malpractice, the court said:

> Vanderbilt hastily embarked on a vague and ill-defined doctoral studies program when it knew or should have known that it did not have the resources to operate the program. Vanderbilt received something of value from these plaintiffs and gave little to nothing in return.[36]

The court concluded that "the university did not discharge its duty reasonably or consistently. It did not provide a high quality of academic training, and consistent standards and procedures. . . . In short, the GSM doctoral program ceased to function at all."[37]

The *Lowenthol* decision and the *Jacobsen* ruling are more than fifty years old, but they illustrate the legal problem that arises when students sue their colleges for a tuition refund. Are students complaining about the quality of instruction? If so, their complaint is an educational malpractice claim that should be summarily dismissed. Or are students claiming that their institutions breached a promise to them—either express or implied? If their cause of action is categorized as a contract dispute, then their lawsuit can move forward for a judicial ruling on the merits.

In *Metzner v. Quinnipiac University*, one of the recent tuition-refund cases arising from the COVID-19 pandemic, Judge Kari A. Dooley rejected Quinnipiac University's argument that students' tuition-reimbursement claims should be dismissed under the educational malpractice doctrine.[38]

"Here," Judge Dooley wrote, "the promise alleged to have been breached is not a promise to provide an effective or adequate education but instead to provide an in-person education."[39] In Judge Dooley's view, the plaintiffs had "pled the breach of a specific contractual promise" and these claims could be resolved without requiring "subjective assessments of educational quality."[40]

In an analysis of tuition-refund cases decided by New England courts during 2020 and 2021, Fossey and DeMitchell found that most judges ruled similarly to Judge Dooley when analyzing a university's educational malpractice defense. In other words, they declined to dismiss students' lawsuits on the grounds they amounted to educational malpractice complaints and thus were nonjusticiable. Instead, they determined that these suits were grounded in contract theory or were claims for unjust enrichment.

The following cases explore the application of educational malpractice to pandemic tuition-refund litigation. While few if any plaintiffs assert educational malpractice as a cause of action, given the precedential value of *Peter W.* and *Ross v. Creighton University*, several universities sought to dismiss these lawsuits on the grounds that the allegations were nothing more than disguised educational malpractice claims.

Gociman v. Loyola University of Chicago[41]

In an Illinois case, five students, acting individually and on behalf of all others similarly situated, sued Loyola University of Chicago for breach of contract and unjust enrichment.[42] Both of these causes of action were being asserted in many of the over 300 suits that were filed in 2020.[43]

Loyola filed a motion to dismiss the lawsuit, arguing that the students' claims amounted to educational malpractice which is "not cognizable under Illinois law," without regard to "whether they sound in contract or tort."[44] The plaintiffs sought to sidestep this "flaw" by alleging that the university "failed to perform the educational service 'at all.'"[45] Unfortunately for the students, their argument did not prevail.

U.S. district court judge Gettleman held that the underlying claim was that online instruction was "worth significantly less than the value of live classes."[46] Consequently, the court, in order to resolve the issue, would have to venture into territory in which it asserted that it was not equipped to operate—judgments about the "quality and value" of the online instruction.[47] This is the territory of educational malpractice, which the court noted had been rejected in Illinois and throughout the nation. The plaintiffs lost their breach of contract argument[48] as well as their unjust enrichment[49] argument, which were dismissed with prejudice.

In *Gociman*, the court squarely held that the foundation of the complaint was that online instruction is of lesser quality than in-person instruction. If students perceived that online instruction was comparable to in-person and the difference was just another acceptable delivery system, there would not be a controversy.

Consequently, the value of the instruction must be weighed at some point to ascertain how much the student's education was damaged by online instruction in order to fashion a reasonable remedy. Basically, the *Gociman* court cut to the chase and aligned its decision with decisions that framed students' complaint about the quality of education they were receiving as educational malpractice claims, which courts have universally rejected.

On appeal to the Seventh Circuit, a three-judge panel in a split decision vacated part of the district court's ruling that dismissed the students' lawsuit and allowed the plaintiffs to state a claim for a breach of an implied contract.[50] The Court of Appeals rejected the lower court's finding that the plaintiffs' lawsuit was a complaint about the quality of the education they received, asserting that the plaintiffs were not complaining about the quality of Loyola's remote instruction but instead were arguing that Loyola had breached an implied contract to provide in-person learning. Consequently, the Seventh Circuit panel reversed the district court's ruling that the students' lawsuit was essentially a malpractice claim that was barred under the educational malpractice doctrine. However, the Seventh Circuit endorsed the proposition that claims of educational malpractice are barred in Illinois.

Michel v. Yale University[51]

Jonathan Michel, a Yale undergraduate, filed a lawsuit over Yale's decision to cease in-person instruction on March 20, 2020, in response to the COVID-19 pandemic with five weeks left in the semester. Michel alleged that his tuition and fees were accepted by Yale in exchange for in-person instruction and use of the university's various facilities.

The court first discussed Yale's motion to dismiss based on educational malpractice. Yale argued that the plaintiff's claim essentially rested on the theory that online courses were inferior to in-person courses. Yale cited *Gupta v. New Britain General Hospital*, which held that claims for breach of contract based on inadequate educational services are not cognizable in Connecticut.[52]

However, the court denied Yale's motion to dismiss based on the university's educational malpractice argument, stating that it "agrees with the weight of authority on this question and, at this stage of the case, concludes that Michel's claims do not implicate the educational malpractice doctrine."[53]

The court concluded that Michel's claim did not challenge the adequacy of the online learning he received. Consequently, it did not require the court to determine what constitutes a reasonable educational program and then ascertain whether the standard had been breached. This argument closely tracks the concerns of both *Peter W.* and *Ross*. However, in the court's view, the issue of entering the territory of review of educational decisions surfaces in the analysis of damages; what value was lost in the move to online learning? Instead of front-loading the court's analysis of Yale's educational decisions, the court deferred the analysis until the damages phase of the litigation.

Having decided that educational malpractice did not bar the suit, the court reviewed Michel's pleadings on the other grounds. Unlike the ruling on educational malpractice, Michel's other pleadings failed. There was no breach of contract claim, the court concluded, because Michel failed to demonstrate that students were promised in-person instruction. In fact, Yale's Suspension Provision in the undergraduate regulations stated that in its "discretion and judgment" it retained the right to temporarily suspend its operations in response to emergencies, including health emergencies.

"Thus," the court asserted, "Yale's decision to suspend in-person education in light of the COVID-19 pandemic represents an exercise of authority expressly reserved to the University, and the exercise of that authority cannot constitute a breach."[54] The regulation also vested the sole right of reimbursement to the university. Thus, the students' breach of contract complaint failed, as did their claim for damages based on Yale's alleged unjust enrichment.

Even though Judge Hall held that Yale could not use educational malpractice to dismiss Michel's lawsuit, Michel's tuition-refund complaint failed to show that Yale had breached a contract with its students. Consequently, the court had no reason to rule on damages or to determine whether online instruction was inferior to face-to-face teaching.

Hassan v. Fordham University

As seen earlier in two different court decisions, malpractice was found in one and not the other. This last case found no malpractice but no breach of contract either. For example, the Southern District Court of New York's discussion of educational malpractice in *Hassan v. Fordham University*[55] stated that courts should show restraint in educational areas reflecting the "peculiar capabilities" of educational professionals to make the "appropriate and necessary" decisions for their institutions. Consequently, they should avoid situations in which they are reviewing the wisdom of educators' choices.[56]

Fordham University argued that the complaint was premised on the idea that online learning was "subpar." This would require the court to evaluate and decide whether the University's decision to move to online learning was indeed subpar. Plaintiffs assert that the issue was whether the University promised to "provide services and failed to do so."

The court held in response to the defendants' petition to dismiss the complaint on the basis that it was essentially a malpractice complaint, writing:

> New York's public policy does, however, preclude lawsuits that are predicated on claims of "educational malpractice." If the "essence of the complaint is that the school breached its agreement to provide an effective education," or if a court is asked to "evaluate the course of instruction" or "review the soundness of the method of teaching that has been adopted by an educational institution," those claims should be dismissed.[57]

The *Hassan* court deferred to educational officials when making educational decisions. The language of *Hassan* is consistent with the *Michel* court that courts should not venture into the territory of assessing educational policy decisions for which they are not prepared to traverse.

While rejecting the university's educational malpractice defense, the court dismissed all claims for a failure to state a claim for each of the grounds. However, the student then submitted a Proposed Second Amended Class Action Complaint.[58] This amended complaint did not contain any assertion of educational malpractice. The court allowed a breach of contract claim to move forward regarding the technology access fee, which provided computer access to on-campus facilities.

However, the court rejected the student's breach of contract claim regarding the switch to online instruction. The court ruled that the university had made no explicit promise to provide in-person instruction. The court threw out the student's unjust enrichment claim as well. The student was only allowed to proceed with his demand for partial reimbursement of the university's technology access fee.

TUITION-REIMBURSEMENT CLAIMS AND THE *STATUS QUO* OF EDUCATIONAL MALPRACTICE IN HIGHER EDUCATION

TEXTBOX 5.4

Courts cannot and should not attempt to be the forum to litigate all potential implied promises between the educating institution and the student. Courts can, however, use good faith and fair dealing as a framework to protect institutional autonomy, accord substantial deference to educators and administrators, while protecting student rights and providing some accountability to higher education.

Miller v. Loyola University of New Orleans, 829 So.2d 1057, 1065 (La. Ct. App. 2002) (Plotkin, J., dissenting).

Prior to the COVID-19 pandemic, courts across the United States had firmly rejected the tort of educational malpractice as a viable cause of action against colleges and universities.[59] Courts flatly refused to recognize a cause of action for damages based on students' claims that they were negligently educated.

However, in the aftermath of the COVID-19 pandemic, educational malpractice resurfaced in the context of students' lawsuits for tuition refunds, which were mostly framed as actions for breach of contract or unjust enrichment.[60] In this wave of litigation, however, higher education institutions defended against tuition-refund claims by arguing that plaintiff students were arguing about the quality of the online education they had received and thus their complaints were properly categorized as educational malpractice claims, which were not judiciable in the courts.

A few courts agreed with the universities' arguments and dismissed students' tuition-reimbursement lawsuits on the grounds that they were grounded in educational malpractice. The *Michel* decision and the *Gociman* ruling, which were discussed in this chapter, are examples of rulings by courts that took this view.

Most courts, however, concluded that the students were not complaining about the quality of their education. Instead, they were asserting that the universities promised to provide students with face-to-face instruction in classrooms and they breached those promises when they switched instruction to an online format. For example, a Florida federal court wrote that the "resolution of the plaintiff's claims [does] not require the court to examine the educational value or academic adequacy of the online instruction by the university."[61]

A few takeaways can be sketched from the analysis of the application of educational malpractice to college reimbursement litigation. This analysis provides a unique perspective on educational malpractice, in that instead of viewing malpractice from the standpoint of an individual student's alleged harm with all of the confounding variables of causation, it looks at the instructional decisions of the university—not just what shall be taught, but how it shall be taught.

1. First, courts across the nation are unwilling to recognize educational malpractice claims against colleges and universities. Thus, students who brought tuition-refund lawsuits against postsecondary institutions in the wake of the COVID-19 pandemic did not assert educational malpractice. Instead, they largely sought tuition refunds based on their arguments that institutions breached contractual obligations to them or unjustly enriched themselves by switching their teaching format from classroom settings to online instruction.
2. Traditionally, courts have expressed deep reservations about intruding into the day-to-day operations of the university. For example, the U.S. Supreme Court in *Regents of the University of Michigan v. Ewing* noted the role of judicial deference to institutions, writing, "considerations of profound importance counsel restrained judicial review of the substance of academic decisions."[62] Most courts recognize that the analytical tools of the judiciary are not easily adapted to pedagogy.
3. Courts that have rejected educational malpractice as a valid theory of recovery have expressed concern about causation. How can causation be determined, and who is responsible when a student's learning outcomes are subpar?

4. Several courts have been willing to allow students' tuition-refund claims to be heard as claims for breach of contract, but most universities have been able to defeat breach-of-contract claims on the ground that they never promised students they would be taught live in a classroom setting. Some colleges have pointed to boilerplate language in their curriculum documents that specifically gave the schools the unilateral right to change the mode of instruction at their sole discretion.

5. Interestingly, no court has considered the impact of tuition-refund lawsuits on universities' academic freedom. In its *Ewing* decision, the Supreme Court recognized the courts' responsibility "to safeguard [educational institutions'] academic freedom."[63] An academic freedom analysis would most likely conclude that colleges have the right to determine the instruction that best fits their pedagogical goals[64] and to adapt their instructional formats when necessary to respond to unanticipated challenges such as the COVID-19 pandemic.

   Thus, it would appear that a court ruling that a college made a hard-and-fast promise of in-person instruction would be negating the ability of professors to offer hybrid courses that involve both online and in-person instruction. As the court in *Miller v. Loyola University of New Orleans* noted, it is generally understood that instructors may change their course descriptions in response to students' need for additional instruction on a particular topic and to teach on pertinent topics that may arise even if those topics were not originally included in the syllabus (the teachable moment). As the court observed in *Miller*, "Education must be flexible to accommodate changing circumstances."[65]

6. Finally, given the enormous amount of litigation that arose when colleges closed their campuses in response to the COVID-19 pandemic, institutions of higher education would be well served by critically reviewing their documents to ensure that they are not promising what they cannot deliver. In 2022, the District of Columbia appellate court in a COVID tuition-refund case agreed with two lower courts that held that there was no explicit offer of in-person instruction, thus there was no express contract. However, the students made plausible claims that the university breached an implied-in-fact contract of in-person instruction. Repeated university references to on-campus instruction through numerous communications (e.g., "hands-on training" in workshops and "hands-on laboratory experience using laboratory facilities")[66] was cited by the court to support its decision to allow this claim to proceed. Marketing materials should not make promises—either express or implied—that all teaching will take place in a traditional college classroom.

In sum, the tort of educational malpractice remains a much-discussed legal theory but not a theory that courts have been willing to recognize. The

COVID-19 pandemic, which gave rise to hundreds of lawsuits against colleges that closed their campuses in the spring of 2020, gave the courts an opportunity to reexamine this tort and to breathe new life into a doctrine that had been firmly rejected in pre-pandemic decisions. Perhaps everyone in the academic community—students, professors, and college leaders—is best served by the fact that educational malpractice is still a theory that the courts refuse to embrace, given the extent of the known and unknown consequences of such a tort and the unique circumstances of higher education.

NOTES

1. Author, "Education and Litigation Alert: COVID-19 Lawsuits against Colleges for Opening or Closing during the Pandemic," *Hancock Estabrook* (August 28, 2020), https://www.hancocklaw.com/publications/education-and-litigation-law-alert-covid-19-lawsuits-against-colleges-for-opening-or-closing-during-the-pandemic/.

2. *Miller v. Lewis University*, Case No. 20 C 5473 (N.D. Ill. April 11, 2021).

3. For a discussion of force majeure and COVID-19, see "Perspectives, COVID-19: Force Majeure Event?" *Shearman & Sterling* (March 12, 2020), https://www.shearman.com/Perspectives/2020/03/COVID-19—Force-Majeure-Event.

4. Greta Anderson, "Feeling Shortchanged," *Inside Higher Ed* (April 13, 2020), https://www.insidehighered.com/news/2020/04/13/students-say-online-classes-arent-what-they-paid. Similarly, a graduate student at the Harvard Kennedy School of Government stated, "Earning a master's is not just about what you're learning in class, but it's about meeting new people and being in a community and engaging with faculty and guest speakers and conferences—and all of that's obviously gone now." Abigail Johnson Hess, "Students Are Suing Their College for Coronavirus-Related Refunds," MAKEIT (April 14, 2020), https://www.cnbc.com/2020/04/13/students-are-suing-their-colleges-for-coronavirus-related-refunds.html.

5. For discussions of these COVID-19 refund lawsuits, see, e.g., Richard Fossey & Todd A. DeMitchell, "COVID-19, Online Learning, and Students' Demands for Tuition Refunds. An Overview of Litigation in the Federal Courts and Call for Statutory Immunity for Universities," *Education Law Reporter* 384 (2021): 608–619; Richard Fossey & Todd A. DeMitchell, "'In re: Boston University COVID-19 Refund Litigation—Federal Court Refuses to Dismiss Students' Lawsuit for Tuition Refunds," *ED LAW* Update 1, no 2 (May 2021): 11–12 (Education Law Association); Richard Fossey & Todd A. DeMitchell, "Students, the COVID Pandemic, and Academic Dislocation: Tuition Reimbursement Lawsuits in New England," *ED LAW* 1(4) (July 2021): 15–17 (Education Law Association).

6. 957 F.2d 410 (7th Cir. 1992).

7. 740 F. Supp. 1319, 1327 (N.D. Ill. 1990), *aff'd in part*, 957 F.2d 410 (7th Cir. 1992).

8. Ibid., 411.

9. Ibid., 412. For a discussion of the legal challenges confronting college athletics, see Timothy Davis, "A Thirty-Year Retrospective of Legal Developments Impacting College Athletics," *Marquette Sports Law Review* 30 (2020): 309–345.

10. Ross, in addition to his educational malpractice claim, brought a negligent admission claim aimed at underprepared student athletes who are not assisted in taking advantage of the institution's many educational opportunities. Also, Ross brought a claim for breach of contract for a failure to provide him with meaningful educational opportunities. Both the district court and the Seventh Circuit of Appeals denied relief for both of these claims. For the negligent admissions claim, the courts found that establishing a duty of care would be difficult and if found that the court could become enmeshed in the admissions decisions of the institution. The breach of contract claim was considered as essentially a restated educational malpractice claim. The Appellate Court applied the same reasoning used in educational malpractice cases. However, it did allow that breach of contract claims may be based on specific promises were made but not kept. Ibid., 415–417.

11. The Court of Appeals wrote, "A party fails to state a claim upon which relief may be granted only if that party 'can prove no set of facts upon which relief may be granted.'" Ibid., 413.

12. Davis, *supra* note 9, 59.

13. *Ross v. Creighton University*, 957 F.2d 410, 414.

14. Noted educational researcher, Eric Hanushek writes, "First, teachers are very important; no other measured aspect of schools is nearly as important in determining student achievement," *The Economic Value of Higher Teacher Quality* (Washington, DC: National Center for Analysis of Longitudinal Data in Education Research, Calder The Urban Institute, 2010): 3. See also President Barack Obama's statement on the importance of the teacher: "From the moment students enter a school, the most important factor in their success is not the color of their skin or the income of their parents, it's the person standing at the front of the classroom." Barack Obama, "Remarks to the United States Hispanic Chamber of Commerce" (March 10, 2009), http://www.whitehouse.gov/the_press_office/ Remarks-of-the-President- to-the-United-States-Hispanic-Chamber-of-Commerce/.

15. *Ross v. Creighton University*, 957 F.2d 410, 414, citing to *Donohue v. Copiague Union Free School District*, 391 N.E.2d 1352, 1355 (1979).

16. *Paladino v. Adelphi University*, 454 N.Y.S.2d 868, 873 (1982).

17. *Ross v. Creighton University*, 957 F.2d 410, 415.

18. Ibid., 417.

19. Ibid.

20. Ibid.

21. *Miller v. Loyola University of New Orleans*, 829 So.2d 1057 (La. App. 2002).

22. Higher education cases may also attach other substantive theories such as misrepresentation to their complaint (Timothy Davis, "Examining Educational Malpractice Jurisprudence: Should a Cause of Action Be Created for Student-Athletes?" *Denver University Law Review* 69 (1992): 57–96, 67).

Cases that have an element of instructional practice associated with it may be more susceptible to being recast as an educational malpractice suit. The dissent in *Wickerstrom v. North Idaho College*, 725 P.2d 155 (1986), discussed the difference between educational malpractice and breach of contract claim. Chief Judge Donaldson's dissent asserted that if the inquiry involves the adequacy of instruction, the "education function, then the complaint lies with educational malpractice." Ibid., 160.

In contrast, the plaintiffs in *Peretti v. State of Montana*, 464 F. Supp. 784 (1979), won their suit for breach of contract against a postsecondary institution the Montana State Vocational Education Center when the course of study was interrupted part-way through the students' program due to a cut in legislative appropriations. The District Court held that there was an implied contract thus allowing the plaintiffs were entitled to relief. The contract held that the students who paid all required fees, maintained the prescribed academic level, and adhered to the disciplinary regulations would be allowed to pursue the course of study and to award a diploma for completion.

23. *Dixon v. Alabama State Board of Education*, 294 F.2d 150 (5th Cir. 1961).

24. *Piazzola v. Watkins*, 442 F.2d 284 (5th Cir. 1971).

25. 612 F.2d 135, 138 (3rd Cir.1979).

26. *Gally v. Columbia University*, 22 F. Supp. 2d 199, 208 (S.D.N.Y. 1998).

27. *Lawrence v. Lorain County Community College*, 713 N.E.2d 478 (Ohio App. 9 Dist. 1998).

28. *Mooers v. Middlebury College*, Case No. 2:20-cv-00144, 2021 WL 4225659, at *5 (D. Vt. September 16, 2021)

29. John Collis, *Educational Malpractice: Liability of Educators, School Administrators, and School Officials* (Charlottesville, VA: The Michie Company, 1990): 236.

30. *Trustees of Columbia University v. Jacobsen*, 53 N.J. Super. 148 A.2d 63 (1959).

31. Ibid., 64

32. Ibid., 66. "Wisdom is a hoped-for end product of education, experiencing and ability which many seek and many fail to attain." Ibid.

33. Ibid.

34. *Paynter v. New York University*, 314 N.Y.S.2d 676, 680 (1970).

35. *Lowenthol v. Vanderbilt University*, Chancery Court for Davidson County, Part Three, Nashville, Tenn., No. A-8525 14 (1976).

36. Ibid., 39.

37. Ibid., 17.

38. *Metzner v. Quinnipiac University*, Case No. 3:20-cv-00784 (KAD), 2021 WL 1146922 (D. Conn. March 25, 2021).

39. Ibid., *8.

40. Ibid. Similarly, in another New England tuition reimbursement case, *In re Boston University COVID-19 Refund Litigation*, Judge Richard G. Stearns declined an invitation to dismiss tuition-refund claims against Boston University under the educational malpractice doctrine. "The court is not convinced that plaintiffs' contract claim is a disguised educational malpractice claim, as BU implies," Judge Stearns wrote, "rather the students appeared to be challenging the fact of the switch from in-person to online instruction, not the *quality* of the online education BU provided."

In re Boston University COVID-19 Refund Litigation, 511 F. Supp. 3d 20, 21 n.3 (D. Mass. 2021). See also *Florez v. Ginsberg*, 57 Kan. App. 2d 207, 214 (Kan. App. 2019), which asserted that the plaintiff's claim that the Kansas University School of Education knowingly placed false information on its website regarding whether a program of study led to an initial teaching license was not a challenge to classroom methodology, theories of education, or the quality of the education he received. His claim is unrelated to academic performance or the lack of expected skills. His claim does not bring into question internal operations, curriculum or academic decisions of an educational institution, or any assigned function of a school under state law. The court remanded the case rejecting the lower court's dismissal based on educational malpractice.

41. *Gociman v. Loyola University of Chicago*, 515 F. Supp. 3d 861 (N.D. Ill. 2021).

42. For examples of other lawsuits that assert breach of contract and unjust enrichment among other theories, see *Lindner v. Occidental College,* Case No CV-20–8481-JFW(RAOx) (C.D. Calif. December 11, 2020); *Saroya v. University of Pacific*, Case No. 5:20-cv-03196-EJD, 2020 WL 7013598 (N.D. Calif. November 27, 2020); *In re Boston University COVID-19 Refund Litigation*, C.A. NO. 20–10827-RGS, 2021 WL 66443 (D. Mass. January 7, 2021).

43. Doug Lederman, "Courts Skeptical on COVID-19 Tuition Lawsuits," *Inside Higher Education* (May 6, 2021), https://www.insidehighered.com/news/2021/05/06/courts-view-covid-19-tuition-refund-lawsuits-skeptically.

44. *Gociman v. Loyola University of Chicago*, 515 F. Supp. 3d 861, 867. Judge Gettleman cited a number of cases that held that educational malpractice is not a viable tort. For example, demonstrating the broad acceptance of this position, Judge Gelleman cited *Ross v. Creighton University*, 957 F.2d 410, 416 (7th Cir. 1992) (writing following the "great weight of authority . . . bar[ring] any attempt to repackage an educational malpractice claim as a contract claim"). Furthermore, the court noted the great reluctance the courts have in asserting itself in matters of pedagogy second-guessing educators. For example, the court cited the U.S. Supreme Court in *Board of Curators of University of Missouri v. Horowitz*, 435 U.S. 78, 96 n. 6 (1978) (writing, "University facilities must have the widest range of discretion in making judgments as to the academic performance of students and their entitlement to promotion or graduation") (Powell, J., concurring).

45. Ibid.

46. Ibid.

47. Ibid.

48. In addition to losing the breach of contract claim on the basis of the underlying educational malpractice argument, the court also denied the claim, writing that the plaintiffs failed to identify a specific "promise made to provide in-person instruction and in-person services." Ibid., 869 Thus, they did not state a claim for breach of contract.

49. Because the unjust enrichment cause of action is predicated on a contract and the "the unjust enrichment claim would still fail because the breach of contract claim fails." Ibid., 870.

50. *Gociman v. Loyola University of Chicago.*, No. 21–1304,— F.4th —2022 WL 2913751 (7th Cir. July 25, 2022). Judge St. Eve concurred with the majority that the students' claim was not educational malpractice. The Judge dissented, however, with the finding that the plaintiff's had a viable breach of contract claim and would affirm the judgment of the district court.

51. *Michel v. Yale University*, Case No. 3:20-CV-01080 (JCH), 2021 WL 2827358 (D. Conn. July 7, 2021).

52. 239 Conn. 574, 591 (1996).

53. *Michel v. Yale University*, *5 (writing, "Many more courts, however, have concluded that COVID-19 tuition refund suits do not implicate the educational malpractice doctrine"). Ibid.

54. Ibid., *7.

55. 515 F. Supp. 3d 77 (S.D. NY 2021).

56. Ibid., 84.

57. Ibid.

58. *Hassan v. Fordham University*, 20-CV-3265 (KMW) (S.D.N.Y. April 6, 2021).

59. See, e.g., *Montany v. University of New England,* 2016 WL 3566200, at *11 n. 6 (D. Me. June 24, 2016) ("Educational malpractice is a claim that has been rejected in the majority of states that have considered it"); *Bittle v. Oklahoma City University*, 6 P.3d 509, 514–515 (Ct. App. Div. 3 April 21, 2000) (agreeing with "the great weight of authority," the court held that public policy "militates against recognition" of educational malpractice); *Finstad v. Washburn University*, 252 Kan. 465, 477 (1993) (citing that "the public policy concerns expressed in other jurisdictions that previously had considered and rejected educational malpractice as an actionable theory of liability").

60. In addition to breach of contract and unjust enrichment, higher education plaintiffs are also asserting consumer protection claims. "Broad claims of consumer protection violations are typically construed as veiled arguments for educational malpractice. (Kerry Brian Melear, "Contracts with Students," in Richard Fossey & Suzanne Eckes (eds), *Contemporary Issues in Higher Education Law* (Cleveland, OH: Education Law Association, 2015, 3rd ed.): 326). See, for example, *Florez v. Ginsberg,* 57 Kan. App.2d 207, 216–18 (Kan. App. 2019).

61. *Rhodes v. Embry-Riddle Aeronautical University Incorporation*, 513 F. Supp.3d 1350, 1356 (M.D. Fla. 2021). See also *Miller v. Lewis University*, Case No. C 5473 (N.D. Ill. April 11, 2021), in which the federal Northern District Court of Illinois did not accept the University's assertion that the plaintiff's suit was educational malpractice and not breach of contract. The court wrote:

> To summarize, Miller's breach-of-contract claim does not sound in educational malpractice because her complaint does not challenge the adequacy of the education she received, and the resolution of her claim would not require "second-guessing the professional judgment of the University faculty on academic matters. Ibid., *5.

62. 474 U.S. 214, 225 (1986).

63. Ibid., 226.

64. See *Sweezy v. New Hampshire*, 354 U.S. 234, 263 (1957) (Frankfurter, J. concurring), writing:

> It is the business of a university to provide that atmosphere which is most conducive to speculation, experiment and creation. It is an atmosphere in which there prevail 'the four essential freedoms of a university—to determine for itself on academic grounds who may teach, what may be taught, how shall it be taught, and who shall be admitted to study'."

65. *Miller v. Loyola University of New Orleans*, 829 So.2d 1057, 1062.
66. *Shaffer v. George Washington University*, 27 F.4th 754, 764 (D.C. Cir. 2022).

Section III

EDUCATIONAL MALPRACTICE

A Viable Tort? Law and Policy Responses

Chapter 6

Are Cracks Forming in the Educational Malpractice Wall?

Viability, Gag Orders, and VAM

> This brave new world of data on teacher effectiveness requires courts to revisit the initial rationales used to reject education malpractice claims, and why as a result a properly framed complaint may succeed today.[1]

As we explained in earlier chapters, the courts have erected a sturdy judicial wall that prevents educational malpractice lawsuits against educational institutions. Almost unanimously, judges toss these cases out, not even allowing an educational malpractice claim to go to trial.

Are cracks forming in the wall of educational malpractice? From the *Peter W.* decision in 1976 to the second decade of the twenty-first century, the wall has held. Courts have invariably found that plaintiffs' causes of action for malpractice face insurmountable hurdles regarding the essential elements of a tort claim: a legal duty owed to a plaintiff student, proof of injury, and causation.[2]

However, the chief barrier to an educational malpractice claim is strong public policy concerns. "In fact, in most jurisdictions, a suit for educational malpractice is against public policy."[3] Thus, policy arguments against educational malpractice form the cement in the barrier against educational malpractice claims. Cracks may be forming in the wall, but until the inertia of public policy against educational malpractice shifts, the wall will likely hold.

But for how long? As we explain in this chapter, recent scholarly and legislative developments provide new arguments in favor of recognizing educational malpractice as a viable tort—a tort that can form the basis for money damages.

A policy[4] often solves a problem, clarifies a situation, or directs behavior that seeks consistency. However, the public agenda is always crowded. The number of partisan issues clamoring for a place on the public agenda is large.

Neither government nor public schools can address all of the issues that parents, citizens, and educators want to be solved. Consequently, the agenda-setting process narrows a wide range of conceivable policy issues to the set that actually becomes the focus of attention of government officials.

So, how does an issue get on the public agenda for attention and resolution? John W. Kingdon's classic work on policy streams and policy windows provides a framework for understanding how issues get on the public agenda and become public problems for public resolution. He starts his work with the question, "How does the public know that an idea's time has come?[5]

Kingdon identified three streams that are constantly flowing and that occasionally converge to open a policy window. First, there is the problem stream; gaining public recognition for your problem is important. This often occurs when critical or prominent events, influential people, or data/research help focus attention on a problem.

Second, there is a stream of proposals seeking problems to which they can become attached so that they can be implemented.[6] The last stream is politics, the ongoing search to gather scarce resources through competition and coalition-building. This stream consists of political factors and actors who gain power and judge the political climate and mood, and voices of advocacy and voices of opposition.[7]

When these streams converge, a window of opportunity opens. Open windows allow solutions to be grafted onto problems so that a new policy can be developed and an old one revised. These policy windows do not stay open for long and advocates must rush to take advantage of the opening.

As we will discuss in this chapter, a window may be opening that may frame educational malpractice as a public policy problem—a problem that can be remedied by the courts. In other words, cracks are appearing in the judicial wall first erected in *Peter W.* against educational malpractice.

We will start by reviewing research that has probed the viability of educational malpractice. Next public policy and educational malpractice will be explored. Selected legislation allowing parents to sue school districts for damages based on allegations that instruction or curriculum was negligently provided will be discussed. These statutes provide a private cause of action for students/parents to sue for statutory violations of professional responsibilities owed to students and parents. The last section discusses VAM and causation.

PERCEPTIONS OF LEGAL SCHOLARS ON THE EMVS

There is little published research on educational malpractice. Commentators have expressed their positions on the topic which has been briefed and analyzed, but there is a dearth of data on the topic of educational malpractice.

To address this issue, we review a recent exploratory quantitative and qualitative mixed methods survey using a sampling method to determine the perceptions of knowledgeable stakeholders about educational malpractice (EMVS).[8]

This exploratory study was developed from an examination of educational malpractice cases. The study used judgmental or expert sampling, which is a nonprobability sampling technique in which the researcher(s) select potential respondents based on their knowledge and professional judgment—not a random sample of participants. This judgmental sample consisted of school law attorneys and school law professors.

The exploratory research posited that a population of school law experts could best respond to Likert-style questions regarding the viability of educational malpractice lawsuits, various factors impacting these lawsuits, and the individuals and entities that would most likely be held liable for malpractice. It also asked open-answer questions that requested survey-takers to respond to two prompts on strategies and defensive responses to a malpractice case. This section of the study will be discussed in chapter 7.

Three nationally known school law professors who have experience as school law attorneys and hold law degrees as well as either a PhD or EdD in education from R1 research-intensive universities juried the instrument. The instrument was then finalized based on their analyses.

Results were analyzed using descriptive statistics because the response rate was too low in this exploratory study for more robust statistical treatments. Caution is urged by the three authors of the study as well as the co-authors of this book to be careful not to generalize beyond this small sample. Nevertheless, the findings are interesting and will hopefully lead to further research that will be useful to classroom educators, school principals, and district-level school administrators as well as policymakers.

The survey contains eight Likert-style questions, two open-answer questions (which will be discussed in chapter 7), and six demographics questions, which collected information on each participant's professional position (law professor or practicing attorney), education, and prior experience in K–12 education and malpractice suits. A list of potential participants was developed from an examination of law reviews and professional journals, membership lists from the Education Law Association, and internet searches of law firms that advertise their expertise in handling malpractice claims.

Demographics

The survey was sent to 200 identified school law professionals. Forty-three school law experts out of 200 responded from twenty different states; the response rate was 21.5 percent. The sample included seven (16.3 percent) practicing school law attorneys, 34 (79.1 percent) school law professors, and two (4.6 percent) respondents who were both. All respondents held either a JD or PhD/EdD, while seventeen (39.5 percent) of the respondents held both terminal degrees. Eleven (25.6 percent) respondents had been involved in professional malpractice suits (medical, legal, etc.). A total of 72 percent of the participants served as teachers and 44 percent served as administrators.

The following analysis of the Survey Questions is organized according to three of the thematic constructs embedded in the survey instrument. Each theme is discussed next.

Viability of a Tort for Educational Malpractice

Two of the eight survey questions focus on the perceived viability of torts for educational malpractice. The first ($N = 43$) asked, "At this point in time, I believe that instructional educational malpractice suits are viable causes of action." When the five categories were collapsed, just over three-quarters (76.7 percent) Disagreed/Strongly Disagreed with the statement. With no responses of Agree, 18.6 percent of the responses were Strongly Agree. Only two respondents (4.7 percent) were not sure. When the two Not Sure responses are removed from the calculation, resulting in a forced choice of disagree or agree, 80 percent of the school law respondents believe that educational malpractice is not currently a viable cause of action.

The second viability question shifted from the present to the near future. The question asked was: "In the near future, instructional educational malpractice is likely to become a viable cause of action." The Disagree/Strongly Disagree responses declined when pushing the date of viability out from the present (53.5 percent) with a decrease of 23.2 percent. The Agree/Strongly Agree responses (23.3 percent) only increased by 4.7 percent. However, the "Not Sure" (23.3 percent) increased by 18.6 percent.

This is a large swing in responses. Of the twelve school law respondents who moved from current viability to near future viability, ten moved to Not sure and two to Agree. Overall, there was a migration of ten respondents (23.3 percent) from Disagree/Strongly Disagree to either "Agree" or "Not sure." The majority moved to Not Sure, which may be an indication that the factors that have militated against the viability of this tort are in decline. Given the ambiguity of "in the near future," the researchers could not draw any conclusions about how respondents interpreted this window of time. Nevertheless, nearly a quarter of the respondents foresee a possible shift.

A majority of surveyed school law experts disagree that educational malpractice suits are viable now, but fewer disagree that it will be viable in the near future, and more are uncertain. (*n*=43)

■ Viable Now   ▓ Viable in the Near Future

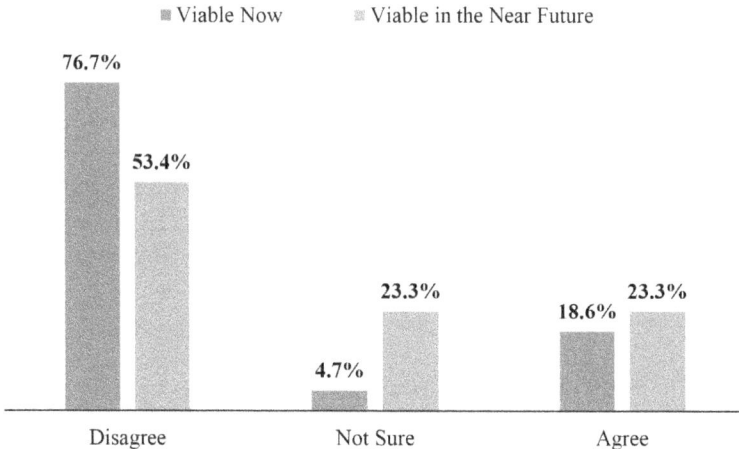

Source: DeMitchell, King, & DeMitchell, *Educational Malpractice Viability Survey* (2022)

Figure 6.1   Collapsed Strongly Disagree/Disagree and Strongly Agree/Agree Responses. *Source*: DeMitchell, King, and DeMitchell, Educational Malpractice Viability Survey (2022).

Factors Impacting Educational Malpractice

The following four survey questions focused on factors that may have an impact on the viability of educational malpractice suits. Three of the factors reflect the legal arguments advanced for denying this tort—research that defines instructional practices (the duty owed), establishing causation for student outcomes of instruction, and a change in public policy. The survey directions for these three questions stated as follows: "For the next three questions, please rate how much impact each underlined piece of information has on the viability of instructional educational malpractice as a tort."

The fourth question asked a query posed by the *Peter W.* court: "Are there established teaching standards?" This question is similar to the question posed in figure 6.2(a). However, the question in figure 6.2(a) focuses on the research on instructional practices, while this question focuses on the practical application of standards-based instruction. We start with the impact questions.

The following figures display the responses to each of the three impact questions, designed to assess the respondents' perceptions of specific factors that have impacted educational malpractice suits.

- Figure 6.2(a) asked: "Educational research has been identifying instructional practices that are effective. This research has the following impact on the viability of instructional educational malpractice suits."
- Figure 6.2(b) asked: "VAM, which purports to measure student achievement and then attribute expected gain or lack of gain to a specific teacher, is currently being used in teacher evaluations. This practice has the following impact on the viability of instructional educational malpractice suits."
- Figure 6.2(c) asked: "Public policy has been moving toward greater accountability for student learning. This emerging policy has the following impact on the viability of instructional educational malpractice suits."

A clear majority of the respondents believe that these three factors impact the viability of malpractice. To gauge the degree of impact, we collapsed No Impact and Slight Impact into one group and Moderate Impact and Significant Impact into another group, calculated the percentage for each group, and excluded "Not Sure" responses from the calculation.

The respondents perceived that public policy has the largest impact on the viability of a tort of educational malpractice (moderate/significant

A. Research Question
Educational research has been identifying instructional practices that are effective. This research has the following impact on the viability of instructional educational malpractice suits.

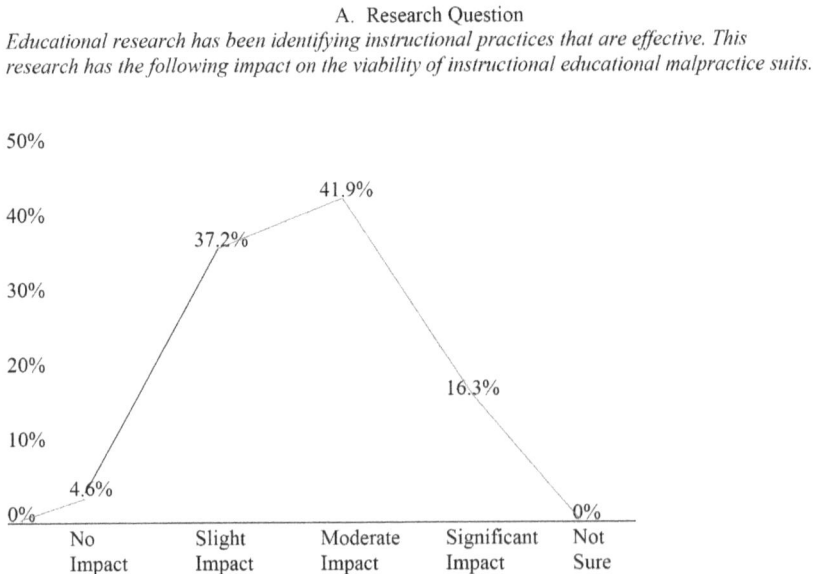

Figure 6.2(a)   **Research Question**

Question
*VAM, which purports to measure student achievement and then attribute expected gain
or lack of gain to a specific teacher, is currently being used in teacher evaluations.
This practice has the following impact on the viability of instructional educational malpractice
suits.*

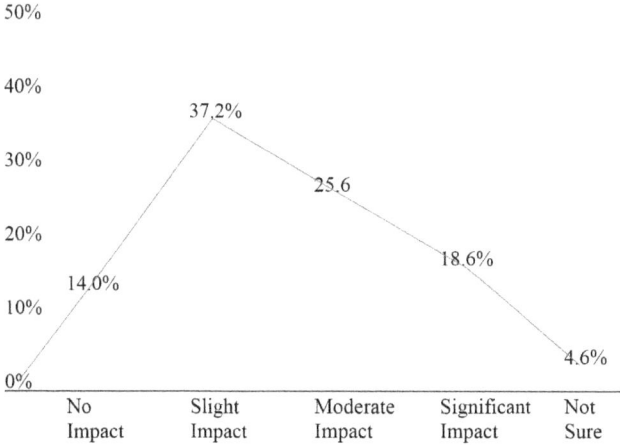

Figure 6.2(b)   Value-Added Modeling

Question
*Public policy has been moving toward greater accountability for student learning. This emerging
policy has the following impact on the viability of instructional educational malpractice suits.*

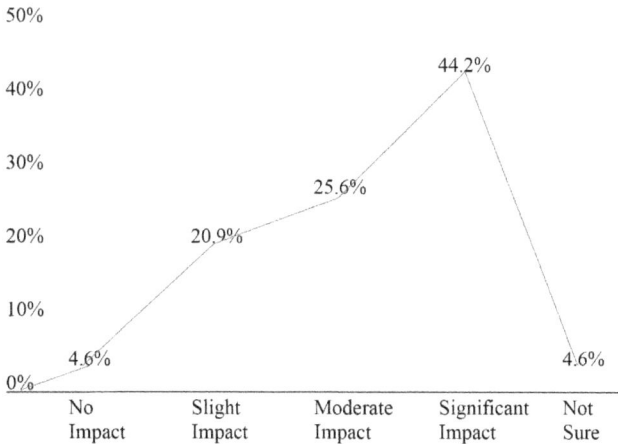

Figure 6.2(c)   Public Policy

impact—69.8 percent, figure 6.2[c]). Public policy has consistently been the basis for the courts' denial of suits for educational malpractice. The survey's public policy question also had the largest number of significant impact responses, which supports the conclusion that school experts perceive that public policy is the most important factor in determining the viability of a tort for educational malpractice.

An analysis of survey responses identified research on effective instructional practice as the second-largest factor impacting the viability of educational malpractice cases (moderate/significant impact—58.2 percent, figure 6.2[a]). It is noteworthy that no respondent marked "Not Sure." Courts have identified a lack of teaching standards as one of the reasons for the failure of educational malpractice suits.

The third-ranked factor impacting the viability of educational malpractice is VAM. Less than half (44.2 percent, figure 6.2[b]) of the respondents selected moderate/significant impact of VAM, with just over half (51.2 percent) describing VAM as having no impact or only a slight impact. Their responses may reflect the controversy regarding the use of VAM on high-stake employment decisions and its reduced level of influence in the broader public policy debate about teacher evaluation. The respondents did not provide strong support for VAM serving as a vehicle for establishing causation between ineffective teaching practices and harm to the student.

The last question asked was, "*I believe there are established standards for teaching that all teachers must adhere to in order to be considered as providing a professional service to their students.*" While the question in figure 6.2(a) asked whether research has been identifying effective instructional practices, this question asks whether there is a set of standards for instruction that the profession recognizes and accepts and operationalizes into expected practice. This question in many ways captures the crux of the instructional duty that educators owe to students.

Figure 6.2(d) shows that almost half (48.8 percent) of the respondents were "not sure" if such instructional standards are established. Of the remaining respondents, just over 30 percent disagreed or strongly disagreed that such instructional standards establish the base level of professional practice for the teaching profession. Only 20.9 percent of the experts agreed or strongly agreed that common instructional standards exist and guide professional practice.

The survey's authors conclude that the respondents of figures 6.2(a) and 6.2(d) "think that research is making progress on developing standards of practice but that they are not yet in place to support educational malpractice as a cause of action."[9] The instructional duty owed according to the respondents has not yet been established.

Question
I believe there are established standards for teaching that all teachers must adhere to in order to be considered as providing a professional service to their students.

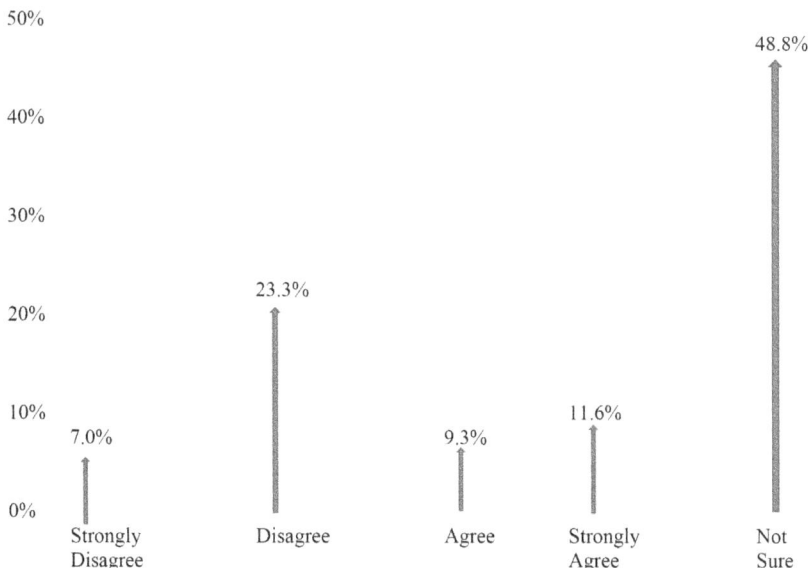

Figure 6.2(d)   Question

Who Should Be Liable for Malpractice, A Teacher, Teachers, a School District?

A persistently thorny issue for supporters of educational malpractice is determining who should be held liable if there is a showing of negligent instruction. Does the plaintiff student select a specific defendant teacher or teachers as a group as causing harm or does the plaintiff select the school district as the entity that is liable for the educational injury? Most likely the school district will be named as at least one of the defendants under the "deep pockets" theory of litigation. In other words, most educational malpractice lawsuits will include the school district as a named defendant because the school district is likely to have adequate insurance coverage to pay a tort judgment.

Any of these potential defendants presents challenges for the plaintiff student. If the student sues a single teacher for educational malpractice, it will be difficult to show that the teacher defendant is the sole actor who acted negligently. On the other hand, students who sue all the teachers with whom they came in contact will find it difficult to apportion liability among all the defendants. Suing a school district raises a different challenge. In many states, school districts are statutorily immune from being sued for the discretionary acts of their professional employees.

The data for the two questions on this topic are displayed next.

- A school district should be held liable when its teachers' professional practice (teaching) falls below the expected standards and a student is harmed by not learning at an acceptable level.
- Educators should be held personally liable when their professional practice (teaching) falls below the expected standards and a student is harmed by not learning at an acceptable level.

Who should be sued is an important question. It not only addresses who is potentially negligent but also addresses what remedies are available. Damage awards may be assessed against the defendant in a successful negligence. This could apply to both the individual and the school district. However, equity issues, such as compensatory services found in special education suits would likely only be available against the governmental defendant.[10] We focus on damage awards such as compensatory and punitive damages.

Approximately 50 percent of the respondents strongly disagree/disagree that school districts should be liable for instructional harm to a student. Only 21 percent agree or strongly agree that the school district should be held liable. This leaves just over 30 percent of the attorneys and professors who are not sure about whether school districts should be liable. When the Not Sure respondents are removed, the disagree responses account for 70 percent of

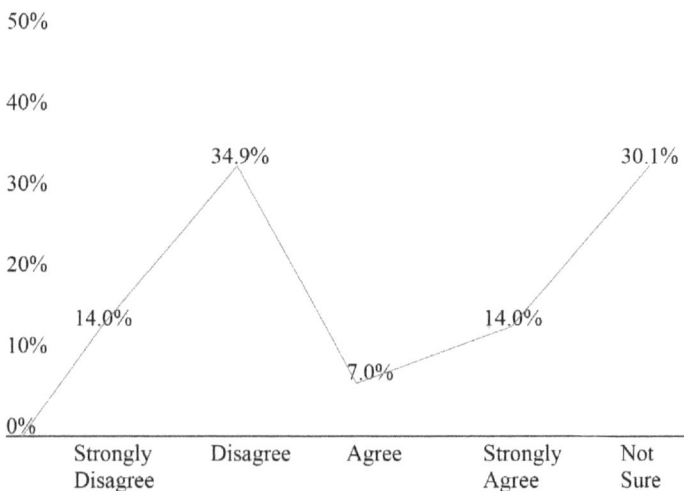

Figure 6.3   Who Should Be Liable? The School District

the responses. The responding attorneys and professors, by a margin of over 2-to-1, do not believe that school districts should be held liable for lawsuits of educational malpractice.

As seen in figure 6.4, respondents clearly lean toward not holding teachers liable for malpractice-type actions. A total of 72 percent Strongly Disagree/ Disagree that teachers should be held personally liable for their professional practice. In comparison, there is a difference of 23.1 percent between holding educators personally liable as opposed to school districts.

The Not Sure responses for teacher liability were half of that for school districts. One survey respondent's comment on educational malpractice probably reflects the position of the majority of the respondents. This commentator stated, "Clearly the act of one particular teacher in the school system cannot cause a student to graduate from school as a functional illiterate."[11]

There was less uncertainty regarding educators' liability versus the liability of a school district. This is consistent with the plaintiff students' selection of defendants in actual educational malpractice lawsuits. In the majority of cases, educators were not named defendants, possibly underscoring the challenge of showing that a specific teacher caused the educational injury. The combined Strongly Agree and Agree responses for the school district and educators showed that the number of respondents willing to hold the school district liable as opposed to educators (21 percent for the school district and 14 percent for educators). In any event, the respondents appear to be less conflicted about not holding educators personally liable for malpractice.

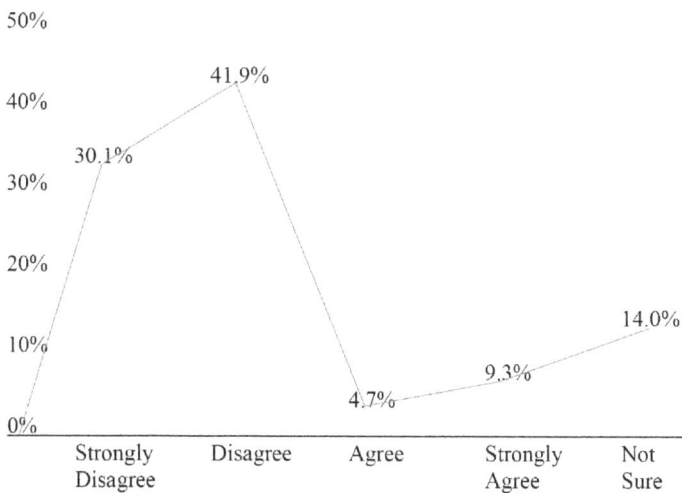

Figure 6.4   Who Should Be Liable? Educators

Taken together, the responses indicated that in the judgment of a small exploratory sample of school law attorneys and professors, educational malpractice is not
currently a viable tort and is unlikely to be viable in the near future. For example,
when asked in the survey whether the professors/attorneys believed that there are
established standards for teaching that must be adhered to, 30.3 percent strongly
disagreed or disagreed and only 20.9 percent agreed or strongly agreed. A near
majority of 48.8 percent were "Not Sure." This reticence in believing in the current
viability of educational malpractice was supported in figure 6.1 in which 76.7 percent of the respondents disagreed that educational malpractice is a viable tort.

The respondents were unsure as to whether a standard of practice to which
teachers must adhere currently exists. However, the respondents noted that
research on instructional practices may impact the development of educational malpractice.

The responses to the two questions about who would be liable for educational malpractice support the conclusion that educational malpractice is not
a viable tort, in that more respondents chose Strongly Disagree/Disagree on
this tort's liability for both the school district and individual teachers. However, the Not Sure response for school liability was quite high.

This leaves the question about who should be named as the defendant in
a malpractice suit. The respondents appear to support the *Peter W.* decision
that educators have not yet clearly articulated the standards of professional
practice upon which an individual's teaching practice can be judged. It is a
work in progress, which until fully established, remains an obstacle to the
viability of an educational malpractice claim.

The respondents also seem to agree with the line of reasoning that public
policy considerations are central to the viability of educational malpractice
tort actions. Currently, public policy concerns are a bar to such suits. Consequently, future plaintiffs must persuade the courts that public policy weighs
in favor of recognizing educational malpractice as a viable tort.

STANDARD OF CARE: GAG ORDER LEGISLATION
AND TEACHER SPEECH

TEXTBOX 6.1

Currently, public policy dictates that educational malpractice is not
recognized as a tort. But public policy does change.

Todd A. DeMitchell & Terri A. DeMitchell, "Statutes and Standards: Has the
Door to Educational Malpractice Been Opened," *Brigham Young University
Education and Law Journal* 2003 (2003): 485–518, 506.

The first prong of a *prima facie* case of negligence requires the plaintiff to demonstrate that the defendant owed a duty to the plaintiff. This must be established by the plaintiff and accepted by the court. Whether a defendant owes a duty to a plaintiff is a question of whether the defendant is under a legal obligation to act reasonably for the benefit of the plaintiff student. As stated, earlier legislation may be one of the vehicles used to establish a duty.

A statute often establishes a standard of care that is owed by the professional while rendering services and therefore impliedly creates a legal duty of due care. Depending upon the jurisdiction, a violation of a statute specifying a standard of care may be considered either as negligence *per se* or merely as evidence of negligence. In a jurisdiction that recognizes a violation of a statute as negligence *per se*, once the breach of a statute is established, negligence is conclusive.[12] In other jurisdictions, the violation of a statute is only evidence of negligence that may be accepted or rejected by the jury.[13]

However, compliance with a statute does not necessarily prove due care. While compliance may be used as evidence that the defendant used due care, a plaintiff might argue that the defendant was negligent because he or she did not do more than what was required by the statute.

Regardless, for a statute to be considered applicable in a malpractice case, the statutory intent must clearly specify the conduct required of the professional and the intent of the statute must be to prevent the type of injury claimed.[14] The statute must also be designed to protect the class of persons who might bring an action for malpractice. Furthermore, municipal ordinances and regulations established by administrative agencies may also establish required behavior and therefore create a duty of due care.[15]

One of the obstacles to educational malpractice suits has been the challenge of proving that a duty to properly educate students was owed to the plaintiff student. Establishing teaching standards of practice recognized by a significant portion of educators is one way to demonstrate that a duty is owed; another way is through legislation.

We next analyze legislative enactments that have either mandate specific instructional practices or (most often) prohibit certain instructional practices. Standards of practice identify practices that must be followed as well as practices that are prohibited. The statement of expectations designates what must be done and the failure to conform may provide the basis for a cause of action for unprofessional practice or malpractice. The obverse is statements of prohibited acts, which, if conducted, may also form the basis for a lawsuit against the professional.[16]

This section focuses on legislation that authorizes a cause of action against school districts and educators by students and/or their parents. This is more akin to malpractice, in that a violation of the duty may lead to court cases for a breach of the duty owed. Chapter 3 noted that the term "instructional negligence" is sometimes used in place of educational malpractice.

The term instructional negligence works well in this discussion. The focus is on instruction. A statute that prohibits teachers from addressing certain topics might be used to argue that a teacher who violates such a statute was negligent, thus opening the door to a cause of action for educational malpractice. Critics of the bills/legislation often point to the vagueness of the language, leaving teachers in a quandary as to what they can say and what they cannot say.[17]

TEXTBOX 6.2

The full scope of a law or policy's censorship should be understood to include not just what expression is prohibited but the extent to which people will self-censor out of fear of punishment. This so-called chilling effect is a well-recognized concept both in American jurisprudence and in anti-censorship research and advocacy.

Jonathan Friedman & James Tager, "Educational Gag Orders," *PEN America* (January 18, 2022): 1–71, 48–49, https://pen.org/wp-content/uploads/2022/02/PEN_EducationalGagOrders_01-18-22-compressed.pdf.

An early example of the use of lawsuits to control classroom instruction through punitive legal remedies is the passage of Proposition 227, "English Language in Public Schools" on June 2, 1998. California voters changed the California Education Code through a ballot initiative, replacing bilingual programs with English immersion. Essentially, the statute states that the educators owe a statutory duty to provide students with a standard of practice that "nearly all classroom instruction is in English."[18] The statute states:

> Any school board member or other elected official or schoolteacher or administrator who willfully and repeatedly refuses to implement the terms of this statute by providing such an English language educational option at an available public school to a California school child may be held personally liable for fees and actual damages by the child's parents or legal guardians.[19]

Proposition 227 may have altered the landscape of educational malpractice. Its grant of a "right of individual recovery for violations of a statutorily defined duty of care may well overcome the policy argument used in *Peter W*."[20] However, several years after the passage of the initiative, another ballot initiative eliminated this potential crack in the wall by repealing Proposition 227.[21] But recent legislation in 2021–2022 revived the concept by authorizing lawsuits against teachers, administrators, or school boards for violations of statutory instructional duties. This legislation, which is discussed later, demonstrates how a statutory instructional duty may lead to a change in public policy.

As beginning points for a discussion of instruction within the context of negligent instruction, we first explore two foundational concepts. The first is teacher speech that forms the basis for classroom instruction. The second is the role of academic freedom in the elementary and secondary schools. This is an important issue, given that the teachers often assert academic freedom when school authorities take action that teachers believe interferes with their right to control their instructional choices, such as "gag order" provisions in recent legislation and bills that seek to control instruction and curriculum through punitive methods.

Teacher Speech

Teachers stand at the crossroads of education. It is chiefly through their efforts that the goals of education are achieved or thwarted. Therefore, what teachers do in their classrooms is central to education.

The dominant instructional activity of teachers inside the classroom is speech. It is the verbal interaction between teachers and students, in which the teaching process is nested. Teachers tend to monopolize communication in the classroom. Ned Flanders's groundbreaking research on teaching styles found that established norms in schools are 80 percent teacher talk. This is the prevalent scenario in our present educational system across the three levels of primary, secondary, and higher education.[22] A teacher's instruction is the primary way that educational institutions impart the curriculum to students.

Although it is well settled that state legislatures have the authority to mandate curriculum content through legislation, teachers must deliver that curriculum content in their classrooms.[23] Thus, the professional service of instruction that is rendered by teachers centers on their speaking to students. Consequently, restrictions on teacher classroom speech implicate the core of what a teacher does daily.

Academic Freedom of K–12 Teachers

TEXTBOX 6.3

If teachers must fear retaliation for every utterance, they will fear teaching.

Ward v. Hickey, 996 F.2d 448, 453 (1st Cir. 1993).

Public education is a federal interest, a state responsibility, and a local function. Essentially, this means that the control of public education is vested in the state legislatures. However, this plenary power must be exercised in accordance with the mandates of individual state constitutions and the U.S. Constitution. Consequently, the states may direct what shall be taught as well as what may not be taught. State mandates are actualized at the school district level.

In *Keyishian v. Board of Regents*, Justice Brennan stated that "the classroom is peculiarly the 'marketplace of ideas.'"[24] This marketplace has two core elements: the selection of the curriculum (what shall be taught) and instruction (how it shall be taught). Vanessa Wernicke framed the marketplace of the public school classroom in the following way:

> If students in public schools are to be exposed to a "marketplace of ideas," teachers must be able to express and facilitate these ideas in the classroom. At the same time, it is the traditional province of school administrators and local school boards, as representatives of the community, to determine the curriculum that students will be taught and to operate schools efficiently.[25]

As stated earlier, two major educational activities have been the subject of intense public debate: teacher control of the curriculum and teacher control of their instruction. Most courts give teachers some measure of freedom over the selection of instructional practices and less to no control over the curriculum.

An *en banc* decision, the Washington State Court of Appeals decided a case about course offerings that demonstrates the courts' bifurcated view of academic freedom in the public schools. On the issue of control over the curriculum the court wrote, "Course content is manifestly a matter within the board's discretion."[26] However, the same court also held that the "teachers should have some measure of freedom in teaching techniques employed."[27]

Similarly, the Second Circuit Court of Appeals in a 1977 decision confirmed that school boards have considerable discretion as to the substantive content of what is taught in order to inculcate basic community values. However, this discretion may not be extended to the "teaching process itself. There is, as we see it, a sharp distinction between the content of curriculum and pedagogical methodology."[28] The court stated that, as long as the substantive values that the board seeks to inculcate are not subverted, the teacher's choice of teaching materials should be "weighted in the constitutional scales."[29]

In other words, the courts acknowledged that what is taught is controlled by the political processes determined by elected school boards and state legislators. But the contours of a teacher's freedom of choice over instructional practices to teach the curriculum are not always clear.

While teachers retain their right to speech inside the schoolhouse gate, that right cannot be exercised in all school situations. As discussed earlier, teacher speech is the core of instruction for the curriculum. The Seventh Circuit Court of Appeals stated in *Mayer v. Monroe County Community School*: "The school system does not "regulate" teachers' speech as much as it hires that speech. Expression is a teacher's stock in trade, the commodity she sells to her employer in exchange for a salary."[30] At least one appellate court in a concurring opinion suggested as follows:

> The school district bears responsibility for the speech, and for First Amendment purposes it therefore is the speaker and it therefore has the right to retain control of the speech—or, more precisely, to retain control over what is being taught in the classroom.[31]

However, the courts have not acted uniformly regarding an elementary or secondary teacher's right to academic freedom. In fact, the case law in both state and federal courts generally does not support the argument that teachers have a robust right to academic freedom, especially when it comes to establishing the curriculum.

As school law scholar Julie Underwood observed, "School boards set the curriculum for schools, and they have the legal right to decide what materials and speech are appropriate for the classroom."[32] Justice Black, concurring in an Establishment Clause case, expressed the judicial philosophy of most courts, when he wrote, "I am . . . not ready to hold that a person hired to teach school children takes with him into the classroom a constitutional right to teach sociological, economic, political, or religious subjects that the school's managers do not want discussed."[33]

The courts are typically protective of the school board's authority to make curricular decisions based on community values. For example, in *Zykan v. Warsaw Community School Corporation*, the Seventh Circuit Court of Appeals stated that the school board "has a legitimate, even a vital and compelling interest 'in the choice [of] and adherence to a suitable curriculum for the benefit of our young citizens.' "[34] Similarly, the National School Board Association in an *amicus curiae* brief for a Colorado school district wrote, "The court misses the point. Teachers do not have First Amendment rights to exercise state power in a manner of their own choosing through their teaching methodologies."[35]

A teacher's academic freedom is at its nadir when it comes to controlling the curriculum, but some courts have recognized the need for teachers to exercise some control over their instructional decisions. For example, in an early and often quoted case involving a teacher's decision to have her high school English class read Kurt Vonnegut, Jr.'s *Welcome to the Monkey House*, the teacher's decision was protected as academic freedom.[36] A later Sixth Circuit panel held that teachers have academic freedom rights "to exercise professional judgment in selecting topics and materials for use in the course of the educational process."[37]

Likewise, a Texas federal district court offered a strong endorsement of academic freedom when it asserted that "a teacher has a constitutional right protected by the First Amendment to engage in a teaching method of his or her own choosing, even though the subject matter may be controversial or sensitive."[38]

However, it would be a mistake to assume that public school teachers have a robust right to control their instructional decisions in the classroom. A New York federal district court wrote, "Although teachers do not relinquish their First Amendment rights at the 'schoolhouse gate,' their constitutional freedom may be curtailed by school policies that are reasonably designed to adjust those rights to the needs of the school environment."[39] Although the language used by the courts in these cases varies, it is clear that academic freedom in the public school setting is limited. As the Tenth Circuit of Appeals noted in a 1991 decision, "The case law does not support [the] position that a schoolteacher has a constitutional right to academic freedom."[40]

In short, the control of the curriculum resides with the school board. "Classrooms are the place where the school boards speak; the curriculum is their message."[41] Consequently, malpractice claims that target an inadequate curriculum would most likely be directed at the school board.

However, a lawsuit that targets an individual teacher's instruction would almost certainly name the teacher as a defendant. Moreover, a teacher who fails to teach the curriculum or negligently teaches the curriculum could also face district charges of incompetence and/or unprofessional conduct in addition to being a named defendant in a malpractice lawsuit.

This leads to the next part of the discussion: Does the spate of legislative enactments and pending bills create a legislative duty owed to students to

NOT teach a particular subject? If so, the duty not to teach may be breached if a teacher teaches a banned topic—sex education, for example. Injury can be inferred from the legislative statements, indicating that the legislation is designed to protect students from a particularized harm, with causation connected to the instruction on the banned topic.

It is reasonable to argue that the elements of a malpractice suit may be met, and the public policy constraints overcome by demonstrating that the legislative intent to identify a duty along with a judicial remedy for parents and students at least implicitly recognizes the tort of educational malpractice. Since these legislative initiatives to ban the teaching of certain topics do not contain safe harbor provisions that protect teachers or school districts from malpractice suits, malpractice may become viable without legislation specifically designating that teaching a banned topic constitutes malpractice.

In short, the so-called divisive-content legislation may have created a new crack in the malpractice wall. The wall may have been breached by legislation that bans the teaching of certain topics, thus advancing the argument that the legislation serves as the vehicle by which parents and students can bring a cause of action for educational malpractice and seek monetary damages.

Legislative Actions Restricting Teacher Speech

In many ways the power over the curriculum—what is taught and what is learned—shapes the future;[42] it may well be the lever that moves the Nation in a particular direction. Consequently, the public school curriculum is contested territory, not only by political parties and special interest groups but also by parents seeking to make sure that the education of their children reflects their ideological, political, or religious views.[43] One of the most consequential school controversies of the early part of the third decade of the twenty-first century focuses on issues of race, sexual orientation, and sex, topics that frequently overlap with the debates about COVID masks, public health, and medical freedom demonstrations.

These controversies tend to coalesce around the right of parents to direct the upbringing of their child,[44] the duty of the school board to direct what should be taught for the public benefit, and the students' right to learn. These rights and responsibilities are often in conflict. They have also resulted in a number of legislative actions aimed at controlling what is taught and what is read in public schools. The search to root out books deemed offensive and restrict what can be taught in the schools, specifically legislation targeting critical race theory, has taken on the form that some have called a "moral panic."[45]

For example, several states passed laws and administrative rulings that prohibit instruction about critical race theory.[46]

> The majority of these bills target discussions of race, racism, gender, and American history, banning a series of "prohibited" or "divisive" concepts for teachers and trainers operating in K–12 schools, public universities, and workplace settings. These bills appear designed to chill academic and educational discussions and impose government dictates on teaching and learning. In short: They are educational gag orders.[47]

Aligned with this focus of the "gag orders" are laws that Sachs, Young, and Friedman have characterized as "compulsory patriotism" that "censor" any topics/events that could be considered "anti-American."[48]

A report from *Pen America*, a research organization that explores the impact of government policy and social trends on free expression, identified 175 bills introduced in forty states since January 2021, with fifteen becoming laws in thirteen states, with three becoming law in March 2022 (Florida, Mississippi, and South Dakota). The pending bills target K–12 schools and higher education.[49]

For the purposes of this discussion, fifty-seven of the pending bills and adopted legislation include punishment for educators (employee discipline, including revocation of teaching credentials) and punishment for school districts, including exposure to lawsuits filed by private individuals, loss of state financial support, and loss of state accreditation.[50]

Some examples of these restrictive bills include Tennessee's divisive-content legislation, which identified fourteen concepts deemed "cynical or divisive" and which are banned from being taught or included in the curriculum.[51] Similarly, a Virginia bill filed on January 12, 2022, defines, in part, prohibited divisive concepts as those that elicit feelings of "discomfort, guilt, anguish, or any other form of psychological distress on account of the individual's race, religion, ethnicity, or sex."[52] Section (H) states that violations of the legislation are misdemeanor and can form the basis for termination and licensure revocation.

A high-profile, controversial Florida bill (HB 1557), which critics have dubbed the "Don't Say Gay" bill, was passed in March 2022. The contentious section of the legislation states, "3. Classroom instruction by school personnel or third parties on sexual orientation or gender identity may not occur in kindergarten through grade 3 or in a manner that is not age appropriate or developmentally appropriate for students in accordance with state standards."[53]

The bill's advocates argue that it does nothing more than ban the teaching of sexual topics to children in the third grade or younger. Many parents would agree that the introduction of sexual matters to very young children is not developmentally appropriate.

Critics, however, assert that the bill is vague.[54] Vague rules fail to provide adequate notice of what is impermissible, and they invite uneven, biased, and variable application.

What constitutes "instruction," for example? Concomitantly, are all conversations with students considered instruction? What is developmentally appropriate material? Do teachers receive proper notice of what conduct may result in adverse employment decisions and potential lawsuits. These laws prohibiting instruction carry consequences and may "chill" teacher instruction in ways that impact students.[55]

As part of a classroom sharing lesson, does the sharing of a family event that reveals that a student's family has two mothers or two fathers constitute a violation of the Florida legislation? Similarly, age-appropriate and developmentally appropriate are not defined in the legislation, and yet legislative prohibitions extend to all grades.

Not only is the curriculum being scrutinized to purge divisive content, but scrutiny also intrudes into the classroom to identify and remove any "objectionable" instruction. In Florida, Republican legislators as part of their anti-CRT legislation considered a bill that would require teachers to wear microphones "in class so that parents could monitor the lessons they're teaching students."[56]

An Iowa bill (HF 2177) was filed on February 1, 2022, requiring school districts to place Internet-connected cameras in all classrooms to provide live footage of the classroom, thereby giving parents the ability to "view live footage of their children" and all of the children in the classroom as well as the teacher.[57] An employee "who intentionally obstructs, disconnects, or otherwise causes a camera or online site not to function" is guilty of noncompliance.[58]

The legislation provides penalties for noncompliance starting with an oral reprimand followed by a fine equivalent to 1 percent of the employee's weekly salary. For a third offense, 5 percent of the weekly salary is levied against the employee.[59]

A Florida superintendent who "fails to cause an employee" to comply with the requirements of the law shall be subject to a "fine equivalent to five percent of the superintendent's weekly salary each time an employee" is fined for a third offense.[60] These types of financial penalties are unusual for human resource actions in education.

The Florida legislation clearly signals that open access into classrooms, which historically have been considered a closed forum for speech purposes, is a high-stakes initiative intended to allow parents to surveil teachers closely.[61] Legislation that proposes to require teachers to wear microphones or which authorizes teachers to be videotaped is an indication of a moral panic. Clearly, some state legislatures are moving toward the establishment of a new public policy under which teachers can be scrutinized to prevent harm to students, whether real or imagined.

The New Hampshire Experience

In some states, teachers and their unions are pushing against divisive-content legislation. For example, the American Federation of Teachers of New Hampshire and a few other plaintiffs recently brought a suit (December 13, 2021)[62] against the New Hampshire State Commissioner of Education and other state officials seeking declaratory and injunctive relief from a recently enacted series of statutes (HB 2), commonly called the "Divisive Concepts Statute."[63] A week later (December 20, 2021), the National Education Association, New Hampshire, and several school administrators, joined by the American Civil Liberties Union, filed a similar lawsuit.[64] Both lawsuits assert a concern about the vagueness of the legislation as to what can or cannot be taught. This vagueness has left many teachers "scared of the repercussions for guessing wrong."[65]

Specifically, the Prohibition on Teaching Discrimination section allows individuals to bring a civil suit against school districts alleging a violation of the new law and seeking legal and equitable relief.[66] In addition, the statute states that educators who violate this section shall be considered as violating the educator code of conduct, which "justifies disciplinary sanction by the state board of education."[67] The New Hampshire Department of Education created a website in which "those who believe that they, or their child, was discriminated against because their child's school was teaching and/or advocating" subjects prohibited by the New Hampshire law, can file a complaint.[68] New Hampshire AFT president characterized the New Hampshire Department of Education as declaring a "war on teachers."[69]

After this legislation was enacted, the Moms for Liberty (NH) tweeted (November 12, 2021) an offer of a bounty of "$500 for the first person that successfully catches a public school teacher breaking the new law. Students, parents, teachers, school staff . . . . We want to know! We pledge anonymity if you want."[70]

Peter Greene, in a *Forbes* article, stated that the use of "bounty" was not hyperbole. He cited a tweet (November 12, 2021, 11:27 AM) in which the Moms for Liberty responded to a query stating that people wishing to make donations to the fund through PayPal should mark their contribution as "CRT BOUNTY" in the notes.[71] Greene observed that, while other states also have vague anti-CRT laws, "New Hampshire has added another layer guaranteed to chill classroom speech."[72]

These laws, with their implicit threats of teacher discipline, including licensure revocation, financial penalties issued by state departments of education, and compensatory damages, may well chill classroom instruction. Thus, divisive-concepts legislation raises the constitutional question as to whether these laws are void for vagueness. Do the statutes give proper notice to the reasonable teacher about what instruction is prohibited?[73]

New Hampshire school law attorney David Wolowitz, commenting on the recently passed New Hampshire Right to Freedom from Discrimination in Public Workplaces and Education Act (2021), opined, "Classroom discussions present a particular risk because a teacher cannot predict what students might say and because the definition of 'taught' is so broad."[74] Jacob A. Bennett commented on the reach of New Hampshire's legislation, writing:

> The Live Free or Die state's version [of divisive-content legislation] is unique in that it places state authority to discipline teachers under existing human rights prohibitions on discrimination, and also creates a private right of action for "any person claiming to be aggrieved" by teachings they believe violate the ban.[75]

A Shift in Public Policy?

A major argument that the courts have used to dismiss educational malpractice suits is that such an award would violate public policy by subjecting public education to an incalculable number of lawsuits with money damages that could create havoc with the public budget. However, the national moral panic over what is taught in public schools and what books are available to students may create a shift in public policy. Table 6.1 indicates that an exploratory sample of school law experts (attorneys and professors) stated that public policy had the most influential impact (moderate/significant) on educational malpractice cases.

Approximately a dozen states have established a public policy that grants individuals the right to sue educators and/or school districts for violating a legislatively defined duty owed to students (see table 6.2). The requirement to not teach certain subjects or topics essentially establishes an instructional duty owed to students who may claim a private right to obtain monetary relief

Table 6.1   Comparative Impact of Factors (Excluding "Not Sure" Responses)

Factors	No Impact/Slight Impact	Moderate Impact/Significant Impact
Figure 6.2(a) Research Question	41.9% (N = 18)	58.1% (N = 25)
Figure 6.2(b) VAM	53.7% (N = 22)	46.3% (N = 19)
Figure 6.2(c) Public Policy	26.8% (N = 11)	73.2% (N = 30)

from individual teachers, the school district, or both. It can be reasonably argued that a duty has been established and that the breach of this duty provides monetary relief to the injured plaintiff much like damages are awarded in cases alleging medical and legal malpractice. The plaintiffs may recover attorney's fees, damages, and equitable forms of relief.

While the legislation on parental rights and anti-teaching restrictions related to race and sex do not specifically describe statutory violations as malpractice, a template for a private action for educational malpractice may have been established. In the rush to pass legislation and in some cases multiple pieces of legislation that place boundaries on subjects that can be taught, legislators may have implicitly created a tort that cracks the educational malpractice wall.

Table 6.2 demonstrates the potential extent of a change in policy regarding the viability of an educational malpractice tort that might occur in response to legislation that prohibits educators from teaching particular subjects and which includes punitive provisions. An individual remedy is being made available to potential plaintiff students in addition to the administrative

Table 6.2   Legislation Allowing Private Individuals to Bring Lawsuits against Educators and School Districts.

Bills/Legislation Status		
State	*Bill/Legislation*	*Status*
Florida	HB 1557	ENACTED
Georgia	HB 888	PENDING
Idaho	HB 488	PENDING
Illinois	HB 5494	PENDING
Kansas	HB 2662	PENDING
Kentucky	HB 18	PENDING
Kentucky	HB 487	PENDING
Kentucky	HB 706	PENDING
Missouri	HB 2189	PENDING
Missouri	HB1995	PENDING
Missouri	SB 645	PENDING
Missouri	HB 2827	PENDING
New Hampshire	NH RSA 193.40(I)	ENACTED
New Hampshire	HB 1532	PENDING
Pennsylvania	HB 1532	PENDING
Wisconsin	SB 409/AB 413	PENDING
Wisconsin	SB411/AB411	VETOED

Source: Adapted from the Pen America Index of Educational Gag Orders. It lists pending bills and enacted legislation that allows private individuals to bring lawsuits against educators and school districts as of March 30, 2022. See https://docs.google.com/spreadsheets/d/1Tj5WQVBmB6SQg-zP_M8uZsQQGH09Tx-mBY73v23zpyr0/edit#gid=1505554870.

Note: The clear majority of bills originate in the House of Representatives. Only one bill originated in the Senate. Several states used a private right of action for more than one piece of legislation.

punitive actions associated with unprofessional conduct (dismissal,[76] suspension/revocation of teaching credentials, or a ban from public school employment).

An emerging public policy that allows a private right to bring suit over teaching is changing the landscape of public education. It may provide a missing puzzle piece for proponents of educational malpractice—an instructional duty owed.

CAUSATION: IS VAM THE ANSWER?

TEXTBOX 6.4

Teachers are paid to adhere to a curriculum; their speech is government-subsidized speech, and the Constitution leaves school boards free to regulate that speech.

R. Weston Donehower, "Boring lessons: Defining the Limits of a Teacher's First Amendment Right to Speak through the Curriculum," *Michigan Law Review* 102 (2003): 517–541, 540.

Establishing causation has also been a major stumbling block in educational malpractice cases along with public policy considerations. In *Peter W.*, the court stated that a student's achievement or failure to achieve literacy development is influenced by numerous factors beyond the education received, thus making causation difficult to establish.[77] These factors include physical, neurological, emotional, cultural, and environmental factors. The *Donohue* court, in a concurring opinion, supplemented this list with the following factors: student attitude, motivation, temperament, past experiences, and home environment.[78]

The court in *Donohue* acknowledged that proving causation might be difficult or even impossible in some instances. But it assumes too much, the court asserted, to conclude that causation can never be established.[79] Central to establishing causation for malpractice is the practice of the teacher; what the teacher does or doesn't do when instructing students.

Who Shall Teach Our Children?

Given the importance of education to our Nation and the American people, staffing classrooms with highly qualified teachers is a critical national concern. As Jennifer Rice, dean of the College of Education at the University of

Maryland, commented "Teacher quality matters. In fact, it is the most important school-related factor influencing student achievement."[80]

Consequently, "quality teaching plays a major, if not the most important, role in shaping students' academic performance."[81] What teachers do in their classrooms is central to the effectiveness of the state's system of public education as well as private education. Teachers stand at the crossroads of education. Therefore, excellence in schools is most directly related to the performance of teachers acting in concert with one another and individually. Consequently, who is hired to teach and who is retained is critical to student achievement.

While teacher effectiveness varies, current systems of evaluation do not sufficiently differentiate among teachers. Evaluating teachers is a critical component in the delivery of quality education to students. However, teachers have both the right and the need to have accurate and fair feedback. Therefore, building effective, professional teacher evaluation system is a critical policy concern and must be built on an ethical foundation.

The purposes of the supervision/evaluation process include developing, improving, and maintaining teaching skills and behaviors that result in students meeting stated outcomes and goals. They also include providing a means for making critical employment decisions, such as granting tenure and identifying and resolving problems in work performance, up to and including non-retention or dismissal. Finally, the personnel evaluation process must comport with the accepted standards of propriety, utility, feasibility, and accuracy, as articulated by the Joint Committee on Standards for Educational Evaluation.[82]

Teacher evaluations serve to define the essential elements of competence.[83] They hold individuals accountable for their practice and help them to improve. Failure to improve may lead to dismissal or contract nonrenewal. In other words, a negative evaluation might indicate that the teacher did not meet the accepted standards of practice of the teaching profession.

A nationwide call for accountability in education focused on teachers at the start of the twenty-first century. Efforts to diminish tenure rights and the shift to the teacher's failure to teach with a concentration on teacher evaluation surfaced.[84] DeMitchell, DeMitchell, and Gagnon, commenting on teacher accountability, observed that the "nexus between teacher effectiveness and large-scale student testing is gaining acceptance by many policymakers and researchers."[85]

During this time a statistical model emerged. VAM purports to determine whether the standards of practice for classroom instruction have been met by measuring student achievement and then attributing expected student gain or lack of student gain to a teacher. If standards of practice are established through evaluations and the outcomes of the practice are measured through

VAM assessments, then an enforceable standard of care and a method for showing causation may be created, thus arguably providing a mechanism for establishing educational malpractice.

Value-Added Modeling

TEXTBOX 6.5

VAMs are an enduring elixir. They satisfy our thirst for "data driven" metrics and need to attribute education results to a school or a particular teacher for accountability purposes.

Mark A. Paige, *Building a Better Teacher: Understanding Value-Added Models in the Law of Teacher Evaluations* (Lanham, MD: Rowman & Littlefield, 2016): x.

VAM is an inclusive term for a collection of complex statistical techniques that calculate the value a teacher adds to the education of a student through the use of multiple years of a student's test score data. Mark Paige writes, "Purportedly they can ascertain a teacher's effectiveness by predicting the impact of a teacher on a student's test scores. Because test scores are the *sin qua non* of our education system, VAMs are alluring."[86] VAM is used to measure the effectiveness of teachers.

VAM is an inclusive term for statistical models that calculate the value a teacher adds to the education of a student. Proponents of VAM assert that non-school-related factors that influence a student's achievement are controlled by using multiple measures over time. Researchers, including William Sanders, who developed VAM, assert in response, "Because the value-added method measures gain from a student's starting point, it implicitly controls for socio-economic status and other background factors to the extent that their influence is already reflected in the pre-test scores."[87]

Proponents of VAM assert that the score captures the effectiveness of an individual teacher's instruction of his or her students as measured by standardized test scores. Furthermore, some argue that, while VAM is not perfect, it is better than the current system of evaluation, which is often based on a school principal's assessment of a teacher's effectiveness.

An underlying theme of VAM is that you cannot improve what you cannot measure. A significant number of states have accepted this argument and have implemented revised legislation, rules, and guidelines that require the use of student test scores in the evaluation of teachers. Many, if not most, have adopted some form of value-added or growth models to meet that requirement.

However, VAM-type models have not been warmly embraced by some scholars who have raised cautionary flags. Concerns have been raised about validity, reliability (stability of scores), and unintended consequences in using student scores for high-stakes decisions such as compensation, tenure, and promotion.[88] For example, the American Statistical Association issued a statement arguing that school districts should not use VAM to make high-stake personnel decisions.[89] Noted researchers Eric A. Hanushek and Steven C. Rivkin concur, writing:

> The bigger issues with value-added estimates of teacher effectiveness concern their use in personnel compensation, employment, promotion, or assignment deci- sions. . . . Despite the strength of the research findings, concerns about accuracy, fairness, and potential adverse effects of incentives based on limited outcomes raise worries about value added estimates in education staffing and policy.[90]

Furthermore, there is an implicit assumption in the use of VAMs to esti- mate teacher effectiveness that teacher quality is a fixed trait and does not vary based on context. In other words, a good teacher in one setting will be an equally good teacher in another setting, even as students and resources vary.[91] However, critics of using VAMs to evaluate teacher quality assume just the opposite—that context does matter.

Critics argue that VAMs will always be biased estimates of teacher effec- tiveness no matter how many years of prior data are analyzed or how many control variables are used, because students are not randomly placed into classrooms.[92] Thus, while VAMs *can be used* to measure changes in student achievement over time, that growth should not be *attributed* to an individual teacher, school, or program quality.[93]

At best, VAM may reveal how a teacher's students are doing in compari- son to other teachers' students. It may provide comparisons of VAM scores by rank-ordering teachers. But VAM tells us little to nothing about what a teacher is doing well, not doing well, or not doing at all. It provides no data about how a teacher can improve or what specific instructional practice needs to be improved.

A focus on quality teacher evaluation systems is critically important. How- ever, VAM is not that clear-cut in establishing a cause for instructional harm suffered by an individual student. There are legitimate concerns about the limitations of VAM as a tool for making high-stakes personnel decisions, let alone being used for educational malpractice suits.

The use of VAM for high-stakes decisions may be waning due to concerns about the appropriateness of its use. In a 2022 interview, assessment expert Dr. Carla Evans observed:

The use of value-added models in teacher evaluation has definitely waned in recent years. Many states that added VAMs into state legislation based on Race to the Top and other political pressures have since either greatly reduced the weight of VAMs in a teacher's overall rating, or they have completely removed the requirement. I don't know of a single state that is adding requirements related to the use of student achievement data in teacher evaluations at this point in time; however, some states have continued their programs. The landscape around teacher evaluation—especially the use of student achievement data—has definitely shifted since 2009.[94]

Mark Paige also noted the decline in the use of VAM. In his analysis of thirteen court cases (six federal cases and seven state cases) brought against VAM policies for alleged violations of substantive and procedural due process, equal protection, and contract clauses, he stated that his review of the court cases demonstrated that several of these decisions "set certain parameters around their use."[95] Plaintiffs in these cases argued elements of constitutional and statutory law and contract law rather than tort law. Consequently, a lawsuit for educational malpractice would not be bound by these decisions, but they may be used as persuasive authority over the appropriateness of using VAM in demonstrating causation.

School law researchers wrote in their analysis of VAM and educational malpractice that "the means by which professional educators are held liable in a court of law for malpractice must be based on procedures that are valid, reliable, and comport with the usual and customary practices of the profession."[96] For example, Paige's analysis of *Lederman v. King* (2016) noted that affidavits from scholars and practitioners were persuasive in highlighting the statistical issues that the plaintiff contended make the use of VAMs irrational.[97] Consequently, this question arises: Will evidence of causation submitted by a plaintiff student in an educational malpractice suit be able to rely on a VAM analysis to show causation even though the same VAM analysis was ruled to be irrational in an earlier court decision?

ARE THE CRACKS WIDENING?

TEXTBOX 6.6

Value-added assessment is the product of technology; it is also the product of a managerial mind-set that believes that every variable in a child's education can be identified, captured, measured, and evaluated with precision.

Diane Ravitch, *The Death and Life of the Great American School System: How Testing and Choice Are Undermining Education* (New York: Basic Books, 2010): 180.

For almost half a century, plaintiffs who have sought relief through a suit for educational malpractice have failed. A three-pronged defense against an educational malpractice claim has largely prevailed. First, courts have expressed the view that there is no clearly defined duty shaped around a standard of care for expected instructional practices. Second, judges have noted the difficult problem of establishing causation for any failure to adequately educate any particular student. Finally, and perhaps most importantly, courts have expressed strong public policy reservations about recognizing a tort for educational malpractice, including the fear that recognizing this tort would open a floodgate of litigation. Together, these three concerns have served as a bulwark against the viability of a lawsuit for educational malpractice.

Given the pervasiveness of legislative accountability measures, divisive-content laws, and the rising interest in teacher effectiveness, a pathway to educational malpractice may be forming, which should be worrying for educators.[98] The old judicial barrier to educational malpractice may be giving way as a by-product of the wave of accountability.[99]

This chapter explored whether cracks are forming in the a cause of action educational malpractice wall. It started with a review of a recent exploratory mixed methods analysis, the Educational Malpractice Viability Study, which surveyed a national judgment/expert sample of school law professors and attorneys.[100] The respondents listed public policy as having the greatest impact on educational malpractice cases, followed by a lack of defined teaching standards. Just over half (53.7 percent) of the survey respondents reported that VAM had no impact or only a slight impact on the viability of a tort for educational malpractice. This latter finding may reflect the pushback on the use of VAM for high-stakes decisions.

The survey also asked questions about the viability of educational malpractice suits at this time and in the near future. Most of the respondents stated that this tort is not a currently viable course of action. However, respondents were less certain about the viability of educational malpractice in the near future. This uncertainty may be a signal that the judicial hostility toward the tort of educational malpractice may be diminishing. If so, this change in attitude may reflect a different perspective on policy issues and a growing sense that a standard of care for educators can be established and that the question of causation can be reasonably determined.

The second section of this chapter discussed the potential impact of legislative gag orders that prohibit instruction on certain subjects. There is a broad agreement among scholars and professionals that state legislators have plenary power over public education, including the articulation of curriculum standards, so long as legislative restrictions on public education do not infringe on constitutional protections.

Particularly worrying, from the perspective of educators, is the proliferation of divisive-content legislation that authorizes parents to sue teachers and school districts for violating legislative restrictions. Such legislation comes very close to being a suit for instructional negligence. Parents can assert that legislative gag orders create a legally enforceable instructional duty and that the breach of this duty of non-instruction is remediable in private lawsuits in addition to governmental employee disciplinary action.

Implicitly at least, divisive-content laws that authorize private lawsuits articulate a new public policy, allowing negligence suits to be brought against schools as well as teachers. After all, once a state legislature identifies subjects that may not be taught, it is easy to see that a breach of a legislative restriction could be framed as instructional negligence—that is, educational malpractice.

The last section reviewed the impact of VAM on the ability to demonstrate causation for a student's failure to be properly educated. Plaintiffs' difficulty in establishing causation for poor educational outcomes has been a major impediment to the recognition of educational malpractice as a tort. There was great interest in VAM in the second decade of the twenty-first century. Could VAM and its connection to educational accountability form the basis for retrieving educational malpractice from the dustbin of judicial history? Legal scholars have arrived at different conclusions with regard to the application of VAM to educational malpractice suits.

For example, one set of researchers argued that potential advocates for using VAM as a lever for educational malpractice should heed its potential and unanticipated consequences. The use of VAM as part of malpractice "should come with a warning label of potential side effects."[101] They concluded their study with the following admonition: "The means by which professional educators are held liable in a court of law for malpractice must be based on procedures that are valid, reliable, and comport with the usual and customary practices of the profession."[102]

However, Hutt and Tang argue that VAM overcomes the causation prong. They write:

> For if we are correct that recent developments in the realm of educational data truly render plausible the malpractice action in the present day, it must be the case that these developments offer a compelling rebuttal to the initial

logic provided by the courts who ruled against similarly situated plaintiffs some four decades ago.[103]

The authors analyzed the concerns and objections to the use of VAM in high-stake decision-making. They asserted that the new world of data changes the calculus of common law negligence claims.[104] They applied VAM to each of the four negligence elements used in malpractice tort claims: duty, breach of duty, causation, and injury.

Their essential argument is that once VAM identifies a teacher as low-performing, the retention of that teacher by the school district constitutes negligence. VAM, the authors maintain, "addresses the proximate cause concerns that troubled courts in the initial era of educational malpractice litigation."[105]

However, Deborah D. Dye, writing before the rise of VAM, states that the problem of proving proximate cause must take into account so many variables that affect a child's ability to learn that are outside the educator's control and that, until they are controlled, "an educator should not be held liable."[106] The fact that control of external variables has not been resolved by a majority of the assessment scholars should raise a cautionary flag and give the courts pause before establishing causation.[107]

Prior to VAM, Johnny Parker's argument was similar to Hutt and Tang's. He analyzed proximate cause and educational malpractice. Parker asserted that proximate cause was not developed to hinder tort law development. Furthermore, he argued that the judicial unwillingness to recognize the tort provides the teaching profession with "governmental immunity," has been "unfair to persons wronged through incompetence," and fosters professional irresponsibility. Public policy considerations are an integral part of the duty-proximate cause inquiry."[108] Public policy can recognize the significance of the teacher's conduct to the injured student.

Public interests change, new interests emerge, and old ones fade like ancient and obsolete customs. The legislative desire in some states to open public education to a private cause of action for classroom instruction may well lead to a breach in the educational malpractice wall. The drive to hold teachers accountable for their professional teaching practice through accurate, reliable, and defensible measurements are designed to strengthen teacher practices.

Will VAM form the basis for identifying causation in an educational malpractice suit or will its high-stakes "rank and yank" characterization and questionable ability to identify teaching deficits along with concerns about VAM's reliability and validity prevent VAMs from becoming a tool for advancing the tort of educational malpractice?[109]

Our last chapter explores the responses to a tort of educational malpractice and ends with our conclusions regarding this book's central question: Is the wall sturdy or is it crumbling? Should a cautionary flag be raised?

NOTES

1. Ethan Hutt & Aaron Tang, "The New Education Malpractice Litigation," *Virginia Law Review* 99 (2013): 419–492, 428.

2. See, for example, *Bell v. Board of Education of the City of West Haven*, 739 A.2d 321 (Conn. App. Ct. 1999) (duty, standard of care, and reasonable conduct "are difficult, if not impossible, to apply in the academic environment").

3. Terri A. DeMitchell, "Educational Malpractice," in Todd A. DeMitchell, *Negligence: What Principals Need to Know about Avoiding Liability* (Lanham, MD: Rowman & Littlefield Education, 2007): 67–77, 67. See, *Livosi v. Hicksville Union-Free School District*, 693 N.Y.S.2d 617, 617–618 (1999) (as a matter of public policy, such a cause of action cannot be entertained by courts of this State"); *Brown v. Compton Unified School District*, 80 Cal. Rptr2d 171, 172 (App. 2d Dist. 1998). ("Policy considerations preclude 'an actionable duty of care' in persons and agencies who administer the academic phases of the public educational process.")

4. A policy is a set of values issued with authority and expressed in written form or words. It is authoritative when there is sufficient power to induce a shift in behavior toward achieving specified values.

5. John W. Kingdon, *Agendas, Alternatives, and Public Policies* (New York: Longman, 1995, 2 ed.).

6. For example, after the massacre at Sandy Hook Elementary School, a number of advocates, or issue partisans, sought to attach their preferred solution to the issue of intruder violence in the schools. Gun control advocates defined the issue as guns and pushed for policy responses that included banning certain types of high-capacity ammunition clips and bans on certain types of firearms. Others pushed for hardening the school site by arming teachers and school administrators. Other issue partisans sought to define the issue as a mental health problem and called for greater mental health screening for persons seeking to purchase firearms.

7. Joseph P. Overton of the Mackinac Center for Public Policy developed the Overton Window of Political Possibility model of how politicians are limited in the policy ideas they can support. Generally, they only pursue policies that "are widely accepted throughout society as legitimate policy options." The Overton Window is designed to capture the acceptable options from the range of options—options that enhance but do not harm their electoral chances. The options are aligned a continuum with a sliding window that generally indicates acceptability. Policy options/solution proposals using Kingdon's work changes overtime as prohibition laws have demonstrated. Overton posits that "families, workplaces, friends, media churches, voluntary associations, think tanks, schools, and many other phenomena . . . establish and reinforce societal norms," which influence those options within the window. Will the reluctance to hold public schools accountable through malpractice litigation slide into the Overton Window? Author, *The Overton Window* (n.d.), https://www.mackinac.org/OvertonWindow.

8. See Todd A. DeMitchell, Stefanie King, & Terri A. DeMitchell, "Educational Malpractice: Is It a Tort Whose Time Has Come? An Exploratory Mixed Methods Study," *University of Florida Journal of Law & Public Policy 32* (2022): 253–291, 128–138. The authors have given permission for their research to be used in this book.

Chapter 6

9. Ibid., 280.

10. See, for example, *Morales v. Newport-Mesa Unified School District*, 768 Fed. Appx. 717, 719 (9th Cir. 2019) (affirming student's award of forty hours of tutoring, a vocational assessment, and an assistive technology assessment).

11. Kimberly A. Wilkins, "Educational Malpractice: A Cause of Action in Need of a Cause of Action," *Valparaiso University Law Review* 22 (1988): 427–460, 458.

12. *Martin v. Herzog*, 228 N.Y. 164, 126 N.E. 814 (1920).

13. *Allen v. Dhuse*, 104 Ill. App. 3d 806 (1982).

14. *Christou v. Arlington Park-Washington Park Race Tracks Corporation*, 432 N.E.2d 920 (Ill. App. Ct. 1982).

15. *District of Columbia v. White*, 442 A.2d 159 (D. C. App. 1982); *Davis v. Marathon Oil Company*, 64 Ill. 2d 380 (1976).

16. See, for example, American Counseling Association, "2014 ACA Code of Ethics," https://www.counseling.org/docs/default-source/default-document-library/2014-code-of-ethics-finaladdress.pdf?sfvrsn=96b532c_2:

- A.11.d Appropriate Transfer of Services: When counselors transfer or refer clients to other practitioners, they ensure that appropriate clinical and administrative processes are completed and open communication is maintained with both clients and practitioners.
- A.12 Abandonment and Client Neglect: Counselors do not abandon or neglect clients in counseling. Counselors assist in making appropriate arrangements for the continuation of treatment, when necessary, during interruptions such as vacations, illness, and following termination. (p. 6)

17. The Ninth Circuit Court on an appeal of lawsuit seeking to declare Proposition 227 unconstitutional noted three primary reasons why vague statutes are objectionable.

First, they trap the innocent by not providing fair warning. Second, they impermissibly delegate basic policy matters to lower level officials for resolution on an ad hoc and subjective basis, with the attendant dangers of arbitrary and discriminatory application. Third, when vague statutes involve sensitive areas of First Amendment freedoms, they operate to inhibit the exercise of those freedoms. *California Teachers Association v. State Board of Education*, 271 F.3d 1141, 1150 (9th Cir. 2001)

The Appellate Court upheld the constitutionality of Proposition 227.

18. California Education Code Annotated §306(d) (West 2002).

19. California Education Code Annotated §320 (West 2002).

20. Todd A. DeMitchell & Terri A. DeMitchell, "Statutes and Standards: Has the Door to Educational Malpractice Been Opened?" *Brigham Young University Education and Law Journal* 2003 (2003): 485–518, 518.

21. Proposition 227 was repealed by Proposition 58 English Proficiency. Multicultural Education Initiative Statute on November 8, 2016 by a vote of 73.5 percent Yes to 26.5 percent No. Shirley N. Weber, California Secretary of State, General Election—Statement of Vote, November 8, 2016, https://elections.cdn.sos.ca.gov/sov/2016-general/sov/2016-complete-sov.pdf, p. 12.

22. See Veronica Odiri Amatari, "The Instructional Process, a Review of Flanders' Interaction Analysis in a Classroom Setting," *International Journal of Secondary Education* 3 (October 2015): 43–49.

23. See Patrick D. Halligan, "Function of Schools, the Status of Teachers, and the Claims of the Handicapped: An Inquiry into Special Education Malpractice," *Missouri Law Review* 45 (1980): 667–707, 679, writing, "Overall the right of the legislature to designate the program of studies for the public schools of its state is a right rarely questioned."

24. 385 U.S. 589, 603 (1967).

25. Vanessa A. Wernicke, "High School Academic Freedom: The Evolution of a Fish Out of Water. An analysis of *Cockerl v. Shelby County School District*," *University of Cincinnati Law Review* 71(2003): 1471.

26. *Millikan v. Board of Directors of Everett School District*, 611 P.2d 414, 418 (1980) See, *Webster v. New Lenox School District No. 122*, 917 F.2d 1004 (7th Cir. 1990) (the "first amendment is not a teacher license for uncontrolled expression at variance with established curricular content"), 1007. *Kirkland v. Northside Independent School District*, 890 F.2d 794, 795 (5th Cir. 1989), *cert. denied*, 496 U.S. 926 (1990) ("We hold only that public school teachers are not free, under the first amendment, to arrogate control of curricula"). In an earlier case, the Seventh Circuit wrote, "There is a compelling state interest in the choice to adhere to a suitable curriculum for the benefit of our young citizens and society. It cannot be left to the individual teachers to teach what they please" (*Palmer v. Board of Education of the City of Chicago*, 603 F.2d 1271, 1274 [7th Cir. 1979], *cert. denied*, 444 U.S. 1026 [1980]).

27. Ibid. See, *Cary v. Board of Education*, 598 F.2d 535, 543 (10th Cir. 1979) ("We think teachers do have some rights to freedom of expression in the classroom, teaching high school juniors and seniors. They cannot be made to simply read from a script prepared or approved by the Board"). A Texas federal district court offered a strong endorsement of academic freedom, writing, "A teacher has a constitutional right protected by the First Amendment to engage in a teaching method of his or her own choosing even though the subject matter may be controversial or sensitive" (*Dean v. Timpson Independent School District*, 486 F. Supp. 302, 307 (E.D. Tex. 1979).

28. *East Hartford Education Association v. Board of Education of East Hartford*, 562 F.2d 838, 843 (2d Cir. 1977).

29. Ibid., 844.

30. 474 F.3d 477, 479 (7th Cir. 2007).

31. *Evans-Marshall v. Board of Education*, 428 F.3d 223, 235 (6th Cir. 2005) (Sutton, J., concurring).

32. Julie Underwood, "School Districts Control Teachers' Classroom Speech," *Phi Delta Kappan* 99(4) (2017/2018): 76–77, https://kappanonline.org/underwood-school-districts-control-teachers-classroom-speech/.

33. *Epperson v. Arkansas*, 393 U.S. 97, 113–114 (1968) (Black, J., concurring).

34. 631 F.2d 1300, 1304 (7th Cir. 1980) (quoting *Palmer v. Board of Education*, 603 F.2d 1271, 1274 [7th Cir. 1979]).

35. Brief for National School Boards Association as Amicus Curiae Supporting Petitioners, *Board of Education of Jefferson City School District R-1 v. Wilder*, 960 P.2d 695 (Colo. 1998) (No. 97SC92292), http://www.nsba.org/site/print.asp.

36. *Parducci v. Rutland*, 316 F. Supp. 352 (D.C. Ala. 1970).

37. *Fowler v. Board of Education*, 819 F.2d 657, 661 (6th Cir. 1987).

38. *Dean v. Timpson Independent. School District*, 486 F. Supp. 302, 307 (D.C. Tex. 1979).

39. *Romano v. Harrington*, 664 F. Supp. 675, 682 (E.D.N.Y. 1987).

40. *Miles v. Denver Public Schools*, 944 F.2d 773, 779 (10th Cir. 1991). See, also *Chiras v. Miller*, 432 F.3d 606, 618 (5th Cir. 2005), which held that "the use of textbooks in public school classrooms is government speech and not a forum for First Amendment purposes."

41. Todd A. DeMitchell & Vincent J. Connelly, "Academic Freedom and the Public School Teacher: An Exploratory Study of Perceptions, Policy, and the Law," *Brigham Young University Education and Law Journal* 2007(1) (2007): 83–117, 116. The responding teachers in this exploratory mixed methods study perceived the distinction between the right of how to teach a lesson and decisions regarding the curriculum. Ibid., 111.

42. "The public school curriculum is society's primary method of attempting to structure its future." Michael Imber & Tyll Van Geel, *Education Law* (Mahaw, NJ: Lawrence Erlbaum Associates, Publishers, 2000, 2nd ed.): 59.

43. See Michael Apple, *Cultural Politics and Education* (New York: Teachers College Press, 1996): 8, writing:

> Education is deeply implicated in the politics of culture. The curriculum is never simply a neutral assemblage of knowledge, somewhat appearing in the texts and classrooms of a nation. It is always part of a selective tradition, someone's selection, some group's vision of legitimate knowledge.

44. In addition to parental rights laws passed and pending in a number of states, Senator Josh Hawley (R-Missouri) introduced "Parents' Bill of Rights Act of 2021." The bill allows a state attorney general to bring a suit for injunctive relief and for the U.S. Department of Education to withhold 50 percent of the federal education aid to the state; https://www.hawley.senate.gov/sites/default/files/2021-11/Parents%20 Bill%20of%20Rights%20-%20FILED_0.pdf.

45. See Todd A. DeMitchell, Richard Fossey, & Terri A. DeMitchell, "A Moral Panic, Book Banning, and the Constitution: The Right to Direct the Upbringing and the Right to Receive Information in a Time of Inflection," *Education Law Reporter* 397 (2022): 905–928.

46. For a listing of legislative and administrative actions regarding educational gag orders, see Author, "PEN America Index of Educational Gag Orders," *PEN America* (March 30, 2022), https://docs.google.com/spreadsheets/d/1Tj5WQVBmB6SQg-zP_M8uZsQQGH09TxmBY73v23zpyr0/edit#gid=1505554870.

47. Jonathan Friedman & James Tager, "Educational Gag Orders," *PEN America* (January 18, 2022): 1–71, 4, https://pen.org/wp-content/uploads/2022/02/PEN_ EducationalGagOrders_01-18-22-compressed.pdf. "This report chronicles the alarming

spreading of legislative efforts in 2021 to constrict education topics related to race, gender, and American history," Research and Resources, https://pen.org/research-resources/.

48. Jeffrey Sachs, Jeremy C. Young, & Jonathan Friedman, "Educational Gag Orders Seek to Enforce Compulsory Patriotism," *PEN America* (March 30, 2022), https://pen.org/update-educational-gag-orders-seek-to-enforce-compulsory-patriotism/.

49. Ibid.

50. Ibid.

51. Tennessee Code Annotated §49–6-1019(a)(1–14).

52. 2022 Session, VA. House Bill No. 781 1(A)(vii) (January 12, 2022), https://lis.virginia.gov/cgi-bin/legp604.exe?221+ful+HB781. Furthermore, section (I) reads in pertinent part that if a school employee has "knowingly and intentionally" violated the Act, parents of the affected student may request the local school board to provide a "voucher in an amount equal to all sums from any source that the school board received for the education of such student" to be used for the education of the child, ostensibly including private schools.

An interesting response to protecting children from any school materials that cause discomfort was written by Zev (Wisconsin) as a reader comment to Margaret Renki's *The New York Times* op-ed "In Tennessee, the "'Maus' Controversy Is the Least of Our Worries" (February 7, 2022). Zev wrote, "If the idea is to ban texts that make children feel uncomfortable, they would start with algebra," https://www.nytimes.com/2022/02/07/opinion/culture/maus-tennessee-book-bans.html.

53. Florida House of Representatives, HB 1557 Parental Rights in Education, Florida statute §1001.42(8)(3) lines 97–101, https://legiscan.com/FL/text/H1557/id/2541706.

54. See, e.g., *FCC v. Fox Television Stations, Incorporation*, 567 U.S. 239, 253 (2012) (noting that the vagueness doctrine addresses "a fundamental principle in our legal system . . . that laws which regulate persons or entities must give fair notice of conduct that is forbidden or required").

55. For a discussion of the chilling effect on teachers and librarians in response to the numerous current legislative actions regarding parental rights and divisive-content restrictions, see, DeMitchell et al., *supra* note 45, 908–914.

56. Brad Reed, "'It's not their private space': Florida GOP mulls forcing teachers to wear microphones so parents can monitor lessons," *Rawstory* (January 13, 2022), https://www.rawstory.com/florida-schools-2656404070/ (writing on the constant monitoring, Representative Bob Rommel stated, "it's not their private space. It's our children's space too").

57. H.F. 2177, line 8, https://legiscan.com/IA/text/HF2177/2021.

58. House File 2177 by Representative Norlin Mommsen, "An Act relating to parental access to live video feeds of public school district classrooms and providing penalties," §(3)(a), https://www.legis.iowa.gov/legislation/BillBook?ga=89&ba=HF2177. The sponsor of the bill stated that the primary purpose of the bill is to increase the involvement of parents in their children's education. Critics condemned the legislation as designed to censor and intimidate educators and "completely outrageous and

dangerous." Adam Edelman, "Iowa Bill Would Require Cameras in Public School Classrooms," *NBC News* (February 3, 2022), https://www.nbcnews.com/politics/politics-news/iowa-bill-require-cameras-public-school-classrooms-rcna14789.

59. Ibid., §3(b)–(d).

60. Ibid., §4.

61. The bill died in its first scheduled subcommittee meeting. The sponsor did not show up for the meeting. The author of the bill stated that the goal of the bill was to showcase "the great work our teachers do and help to continue that parental involvement that occurred during COVID." Amanda Rooker, "Iowa Bill to Require Cameras in Every Classroom Abruptly Killed," *KKCI*, Des Moines, Iowa (February 9, 2022), https://www.kcci.com/article/iowa-bill-to-require-cameras-in-every-classroom-abruptly-killed-hf-2177/39028617#.

62. *Local 8027, AFT-New Hampshire v. Edelbut*, Case 1:21-cv-01063 (December 13, 2021). A copy of the complaint is in the possession of the first author. Requests for a copy of the complaint can be directed to todd.demitchell@unh.edu.

63. New Hampshire Revised Statutes Annotated §193:40. The original legislation sought to ban discussions of certain "divisive concepts as critical race theory and white privilege." It was recast as the freedom from discrimination act. When Governor Chris Sununu signed the legislation, ten of the seventeen members of the state's Council on Diversity resigned. The resignation letter, stated in pertinent part:

> "You signed into law a provision that aims to censor conversations essential to advancing equity and inclusion in our state, specifically for those within our public education systems, and all state employees. Given your willingness to sign this damaging provision and make it law, we are no longer able to serve as your advisors." Governor Sununu "dismissed the resignations as political."
>
> Jenny Whidden, "Half of Governor's Diversity Council Quits Over 'Divisive Concepts' Restrictions in Budget," *Monanock Ledger-Transcript* (Peterborough, NH) (June 29, 2021), https://www.ledgertranscript.com/Half-of-governor-s-diversity-council-abruptly-quits-41216250.

64. ACLU, "Complaint Challenging NH Divisive Concepts Bill HB2" (December 20, 2021), https://www.aclu.org/legal-document/complaint-challenging-nh-divisive-concepts-bill-hb2.

65. Ibid., *Mejia et al. v. Edleblut et al.*, Case 1:21-cv-01077 (D. N.H. December 20, 2021), at 43, line 109.

66. New Hampshire Revised Statutes Annotated §193:40(II), https://casetext.com/statute/new-hampshire-revised-statutes/title-15-education/chapter-193-pupils/discrimination-in-public-schools/section-19340-prohibition-on-teaching-discrimination.

67. New Hampshire Revised Statutes Annotated §193:40(IV). On January 5, 2022, SB 304 was introduced to repeal the changes made to NH RSA §193:40 and NH RSA 354-A:29 through NH RSA 354-A:34, http://www.gencourt.state.nh.us/bill_status/billinfo.aspx?id=2072&inflect=2.

68. Available at https://www.education.nh.gov/who-we-are/deputy-commissioner/office-of-governance/right-to-freedom-from-discrimination. "Once the completed questionnaire is received, it will be reviewed by the Commission's Intake Coordinator. The Coordinator may need to reach out to gather more information to determine if the individual filing has grounds to file a formal complaint." Ibid.

69. Peter Greene, "New Hampshire and Moms for Liberty Put Bounty on Teachers' Heads," *Forbes* (November 12, 2021), https://www.forbes.com/sites/petergreene/2021/11/12/new-hampshire-and-moms-for-liberty-put-bounty-on-teachers-heads/?sh=21f80aa7a4bf. Greene quoted AFT President Deb Howes stating:

> It was bad enough that the law tried to find a problem that doesn't exist—no teacher in New Hampshire teaches that any group is inherently superior or inferior to another. That false flag has now been made worse with Education Commissioner Frank Edelblut launching a webpage to encourage parents to file complaints against teachers who allegedly teach so-called divisive concepts. . . . Edelblut has declared a war on teachers, a war that the overwhelming majority of N.H. parents will find repulsive.

70. Jaclyn Peiser, "N.H. Governor Slams Conservative Group's $500 Reward for Reporting Critical Race Teachings: 'Wholly Inappropriate'," *Washington Post* (November 19, 2021), https://www.washingtonpost.com/nation/2021/11/19/moms-for-liberty-new-hampshire/.

71. Greene, *supra* note 69, citing to https://twitter.com/Moms4LibertyNH/status/1459196198951264264.

72. Ibid.

73. For a discussion of due process and teacher discipline, Todd A. DeMitchell & Mark A. Paige, *Threading the Evaluation Needle: The Documentation of Teacher Unprofessional Conduct* (Lanham, MD: Rowman & Littlefield, 2020): 21–25.

74. David Wolowitz, "A Proposal to Mitigate the Risk to Public School Teachers' Career From New Hampshire's Right to Freedom from Discrimination in Public Workplaces and Education Act," *McLane Middleton* (August 2, 2021), https://www.mclane.com/thought-leadership/a-proposal-to-mitigate-the-risk-to-public-school-teachers-careers-from-new-hampshires-right-to-freedom-from-discrimination-in-public-workplaces-and-education-act.

75. Jacob A. Bennett, "Commentary: GOP Wages War on Educators—Again," *New Hampshire Bulletin* (March 18, 2022), https://www.researchgate.net/publication/359623817_New_Hampshire_Bulletin_Commentary_GOP_wages_war_on_educators_-_again.

76. See, e.g., Alabama HB 11, which mandates termination for any employee who violates the provisions, banning schools from requiring students "to personally affirm, adopt, or adhere to," outlined tenets allegedly associated with critical race theory, or from doing so *in a course of instruction.*" *PEN America*, *supra* note 46 (emphasis added).

77. *Peter W. v. San Francisco Unified School District*, 131 Cal. Rptr. 854 (Cal. Ct. App. 1976).

78. *Donohue v. Copiague Union Free School District*, 391 N.E.2d 1352, 1355 (N.Y. 1979) (Wachtler, J., concurring).

79. Ibid., 1353–1354.

80. Jennifer K. Rice, *Teacher Quality: Understanding the Effectiveness of Teacher Attributes* (Washington, DC: Economic Policy Institute, 2003): v, http://www.epi.org/publications/entry/books_teacher_quality_execsum_intro/#ExecSum. Site visited February 28, 2019.

81. Jian Wang, Emily Lin, Elizabeth Spalding, Cari L. Klecka, & Sandra J. Odell, "Quality Teaching and Teacher Education: A Kaleidoscope of Notions," *Journal of Teacher Education* 62 (2011): 331–338, 338.

82. Author, "Personnel Evaluation Standards," *Joint Committee on Standards for Personnel Evaluation* (2022), http://www.jcsee.org/personnel-evaluation-standards.

83. Anthony T. Milanoski, Herbert G. Heneman III, & Steven M. Kimball (August 2009). "Review of Teaching Performance Assessments for Use in Human Capital Management," Strategic Management in Human Capital, Consortium for Policy Research in Education (Madison, WI, August 2009): 6, http://www.smhe-cpre.org/download/69/.

1. Attention to Student Standards
2. Use of Formative Assessment to Guide Instruction
3. Differentiation of Instruction
4. Engaging Students
5. Use of Instructional Strategies that Develop Higher Order Thinking Skills
6. Content Knowledge and Pedagogical Content Knowledge
7. Development of Personalized Relationships with Students
8. High Expectations for Students.

84. See No Child Left Behind, 20 U.S.C. 70 §6301 (2002); Todd A. DeMitchell & Joseph J. Onosko, *"Vergara v. State of California*: The End of Teacher Tenure or a Flawed Ruling?" *University of Southern California Interdisciplinary Law Journal* 25 (2016): 589–624.

85. Todd A. DeMitchell, Terri A. DeMitchell, & Douglas Gagnon, "Teacher Effectiveness and Value-Added Modeling: Building a Pathway to Educational Malpractice," *Brigham Young University Education and Law Journal* 2012 (2012): 257–301, 260.

86. Mark A. Paige, "A Legal Argument against the Use of VAMs in Teacher Evaluation," *Teachers College Record* (December 2014), http://www.tcrecord.org ID Number: 17796.

87. Dale Ballou, William Sanders, & Paul Wright, "Controlling for Student Background in Value-Added Assessment of Teachers," *Journal of Educational and Behavioral Statistics*, 29 (2004): 37–65, 38.

88. See Bruce D. Baker, Joseph O. Oluwole, & Preston C. Green, "Legal Consequences of Mandating High Stakes Decisions Based on Low Quality Information: Teacher Evaluation in the Race-to-the-Top Era," *Education Policy Analysis Archives 21* (January 28, 2013): 1–71, 5. They wrote, "This article seeks to bring some urgency to the need to re-examine the current legislative models that put teachers at great risk of unfair evaluation, removal of tenure, and ultimately wrongful dismissal."

89. American Statistical Association, "ASA Statement on Using Value-Added Models for Educational Assessment" (Alexandria, VA, 2014), https://www.amstat.org/asa/files/pdfs/POL-ASAVAM-Statement.pdf.

90. Eric A. Hanushek & Steven G. Rivkin, *Using Value-Added Measures of Teacher Quality* (Washington, DC: National Center for Analysis of Longitudinal Data in Education Research, Calder Institute): 4.

91. Raj Chetty, John N. Friedman, & Jonah E. Rockoff, "Measuring the Impacts of Teachers II: Teacher Value-Added and Student Outcomes in Adulthood," *American Economic Review* 104(9) (2014): 2633–2679.

92. Audrey Amrein-Beardsley, *Rethinking Value-Added Models in Education: Critical Perspectives on Tests and Assessment-Based Accountability* (New York, NY: Routledge, 2014).

93. Ibid.

94. Carla M. Evans, Ph.D., senior associate, Center for Assessment, Dover, New Hampshire, personal interview March 25, 2022.

95. Mark Paige, "Moving Forward While Looking Back: How Can VAM Lawsuits Guide Teacher Evaluation Policy in the Age of ESSA?" *Education Policy Analysis Archives* 28 (April 13, 2020): 1–14, 12.

96. DeMitchell et al., *supra* note 85, 301.

97. Paige, *supra,* note 95, 10.

98. See, e.g., Erin Bohanan's PowerPoint presentation to educators in the Unified School District #475, Grandview Elementary School on educational malpractice. The in-service presentation focuses on how the school district is taking steps to avoid educational malpractice. Erin Bohanan, "Why We Do What We Do At Grandview: From a Legal Perspective" (June 19, 2011), Educational Malpractice, http://www.youtube.com/watch?v=qm2KLZDbOtc.

99. See Melanie Natasha Henry, "No Child Left Behind? Educational Malpractice Litigation for the 21st Century," *California Law Review* 92 (2004): 1117–1171 (asserting that No Child Left Behind can form the basis for educational malpractice).

100. See DeMitchell et al., *supra* note 8.

101. DeMitchell et al., *supra* note 85, 301.

102. Ibid.

103. Hutt & Tang, *supra* note 1, 430. The authors expand on this assertion, writing, "The crux of our theory is the dramatic changes in education policy, learning standards, and data quality witnessed over the last four decades" (p. 491).

104. Ibid., 457.

105. Ibid., 491.

106. Deborah D. Dye, "Education Malpractice: A Cause of Action that Failed the Test," *West Virginia Law Review* 90 (1988): 499–512, 508.

107. See American Statistical Association, *supra* note 89, writing, "VAMS typically measure correlation, not causation: Effects—positive or negative—attributed to a teacher may actually be caused by other factors that are not captured in this model."

108. Johnny Parker, "Educational Malpractice: A Tort Is Born," *Cleveland State Law Review* 39 (1991): 301–320, 314, writing further, "Basic common law principles support recognition of the tort of educational malpractice." 310.

109. For a discussion of some cautionary flags regarding the use VAM for highstake personnel decisions that may impact VAM's use in educational malpractice cases, see, Todd A. DeMitchell, & Douglas Gagnon, "Student Outcomes, Teacher Effectiveness: Raising Cautionary Flags," Policy Brief #11–01, Department of Education, University of New Hampshire, Durham, NH (2011), https://www.researchgate.net/publication/270451671_Student_Outcomes_Teacher_Effectiveness_Raising_a_Cautionary_Flag. The cautionary flags include:

- Does VAM appropriately control student variables?
- Would the use of different VAM models using the same data yield the same results?

- If a teacher is truly effective, shouldn't his or her effectiveness be stable?
- Is there enough data to assess beginning teachers?
- Are VAM scores precise enough to make high-stakes decisions?
- Can VAM be applied fairly to teachers who do not teach subjects that are tested?
- Business uses data to gauge effectiveness: Why can't education?
- Some of the consequences of the use of VAM.

Chapter 7

Raising a Cautionary Flag in Response to Viable Educational Malpractice Lawsuits

> From a public policy perspective, the drive for accountability may well turn a reluctance to recognize a cause of action for educational malpractice on its head. Public policy once shielded school districts from such lawsuits. It is conceivable that legislators and the public will demand greater forms of accountability and may well turn to some limited form of educational malpractice to meet a more compelling social need than financial protection.[1]

A wall protects those within from external forces. Is the malpractice wall sturdy or have cracks appeared that could lead to a judicial recognition of educational malpractice as a viable tort against educators and school districts? If the wall of protection crumbles and educational malpractice becomes a viable tort, will school districts be named as the sole defendants or will individual teachers be sued as well?

Without question, if the tort of educational malpractice becomes a viable tort, school districts as institutions will be vulnerable to lawsuits, not just individual teachers. This is because of the context of education—a professional social/institutional activity rather than just an individual activity—and the cumulative nature of learning. Consequently, the response to educational malpractice should be an institutional response and not just a personal response.

Hutt and Tang assert that a breach of the malpractice wall may have salutary effects. First, school districts would be incentivized to remove or remediate "bad teachers" to protect themselves from litigation. Second, it would provide an incentive for teachers to improve. They write:

> In other words, if our theory is correct, its most important consequence might be to change teacher and school district behavior so that successful educational

175

malpractice suits are actually few and far between. That comports with a fundamental purpose of tort law: to incentivize individuals to act with reasonable care
by deterring wrongful conduct in the first place through the threat of liability.[2]

Recent legislative initiatives that authorize a private cause of action against
school districts that violate statutory prohibitions against teaching particular
topics (usually sex education) are a crack in the judicial barrier against educational malpractice. Likewise, the introduction of VAM as a tool for holding individual teachers accountable for poor education outcomes is another
crack in that wall. Both developments run counter to the judicial reluctance to
recognize educational malpractice as a viable tort on public policy grounds.
In addition, ongoing research about best instructional practices may pave the
way for establishing a broad consensus in the educational community about
what constitutes best instructional practice.

All of these developments make it more and more likely that a plaintiff student who was poorly educated will be able to establish causation and identify
the educator or educational institution responsible for negligent instruction.
Will educational malpractice no longer be a "forlorn hope"[3] for plaintiff students seeking damages for instructional negligence?

This chapter discusses potential responses to a viable tort for malpractice.
It also explores various defenses to a malpractice suit, including potential
school district responses to malpractice claims suggested by a judgmental
sample of school law experts, and the unintended consequences of high-
stakes evaluations. The chapter ends with our cautionary flag about the wisdom of recognizing the tort of educational malpractice.

RESPONSES TO EDUCATIONAL
MALPRACTICE LAWSUITS

TEXTBOX 7.1

Social, economic, emotional, and cultural factors all play an essential
and immeasurable role in learning. In addition to innate intellectual
ability, a child's failure to learn may be affected by home environment,
peer pressure, attitude, motivation, personality, student-teacher interaction, class size, and faculty experience. It will be readily perceived that
many of these factors are beyond the control of schools and teachers.
Some may be uncontrollable by anyone.

Richard Funston, "Educational Malpractice: A Cause in Search of a Theory,"
San Diego Law Review 18 (1981): 743–812, 786.

Since educational malpractice has not been recognized as a cause of action, the issue of defenses has not been adequately addressed in the case law. Chapter 3 discusses the typical defenses to a tort of negligence. However, a discussion of contributing factors impacting causation, such as a student's motivation and home life, which were discussed in chapter 3, could be raised to defeat a *prima facie* case of educational malpractice, as well as raise the defense that external factors beyond the control of the educator are contributing factors to the student's educational injury.

In a policy brief titled "Poverty and Potential: Out-of-School Factors and School Success," Arizona State University researcher David C. Berliner wrote that out-of-school factors play a powerful role in generating achievement gaps. Out-of-school factors common among the poor "significantly affect the health and learning opportunities of children and accordingly limit what schools can accomplish *on their own*."[4] The common six out-of-school factors include:

(1) low birth weight and non-genetic prenatal influences on children;
(2) inadequate medical, dental, and vision care, often a result of inadequate or no medical insurance;
(3) food insecurity;
(4) environmental pollutants;
(5) family relations and family stress; and
(6) neighborhood characteristics.[5]

While few teachers would challenge the notion that their job is to improve student-achievement outcomes, research shows that school-level effects, including teacher effects, only contribute about 10 to 20 percent of all the variances in student test scores.[6] Consequently, a defendant school district may assert that attaching high-stakes consequences such as monetary damages for a student's failure to achieve is unreasonable and unfair since 80 to 90 percent of the factors that influence student outcomes are beyond the control of teachers or the school district.[7]

The classic defense of contributory negligence on the part of the plaintiff would also be available in an educational malpractice suit, just as it is in medical malpractice. It is clear that a physician would not be held liable for damages if a diabetic patient would not take his or her insulin even though it was prescribed and the ramifications of not taking the medication were explained to the patient.

Furthermore, in an action against a physician for the improper diagnosis of appendicitis, the court held the plaintiff contributorily negligent for failing to disclose pertinent information to the physician and for failing to seek further medical attention when her condition worsened.[8] In another case, a patient was determined to be contributorily negligent when her physician told her to return in six months after a lump was found in her breast and she waited fifteen months, resulting in a loss of her survival expectancy.[9]

This defense could also be raised when the student failed to follow the instructions of the teacher, such as not turning in assignments or turning in partially completed assignments, or when a student failed to pay attention in class. An early commentator on educational malpractice wrote:

> The multiplicity of factors affecting the learning process, coupled with the lack of any clear understanding of the impact on learning of any one of those factors, makes it virtually impossible to prove that the educator's negligence was a cause in fact of a student's illiteracy.[10]

Therefore, a student should be required to take reasonable responsibility for his or her own learning.

EMVS: Defenses and Protection[11]

We return to the EMVS, which we discussed in chapter 6. The survey is part of a mixed methods exploratory study by DeMitchell, King, and DeMitchell of case law and the perceptions of educational stakeholders (school law attorneys and school law professors) with expertise in educational malpractice. It uses a judgmental sampling technique to identify individuals who have an interest in the impact of the law on schools.

A short-answer section was included in the survey instrument. Two prompts explore strategies and responses to the viability of a tort of educational malpractice.

This research method is a hybrid. Its purpose was derived from the survey instrument, but the data were not amenable to typical quantitative statistical treatments. Furthermore, the short answers, even though the data appear to be like qualitative data, do not fit into the typical qualitative analyses associated with non-numerical data (case study, grounded theory, phenomenology, Seidman interviewing technique, and so on).

Thomas Schram, a qualitative methods scholar, states that responses to these types of questions "can be helpful in terms of enhancing, illustrating, deepening, and/or extending the other survey responses."[12] Therefore, we used an analysis from previous research that allows us to uncover themes from the data using coding techniques often associated with grounded theory.

First, we had to contend with the limitations of the data. For example, we were unable to "probe" or ask, "What is happening here?"[13] Analysis of open-answer responses is problematic for conducting member checks to support validity or to do theoretical sampling. Furthermore, the one-shot aspect of the short-answer data precluded the "unfolding" of data from in-depth interviewing or multiple sequential interviews.[14]

Two of the researchers independently coded the qualitative responses from the two open-item questions on the survey thematically. The results were examined for inter-rater reliability. Discrepancies were discussed and a mutual resolution was arrived at. Both prompts are explored next. The first prompt focuses on defenses that the respondents would use in a hypothetical educational malpractice case that met the *prima facie* burden of establishing that a duty was owed, that the duty was breached, that the breach was the proximate cause of the injury, and that there was a sufficient injury. The prompt reads as follows.

Prompt # 1: If a plaintiff student prevailed in establishing a *prima facie* case for educational malpractice, what arguments would you explore for the defendant's defense?

Thirty-five (81 percent) attorneys/professors responded to this prompt. Five themes emerged from the iterative analysis of the comments. Multiple respondents' comments were placed within more than one theme. Thus, the total is larger than thirty-five responses.

One overarching theme and several supporting themes emerged that revealed why survey respondents largely believed that an educational malpractice case is likely to fail. These five areas may be asserted in responses to the *prima facie* case as well as a defense to a *prima facie* case, should an educational malpractice claim survive an expected summary judgment motion. We start with the overarching theme.

No Prima Facie *Case: Overarching Theme*

The first theme identified by thirteen respondents asserted that "No *Prima Facie*" case can be established with the logic of "if they can't prove the case, I don't have to defend it." Essentially, these respondents stated that the hypothetical educational malpractice scenario did not form the basis for an educational malpractice claim, because currently a *prima facie* case cannot be demonstrated.

Ten attorney respondents cited "causation" as a missing element to a *prima facie* educational malpractice claim. For example, a professor/teacher wrote, "It seems to me the toughest part of a claim would be to demonstrate that the Defendant's actions caused the injury." One attorney respondent concluded, "I don't believe there is any way to prove proximate cause." And a professor/teacher offered the following rationale, "Cannot establish that a single instructor or at a particular grade level, was wholly accountable for inadequate academic progress." This response is in harmony with the answers to quantitative questions about who is liable for malpractice and underscores the difficulty of establishing a cause of action for educational malpractice.

Standards of Assessment: Validity and Reliability? Theme

If the assessment establishes that a duty was breached, can the lawsuit continue? This theme had several responses aimed at student and teacher assessment and standards. They question the vagueness, reliability, and validity of assessments that attempt to define the instructional duty owed, breach of that duty, and causation. For example, a professor/teacher wrote, "Standardized tests and the related value-added measures lack reliability and validity when applied to students and are of even less value as applied to teachers."

Similarly, a professor and former teacher questioned the reliability of value-added assessments to ascertain teacher quality. Another professor/teacher pointed out that the evidence on VAM was not "strong enough to support causation."[15] These statements tend to be supported by our chapter 6 analyses that showed that the majority of respondents hold that VAM has no impact or only a slight impact on the viability of educational malpractice.

This theme also identifies the lack of articulated standards for teacher instructional practice. For example, a professor/teacher asserts that there is an "insufficient Law/regulations governing teacher performance [and existing laws and regulations are] too vague to define teacher/school culpability." Another professor who had served as a teacher stated, "Lack of certainty of, and appropriate evidence about the standards of similarly situated professionals. Lack of uniformity of acceptable inputs, and lack of direct clear evidence of what inputs work on what types of students." These comments implicitly ask this question: If you don't know what you are measuring, how can you assess the validity of the assessment instrument?

Variables Impacting Student Achievement Theme

This theme has two elements: distributed responsibilities variables and non-educator-controlled variables. The distributed responsibilities element focuses on the distribution of responsibilities for student learning among the major participants: students, teachers, and parents. Thirteen respondents identified students with several identifying contributory/comparative negligence and two cited the role of parents in the education of their children. The *Restatement (Second) of Torts* defines contributory negligence as:

> conduct on the part of the plaintiff which falls below the standard to which he should conform for his own protection, and which is legally contributing cause cooperating with the negligence of the defendant in bringing about the plaintiff's harm.[16]

In other words, the plaintiff has violated the duty to act prudently in furtherance of his or her own education. If the defendant's defense of contributory negligence prevails, damages will not be awarded or will be reduced. While the person who owes a duty must act as a reasonable and prudent person would act, so must the plaintiff. A professor and former teacher captured this concept, writing, "Education is a two-way street, [the] student must put forth effort." Another respondent (Professor/Teacher) observed that parent-teacher communications is an "interactive process," and if parents did not engage in the process, "then the liability should not fall solely to the teacher."

Several respondents explicitly used the legal terms of contributory or comparative negligence. Contributory negligence occurs when the plaintiff's actions or omissions are negligent and contribute to his or her own injury—the plaintiff has a duty to act as a reasonable person. One professor cited a lack of effort and a professor and former teacher stated that "whether the student had been keeping up with the work and participating in class" should be explored as part of the defense.

A defense of contributory negligence in educational malpractice could be raised, as the respondent above notes, for failure to pay attention in class and complete assignments. Consequently, a student would arguably be required to take reasonable responsibility for his or her own learning. This is a critical point. Learning is active and not passive. Students must be engaged in their own learning. Reasonable students cooperate and take part in their education. Failure to act as a reasonable and prudent student will likely jeopardize a malpractice case.

The second element is non-educator-controlled variables. It is similar to the variable of distributed education responsibilities, in that it also deals with factors/actions that typically are not part of the purview or under the control of the teacher but can still impact student learning. Twenty-one responses cover external factors such as "home life," socioeconomic status," and "adequate funding." The following are several of the responses that reflect this defense theme.

- A responding attorney who was also a former teacher captured the impact of these factors, writing, "There are multiple factors that affect student performance that the teacher has no control over and for which the teacher should not be held liable."
- A former teacher and now a professor echoed this statement stating, "Too many external factors (e.g., at-risk factors, lack of level playing field for students in public schools, lack of student effort, poor state and local resourcing, poor parental support) that could account for the inadequate academic progress."

Another respondent summed up this theme by writing, "There are many factors both in and out of school that impact student learning, so how can it be proved that the teacher/district caused the harm rather than one or more of the other factors?" One respondent focused on the variables not controlled by the teacher but instead are controlled by the school/school district. The following variables were identified by the attorney: "discipline in the school," "the tools given to the school district and teachers," "the funding given [to] the school district and teachers," and the "remediation efforts to improve teacher performance."

These two sets of variables may provide an argument that because the number of variables that impact student learning are not subject to the teachers' control, it is difficult if not impossible to establish a clear statement of what errors were committed by an educator or school district. Without establishing what variables contributed to a negative educational outcome, can comparative negligence be established; and, if it can't be established, can any damages be leveled fairly? One professor who is also a former teacher wrote, "Cannot establish that a single instructor or at a particular grade level, was wholly accountable for inadequate academic progress."

The Public Policy Defense Theme

This theme drew ten responses from nine respondents. Four survey respondents listed governmental immunity as a response to a *prima facie* case of educational malpractice. A professor stated, "Depending on the jurisdiction, the first argument should be sovereign immunity. While I don't like the doctrine personally, it would shut down the lawsuit immediately in many states, at least in public schools."

Six responses specifically identified policy as a viable response to educational malpractice suits. An attorney and former teacher offered the following analysis about the policy impact of educational malpractice:

- "There is a public policy argument against educational malpractice in that the money that goes to an individual student who claims harms directly takes away from the education of other students."
- "The availability of such a cause of action would result in increased litigation because it would foster litigation by parents with minor claims[,] thereby increasing legal costs for the district and further reducing the money available to educate students. As a matter of policy, if it was found to be a viable claim, it would throw the public education system into chaos."

Essentially, these respondents stated that if a lawsuit for educational malpractice survives the preliminary pleading stage of litigation, it would still fail if the defendants moved for summary judgment. In other words, even if the obstacles of duty, causation, and injury are overcome at trial, malpractice claims would still flounder, because the elements of tort law do not by themselves overcome the policy objections. There must be public support for educational malpractice—a consensus that the cost of recognizing this tort is justified by larger benefits for society as a whole.

TEXTBOX 7.2

The elements of duty, causation, and damages are going to be central to any defense of an educational malpractice claim. Presumably, the issue of duty would need to be addressed to get to the point of a *prima facie* case. The element of causation will be difficult for plaintiffs to establish because of the difficulty of tying specific classroom practices (or the absence of certain practices) was the proximate cause of a student's poor performance. The element of damages will pose similar problems as plaintiffs attempt to show that specific practices (or the absence thereof) resulted in economic harm to a student.

Attorney and former teacher, EMVS.

Many of the earlier responses echo Richard Funston's comments about the impact of social, economic, emotional, and cultural factors (Textbox 7.1). They continue to resonate forty years later.

The next open response prompt focuses on the preventative measures school districts can take to reduce their exposure to educational malpractice lawsuits. School law professor Nathan L. Essex's conclusion regarding educational malpractice set forth thirty-five years ago is still salient today. He wrote, "The time is ripe for teachers to respond to these challenges. Otherwise, it may be a matter of whether teachers' pay now or pay more later. The choice is ours."[17]

Prompt #2: If educational malpractice is found to be a viable tort, what kinds of advice would you give to school districts to protect themselves from a lawsuit?

Thirty-three professors who also practiced law responded to this open response question on proactive actions that can/should be taken in response to potential for educational malpractice lawsuits. Two were removed from the analysis because they did not offer suggestions.

Document everything is the consistent refrain. One respondent wrote, "Document, document, document" (professor and former teacher). The word "document" is found twenty-three times in the responses. The respondents suggested that the following data be collected: student academic and attendance data; parental involvement data; and teachers' instructional data, including student progress reviews and interventions. An attorney and former teacher captured this overarching theme, writing: "Require teachers to document everything they do in a classroom with every student." Clearly, proper documentation is an overarching theme among almost all participants and nearly all activities.

Using the Human Resource Functions Theme

Two specific themes emerged from the data—Using Human Resource Functions and Establishing Expectations. Fifteen respondents recommended one or more activities associated with typical human relations functions. Four human resource functions emerged from the data as significant actions to take as a prudent response to potential malpractice suits—hiring, professional development, evaluation/supervision, and remediation/dismissal. An attorney wrote in stark terms, "Terminate the employment of every questionable teacher; do not risk attempting to help those who need additional assistance."

Hiring qualified teachers and principals was also identified as an essential strategy. "Put more effort into hiring competent teachers" (Professor/ Teacher). "Adopt tested screening tools before hiring a teacher (to avoid negligent hiring)," a school law professor and former teacher offered. Several respondents identified the importance of professional development to hone and develop new instructional practices.

The most cited strategy was evaluation followed by remediation, and failing success—dismissal. A remediation plan is central to the continuum of evaluation, remediation, and termination. One professor captured these functions by writing, "Effective teacher evaluation system/ individual improvement plans[,] termination of demonstratively ineffective teachers."

Similarly, a professor and former teacher expanded on the remediation function. The professor wrote:

> A teacher who is performing poorly would be put on an improvement plan, which would include professional development focused on instructional strategies, training to identify best practices for optimal learning in [the] classroom, culturally relevant practices to engage learners, and other practices known (from research) to impact student learning and engagement in the classroom.

Professional development is the last factor in this theme. An attorney and former teacher offered the following advice to education leaders: "Engage in extensive training on best practices."

Establishing Expectations Theme

The next theme focused on establishing expectations and drew six responses. A professor called for the establishment of parental expectations, writing, "establish parental expectations[,] provide parent training on ed support for children[,] monitor parent compliance." And one response appears to suggest developing "a statement of outcomes form."

The other four responses focused on expectations for teachers. Respondents emphasized the need for establishing expectations for teachers that are set by the teaching profession to ensure that each teacher has an appropriate credential. For setting expectations locally, a professor/teacher suggests the following:

> Boards devise set criteria for all instructional staff ranging from [the] ability to control/ supervise classes adequately, professionalism in addressing/ dealing with students, to ensuring content knowledge and require teachers to demonstrate ongoing knowledge within their fields much in the way attorneys complete CLE units.

Just over three-quarters of the attorneys and professors responded to the two prompts. For the first prompt identifying defenses to a tort of educational malpractice, the respondents first focused on documenting teacher practices and student learning. Next, their responses tracked tort concepts of contributory negligence and causation, including elements of confounding variables that might account for the student's educational outcomes and the reliability/ validity of the assessments used to establish causation. And the last theme was consistent with the defenses to educational malpractice claims and public policy concerns. The Supreme Court has advised the courts to use caution when considering questions of educational practice and policy.[18]

The second prompt follows the first prompt on defenses by positing that a viable tort for educational malpractice has been established and suggesting how school districts might defend against such a tort. The major takeaway of their advice to school leaders was to step up documentation of the factors related to the *prima facie* case of educational malpractice and the potential defenses to a malpractice claim.

Survey respondents recommended that school leaders use existing human resource functions to ensure that only qualified and competent educators are placed in their classrooms. Second, they emphasized the need to articulate expectations for behavior and update these expectations based on new research on teaching. The experts provided advice for school leaders to consider in response to the viability of educational malpractice lawsuits, but, possibly more important, their advice is relevant to the current daily operations of our nation's schools.

POTENTIAL UNINTENDED CONSEQUENCES OF A
VIABLE EDUCATIONAL MALPRACTICE TORT

TEXTBOX 7.3

The goal of defensive medicine is to ensure that, if the patient later sues, the physician has gone above and beyond what is required. Defensive medicine is directly traced to medical malpractice law—without the threat of litigation, there would be no reason to practice defensively.

Lee Black, "Effects of Malpractice Law on the Practice of Medicine," *AMA Journal of Ethics* (June, 2007), https://journalofethics.ama-assn.org/article/effects-malpractice-law-practice-medicine/2007–06.

The research also captured the responses to prompts about the survey-takers' perceptions of educational malpractice lawsuits making their way through the courts. We now discuss some of the unintended consequences that could result from judicial recognition of educational malpractice. It is not unreasonable to explore potential unintended consequences of allowing malpractice suits in education. In fact, as early as 1977, research signaled potential consequences of malpractice.[19]

As the old saying goes, there is no such thing as a free lunch. It would not be realistic to think that such a major high-stakes change, involving the possibility of personal damage awards for negligent instruction, would not alter practices to conform to the new expectation and that these changes might bring unintended consequences.

For example, Lee Black, in an article in the *AMA Journal of Ethics*, wrote that the mere possibility of medical malpractice liability has altered the practice of medicine. "Regardless, the mere perception of injustice and the danger of liability have fueled physician paranoia and distracted physicians from the goal of providing the best and safest care to patients."[20] Is it not reasonable, then, to expect that educators facing potential personal liability from an educational malpractice suit brought by their students might also be "distracted" from their purpose?

Researcher Newton and colleagues asked whether school systems that use VAM without taking student characteristics into consideration might "create disincentives for teachers to want to work with those students with the greatest needs?" Similarly, would teachers become reluctant to work with difficult students if they feared being sued for educational malpractice?

Improvements in instructional practices so that all children learn and demonstrate the expected level of academic competence: this is the intended benefit of educational malpractice as a public policy. However, as seen in medicine, personal high-stakes situations often result in other changes in practice. Education has also experienced unintended consequences in response to high-stakes testing. Brett D. Jones studied the unintended consequences of high-stakes testing that was implemented with the intention of holding educators accountable for their professional practice. He found that while high-stake testing has had some positive effects, some effects have been negative.[21]

The following are some potential unintended consequences of high-stakes accountability measures.

- An example of the distortion of the educational process in response to high stakes is found in the Governor's investigative report of cheating in Atlanta schools in response to No Child Left Behind testing requirements. Some Atlanta teachers and principals altered student test scores to boost their scores and to give the illusion of transforming struggling schools. The report stated, "Thousands of schoolchildren were harmed by widespread cheating in the Atlanta Public School System. . . . Many of the accolades, and much of the praise, received by [Atlanta Public Schools] over the last decade were ill-gotten."[22]
- Education researchers from the University of California, Berkeley, and Stanford University raised the question as to whether VAM "could create disincentives for teachers to work with those students with the greatest needs."[23]
- Professor Rothstein suggests that the high-stakes testing of VAM could distort the educational process through defensive teaching such as teaching to the test and teachers "lobbying their principals to be assigned the 'right' students who will yield predicably high value added scores."[24]
- Newton et al. found that "English teachers were more highly ranked when they had a greater proportion of girls in their classes, and math teachers were more highly ranked when they had more students in their classes who were on a 'fast track' in mathematics." Additionally, positive correlations were found for proportions of students who were Asian or whose parents were more highly educated. [25]
- Newton also found that, when the models were controlled for student demographics, teacher rankings were "significantly and negatively correlated with the proportions who were English learners, free lunch recipients, or Hispanic."[26]
- And finally, some scholars predict that educational malpractice liability will lead to a narrowing of the curriculum, as teachers search for ways can assure positive evaluations.

The caution of unintended consequences from implementing VAM for accountability purposes include increased exposure to educational malpractice lawsuits fits with the experiences of focused high-stakes assessments in various settings. Brian Strecher and colleagues at RAND found that schools had trouble navigating the tension between using evaluations, which would likely be used in malpractice suits, to help teachers improve their instruction skills while also being used to make high-stakes decisions about compensation and dismissal.[27] Evaluations that are designed to improve teacher performance may also be used to establish instructional malpractice.

These potential unintended consequences speak about human responses to high-stakes situations in which they are thrust. The findings from the study of VAM responses may provide insight into what may occur with a finding that teachers can be sued for malpractice. A change to personal liability for professional practice as measured by student learning is fraught with anxiety-producing effects. While these potential effects may not serve as a bar to viable educational malpractice suits, they certainly can provide opportunities for planning to avoid as many consequences which may derail the policy of recognizing a cause of action for educational malpractice.

Educational malpractice will have momentous consequences for education and the definition of what it means to be a professional educator. Perceptions of what constitutes a problem or a threat often presage a shift in public policy. Concern about discrimination and isolation of students with special needs led to special education legislation. A crash involving a school bus led to legislation that reduces the shield of immunity for school districts. The current push to allow teachers and school districts to be sued for teaching prohibited subjects or retaining banned books in school libraries may be another public policy initiative with unintended consequences.

EDUCATIONAL MALPRACTICE LAWSUITS: RAISING A CAUTIONARY FLAG

TEXTBOX 7.4

Who we place and retain in our classrooms is a challenge demanding an imperative of action for school leaders. It must be undertaken with the application of skills and knowledge, and pursued with a high level of professional responsibility — the consistent demonstration of skill and will.

Todd A. DeMitchell & Mark A. Paige, *Threading the Evaluation Needle: The Documentation of Teacher Unprofessional Conduct* (Lanham, MD: Rowman & Littlefield, 2020): 65.

Has the time come for educational malpractice suits in which students and parents can sue individual teachers and/or the educational institutions for monetary damages on the basis of negligent instruction? For almost five decades, courts have rejected the tort of educational malpractice. Various courts identified problems with establishing a *prima facie* case of negligence. However, the overriding concern was public policy. We likewise raise a cautionary flag about the tort of educational malpractice based on public policy concerns.

Before we lay out our concerns about educational malpractice as an emerging new public policy, we will restate our position about the duty owed by teachers and schools to students and the communities they serve. The U.S. Supreme Court in *Plyler v. Doe* captured the importance of education to the nation when it wrote, "Education provides the basic tools by which individuals might lead economically productive lives to the benefit of us all. In sum, education has a fundamental role in maintaining the fabric of our society."[28] It follows, then, that teachers' actions are central to education, fulfilling this fundamental role.

Teachers occupy an important place in our society in terms of their relationship with parents and the community. Parents trust their children to teachers for about six hours a day, five days a week for approximately 180 days a year. No other professional activity outside of teaching has such extensive control and influence over minors. And they exercise this control and influence over students with the full weight of a government bureaucracy behind them. Consequently, parents and the community have a legitimate concern about the qualifications and actions of their teachers.

Accountability for professional service is a critical component in the delivery of quality education to students. School officials are obligated to place and keep qualified teachers in the schools—and *only* qualified teachers. Quality evaluations seek to improve instructional skills and assist school officials in making critical employment decisions, including tenure, nonrenewal, and termination. Consequently, teachers have both the right and the need to have accurate and fair feedback.

Is Education the Right Fit for the Professional Malpractice Template?

Previously we discussed the concerns voiced by a California appellate court in *Peter W.* and by other courts as well regarding the inability of a plaintiff student to establish a *prima facie* case for malpractice. Moreover, as we previously discussed, courts have repeatedly expressed strong public policy concerns that weigh against recognizing this tort.

We offer two reservations about the public policy implications of recognizing a tort for instructional malpractice. First, because instruction is usually delivered in group settings that attempt to respond to the individual needs of various students, the field of education differs fundamentally from the professions of law or medicine, where professionals owe a duty to individual clients/ patients. Second, in contrast to other professions where a negligent event can be identified with specificity, it is virtually impossible to determine when negligent instruction occurred and when a particular plaintiff student was injured.

Chapter 2 explored professionalism within the context of malpractice. Malpractice is a recognized tort of negligence in various professions such as medicine, law, and architecture, to name a few. But it has not been recognized in education. Holding professionals accountable for the public service they provide is good public policy. Malpractice litigation in the professions of medicine and law has largely molded the application of malpractice law in other professions. Is the current and accepted template for professional malpractice a good fit for the field of education?

The Crowded Classroom Is Not the Office, Examination Room, or the Courtroom

Most professionals usually serve one client at a time. This allows them to focus their efforts on a more or less clearly defined set of variables associated with one patient or client. A surgeon normally operates on one person at a time without having to simultaneously juggle different patients' needs. Likewise, attorneys do not represent multiple clients who have conflicting interests.

In a one-to-one relationship, a professional's full concentration is focused on one person—the patient on the operating table, for example, or the defendant in a criminal case. Likewise, while dentists may have multiple patients in different dental chairs in various stages of procedures, when dentists enter an examination room, there is only one patient who occupies their attention.

Attorneys may have more than one client in a single matter but their conduct toward each client is prescribed by standards of practice. For example, the New Jersey Rules of Professional Conduct for attorneys pertain to the representation of multiple clients in a single matter. Rule RPC 1.7(a)(2) Conflict of Interest: General Rule states that a conflict of interest exists if "(2) there is a significant risk that the representation of one or more clients will be materially limited by the lawyer's responsibilities to another client, a former client, or a third person or by a personal interest of the lawyer."[29]

Representation of more than one client in a single matter must comport with RPC 1.7(b)(2), which states that "the lawyer reasonably believes that the lawyer will be able to provide competent and diligent representation to each affected client."[30] The American Bar Association has also formulated principles for working with multiple clients such as class action suits and wills-and-estate planning. Aside from confidentiality challenges with multiple clients, "the lawyer is required to be impartial between commonly represented clients, [and] representation of multiple clients is improper when it is unlikely that impartiality can be maintained."[31]

While most professions usually serve one client at a time, education serves a classroom of students at the same time. It is not individual service of one student at a time. With the exception of limited one-on-one encounters, instruction is usually delivered to a whole class or small groups, with individual instruction occurring only under specific circumstances. While other professionals can focus on the needs of the one being served, teachers must balance instruction while monitoring the classroom environment for off-task behavior and disruptive conduct.

The complexity of instruction is impacted by large numbers of students in the same place and the difficulties of addressing the differing needs of individual students who are being taught simultaneously. In his seminal study, Jackson wrote, "Teaching is an opportunistic process. That is to say, neither the teacher nor his students can predict with any certainty exactly what will happen next."[32] He referred to classrooms as pupil crowds with negative aspects of "delay, denial, interruption, and distraction."

The classroom is unlike any office, courtroom, or surgical suite occupied by other professionals. It is a place for work conducted in a social environment that is dedicated to instruction and learning. The classroom socializes as well as instructs. Relationships develop that are as important as they are varied. This classroom environment is the responsibility of the classroom teacher as part of his or her instructional duties. The classroom has no real analogy to other professional environments. Jackson studied life in classrooms and determined that "there is a social intimacy in schools that is unmatched elsewhere in our society."[33]

When Was the Duty Breached?

When a patient sues a surgeon for operating on the wrong leg, there is an event when a breach occurs. If an attorney fails to file court documents on time, then there is an identifiable time-defined lapse that determines when the breach occurred. A time frame of a breach can be inferred when a banana falls to the floor in the produce section and is not picked up and a customer slips on it. Even *res ipsa loquitur*[34] has means for inferring negligence that is bounded by time. The injurious and negligent event occurred at a time when the defendant had breached a defined duty to another individual that caused an injury.

However, in education, the issue of the time of the breach is almost always fluid and undefined. For example, in *Peter W.*, the plaintiff did not state when the alleged breach took place, let alone identify the cause of the breach. The stated injury was the inability to read at the end of his twelve years of schooling.

But when did the breach occur? Was it a series of connected breaches or periodic unconnected breaches? Was there a precipitating breach that was the point of origin? Was the duty breached in all subjects that involve reading or just in the elementary grades where students are taught to read and then transition to reading to learn?

The education of a student is cumulative with lessons and experiences building on each other. Prior learning is one of the important factors that influences current learning. *Res ipsa loquitur* likely would not well serve the plaintiff student. A student's education is not under the exclusive control of the defendant teacher or school district. The student can also act negligently by not studying or failing to complete assignments, thus contributing to the learning deficit.

Flying a Cautionary Flag

We raise a cautionary flag about tearing down the judicial wall that bars educational malpractice suits. With a nod to John Kingdon's seminal work on what gets on the public's agenda, the time has NOT come for recognizing a cause of action for educational malpractice. Issues with the *prima facie* case remain. A duty based on an articulated and accepted standard of practice for instruction in the various subjects and grade levels has not been established. While strides have been made in educational research, there is not enough evidence that there is a degree of specificity as to how a subject should be taught that guides practice in the classroom.

Teachers talk of "tricks of the trade" and the "wisdom of practice," and these skills and dispositions are still an important part of the conversation that informs the application of instructional practices. However, the wisdom of practice needs to be guided by the research on what instructional practices work best. One of the cracks in the malpractice wall is the growing body of educational research that informs instruction. But the challenge is whether that research is making its way into the classrooms in a consistent cohesive manner so as to provide a recognized standard of classroom instructional practice.[35]

Without a commonly accepted standard of practice whereby a breach can be established and without a focus on the means of instruction instead of just educational outcomes the breach of a duty to educate cannot be reasonably and fairly established. The documented concerns about the use of the VAM-type assessment tool underscore this point, in that the VAM cannot identify specific instructional deficiencies. Related to this challenge is the difficulty of proving that the breach of duty caused the injury. The factors that impact a student's learning are myriad, with many residing outside the control of the teacher or school.

These cautions have surfaced in various court decisions and will persist until research further unravels the complexity of teaching and learning in the nation's crowded and often overcrowded classrooms. These concerns are also reflected in the open-ended responses of school law professors and attorneys. Unless and until these challenges are addressed a caution about changing public policy to enable lawsuits for educational malpractice is warranted.

This caution is not meant to imply that educators, school board members, and public officials should acquiesce to ineffective teaching. Tools exist to address substandard teaching practices and classroom environments that do not meet the profession's expectations for student learning. These tools must be applied in a fair, consistent, and skillful manner, using the skill and will of school administrators. Teachers, administrators, and school board members must endeavor to keep their houses in order. Current public policy supports and demands that they do so.

The educational malpractice wall has cracks, but these cracks are not yet ready to bring the wall down. The current spate of legislative initiatives that allow school districts and teachers to be sued for instructional and instruction-related decisions should not provide a battering ram for tearing down the wall.[36] Assessments that purport to identify causation must be valid and reliable. And we must continue efforts to define professional practice with more precision and construct clear and valid measures for identifying teachers who fail in their instructional responsibilities. Flying a flag urging caution regarding a change in the public policy that would recognize a tort of educational malpractice is prudent.

NOTES

1. Terri A. DeMitchell & Todd A. DeMitchell, "A Crack in the Educational Malpractice Wall," *The School Administrator* 9 (October 2007): 34–36, 36.

2. Ethan Hutt & Aaron Tang, "The New Education Malpractice Litigation," *Virginia Law Review* 99 (2013): 419–492, 492.

3. A forlorn hope is an "undertaking that seems very unlikely to succeed." It comes from the *Duth verloren hoop*, meaning "lost troop." The phrase has been used to denote the start of a dangerous attack such as an attack to breach the walls of a fort. *Farlex Dictionary of Idioms* (2022), https://idioms.thefreedictionary.com/forlorn+hope.

4. David C. Berliner, *Poverty and Potential: Out-of-School Factors and School Success* (Boulder, CO and Tempe: Education and the Public Interest

Center & Education Policy Research Unit, 2009), 1, http://epicpolicy.org/publication/poverty-and-potential.

5. Ibid.

6. David C. Berliner, "Exogenous Variables and Value-Added Assessments: A Fatal Flaw," *Teachers College Record* 116 (2014): 1–31; Peter Z. Schochet & Hanley S. Chiang (2012). "What Are Error Rates for Classifying Teacher and School Performance Using Value-Added Models?" *Journal of Educational and Behavioral Statistics* 38(2) (2013): 142–171.

7. For an interesting informative study of non-school factors that impact student learning using Michigan data on child maltreatment investigations, see Brian A. Jacob & Joseph Ryan, "How Life Outside of a School Affects Student Performance in School," *Brookings* (March 22, 2018). The article discusses the impact of childhood trauma such as "homelessness, domestic violence, parental drug abuse, neglect and physical or sexual abuse." Ibid.

8. *Carreker v. Harper*, 396 S.E.2d 587 (1990).

9. *Roers v. Engebretson,* 479 N.W.2d 422 (Minn. 1992).

10. Richard Funston, "Educational Malpractice: A Cause in Search of a Theory," *San Diego Law Review* 18 (1981): 743–812, 786.

11. See Todd A. DeMitchell, Stefanie King, & Terri A. DeMitchell. "Educational Malpractice: Is It a Tort Whose Time Has Come? An Exploratory Mixed Methods Study," *University of Florida Journal of Law & Public Policy* 32 (spring 2022). The authors have given permission for their research to be used in this book.

12. Professor and qualitative methodologist Thomas Schram, email communication concerning the method for analyzing open answer data (November 5, 2005). This email is in the possession of Todd DeMitchell.

13. Barney G. Glaser, *Theoretical Sensitivity: Advances in the Methodology of Grounded Theory* (Mill Valley, CA: Sociology Press, 1978).

14. Anselm L. Strauss, *Qualitative Analysis for Social Scientists* (Cambridge, UK: Cambridge University Press, 2010).

15. See Derek W. Black, "The Constitutional Challenge to Teacher Tenure," *California Law Review* 104 (2016): 75–148, 97 and 98. Black questions the use of VAM in teacher evaluations, writing:

> Those states that do not fully account for student demographics in their models are measuring students' preexisting knowledge, aptitude, and familial advantages not teaching effectiveness. . . . In short, value-added models and student growth percentile models, as currently implemented, are more a measure of student demographics and out-of-school factors than teaching effectiveness.

16. Restatement (Second) of Torts §463.

17. Nathan L. Essex, "The Teacher and Malpractice: Ten Ways to Invite a Lawsuit," *The Clearing House* 60 (January 1987): 212–215, 215.

18. See *Board of Education v. Rowley*, 458 U.S. 176, 206 (1982) ("cognizant that judges lack on-the-ground expertise and experience of school administrators, however, we have cautioned courts in various contexts to resist 'substitut[ing] their own notions of sound educational policy for those of the school authorities'"); *Hazelwood School District v. Kuhlmeier*, 484 U.S. 260, 273 (1988) ("[The Supreme Court's]

oft-expressed view that the education of the Nation's youth is primarily the responsibility of parents, teachers, and state and local school officials, and not of federal judges").

19. See Marshall C. Darnell, *A Study Designed to Investigate a New Dimension for Educational Accountability . . . Malpractice* (1977), an unpublished doctoral dissertation (EdD) at the University of Nevada, Las Vegas. The author commented on the "Predictive Consequences of Educational Malpractice."

> Services could be reduced. Any area that was the least bit questionable would be eliminated. Instruction would be reduced to an exact and definable position. It is possible that experimental and exploratory programs would be regulated completely or eliminated altogether. (p. 129)

Darnell also expressed concern about the impact of educational malpractice on the school curriculum:

> Add to these dismal predictions the possibility that the advent of educational malpractice actions might produce a "teacher-proof" educational system. In this instance, the weight of costly malpractice legal actions will continue to the creation of an educational program that will be mechanical in nature and void of the human factor. (pp. 129–130)

20. Saks and Landsman defined defensive medicine as follows:

> In general terms, defensive medicine can be thought of as the practice of ordering medically unnecessary tests and performing needless procedures for purposes unrelated to the well-being of patients. Rather, it is "employed explicitly for the purposes either of averting a possible lawsuit or [if a lawsuit were filed] of providing appropriate documentation that a wide range of tests and treatments has been used in the patient's care." One needn't be a medical expert to recognize this as a "deviation from sound medical practice.

Michael J. Saks & Stephan Landsman, "The Paradoxes of Defensive Medicine," *Health Matrix* 30 (2020): 25–83, 26 and 27, https://scholarlycommons. law.case.edu/cgi/viewcontent.cgi?article=1646&context=healthmatrix, as quoted in Lee Black, "Effects of Malpractice Law on the Practice of Medicine," *AMA Journal of Ethics* (June 2007), https://journalofethics.ama-assn.org/article/effects-malpractice-law-practice-medicine/2007-06.

21. Brett D. Jones, "The Unintended Outcomes of High-Stakes Testing," *Journal of Applied Psychology* 23 (October 2, 2008): 65–86, https://doi.org/10.1300/J370v23n02_05. See also David Berliner, "Rational Responses to High Stakes Testing: The Case of Curriculum Narrowing and the Harm that Follows," *Cambridge Journal of Education* 41 (October 12, 2011): 287–302, https://doi.org/10.1080/03 05764X.2011.607151. Berliner, concluded that the narrowing of the curriculum in response to high-stake testing was "pernicious."

22. Christine Samuels, "Report Details Culture of 'Cheating' in Atlanta Schools," *Education Week* (July 13, 2011), http://www.edweek.org/ew/articles/2011/07/13/36atlanta.h30.html.

23. Xiaoxia Newton, Linda Darling-Hammond, Edward Haertel, & Ewart Thomas, "Value-Added Modeling of Teacher Effectiveness: An Exploration of Stability across Models and Contexts," *Education Policy Analysis Archives* 18(23) (September 30, 2010): 1–23, 18, https://epaa.asu.edu/ojs/index.php/epaa/article/view/810/858.

24. Jesse Rothstein, "Teacher Quality in Educational Production: Tracking, Decay, and Student Achievement," *The Quarterly Journal of Economics* 125(1) ([May 2008] February 1, 2010): 175–214, 211.

25. Newton et al., *supra* note 23, 17.

26. Ibid.

27. Brain M. Stecher et al., "Intensive Partnerships for Effective Teaching Enhanced How Teachers Are Evaluated but Had Little Effect on Student Outcomes," *RAND, Research Brief* (February 11, 2019): 1–8, 7, https://www.rand.org/pubs/research_briefs/RB10009-1.html.

28. *Plyler v. Doe*, 457 U.S. 202, 221 (1982).

29. New Jersey Courts, Rules of Professional Conduct, RPC 1.0 to RPC 8.5, https://www.njcourts.gov/attorneys/assets/rules/rpc.pdf.

30. Ibid.

31. American Bar Association, Center for Professional Responsibility, Models Rules of Professional Conduct, "Rule 1.7 Conflict of Interest: Current Clients—Comment, #29," https://www.americanbar.org/groups/professional_responsibility/pub lications/model_rules_of_professional_conduct/rule_1_7_conflict_of_interest_current_ clients/comment_on_rule_1_7/.

32. Philip W. Jackson, *Life in Classrooms* (New York: Holt, Rinehart & Winston, 1968): 166.

33. Ibid., 11. According to Jackson, the teacher is charged with managing the flow of the classroom dialogue. In elementary classrooms, he writes, "teachers can engage in as many as one thousand interpersonal exchanges a day." Ibid.

34. *Res ipsa loquitur*, meaning the "the thing speaks for itself," uses inference/circumstantial evidence to create a rebuttable presumption that negligence can be presumed without proof, because there could be no other logical explanation. To assert *res ipsa loquitur* the plaintiff must prove the following: (1) The incident was of a type that does not generally happen without negligence; (2) It was caused by an instrumentality solely in defendant's control; and (3) The plaintiff did not contribute to the case. Cornell Law School, Legal Information Institute, "Res Ipsa Loquitur," https://www.law.cornell.edu/wex/res_ipsa_loquitur.

35. See Shana Hurley, "The Remediless Reading Right," *Yale Law & Policy Review* 40 (2021): 276–335, 278, writing, "Scientists have found that *almost all students* can learn to read, provided students are deliberately, systematically, and explicitly taught to identify letters' corresponding speech sounds; blend those sounds into words; and recognize those words in their knowledge base. Even though reading scientists have learned how to prevent children from experiencing a lifetime of functional illiteracy, their findings are not making their way into classrooms."

36. For a discussion of the current criticism and legislative enactments aimed at restricting what can be taught and what students may access, see Todd A. DeMitchell, Richard Fossey, & Terri A. DeMitchell, "A Moral Panic, Banning Books, and the Constitution: The Right to Direct the Upbringing and the Right to Receive Information in a Time of Reflection," *Education Law Reporter* 396(3) (2022): 905–928, 928. "School board members and educators must not be stampeded into eschewing the legal calculus that balances competing interests—access to knowledge is too important for the individual and society for school boards to accede to the moral panic of the day."

Appendix A

Table of Cases

FEDERAL COURTS

Fifth Circuit

Sixth Circuit

Seventh Circuit

Ninth Circuit

Tenth Circuit

Eleventh Circuit

District of Columbia

Alabama

California

Connecticut

Florida

Illinois

Maine

New Hampshire

New York

Texas

Vermont

STATE COURTS

Alaska

Arizona

California

Connecticut

Florida

Georgia

Idaho

Illinois

Indiana

Iowa

Kansas

Kentucky

Louisiana

New Jersey

New Mexico

New York

Virginia

Washington

Wisconsin

ENGLISH CASES

Index

About the Authors

Todd A. DeMitchell (BA, MAT, University of La Verne; MA, University of California, Davis; EdD, University of Southern California; post-Doctorate, Harvard Graduate School of Education) is a professor emeritus of education law and labor at the University of New Hampshire. He previously held the John and H. Irene Peters endowed professor of education and the Lamberton endowed professor of justice studies positions. In addition, he was named distinguished professor at the University of New Hampshire. He also received the Excellence in Teaching Award from the College of Liberal Arts and the University Graduate Mentor Award. Prior to joining the faculty at the University of New Hampshire, he spent eighteen years in the public schools, holding such positions as teacher, principal, director of personnel and labor relations, and superintendent.

Richard Fossey (BA, Oklahoma State University; MA, University of Texas; JD, University of Texas (with honors); EdD, Harvard Graduate School of Education) is a professor emeritus at the University of Louisiana at Lafayette, where he was the Paul Burdin endowed professor of Education. Previously, he was the Mike Moses chair of Education at the University of North Texas. From 2011 to 2021, he was the editor of *Catholic Southwest* and is a fellow of the Texas Catholic Historical Society. Prior to entering higher education, he practiced law in Alaska, where he represented school districts in Aleut, Athabaskan, and Inuit communities.

Terri A. DeMitchell (BA, San Diego State University (with Distinction in English); JD, University of San Diego; MA, University of California, Davis; MEd, Harvard Graduate School of Education) is a former elementary school teacher, school law attorney and university instructor in literacy. She is the author of award-winning historical novels and mysteries for young adult and middle-grade readers and regularly publishes papers on legal issues affecting the teaching profession. Prior to starting her writing career, she worked a legal intern for San Diego Unified School District and practiced law in California representing school districts.

Visit: www.terridemitchell.com.

Other Works of the Authors

TODD A. DEMITCHELL AND RICHARD FOSSEY

The Challenges of Mandating School Uniforms in the Public Schools: Free Speech, Research, and Policy.
Student Dress Codes and the First Amendment: Legal Challenges and Policy Issues.
The Limits of Law-Based School Reform: *Vain Hopes and False Promises.*

TODD A. DEMITCHELL

Teachers and Their Unions: Labor Relations in Uncertain Times.
Educators at the Bargaining Table: Successfully Negotiating a Contract that Works for All.
Labor Relations in Education: Policies, Politics, and Practices.
Negligence: What Principals Need to Know about Avoiding Liability.

TODD A. DEMITCHELL AND MARK A. PAGE

Threading the Evaluation Needle: The Documentation of Teacher Unprofessional Conduct.

www.ingramcontent.com/pod-product-compliance
Lightning Source LLC
Chambersburg PA
CBHW021703210326
41599CB00013B/1503